P9-BAU-729

HOMILIES FOR THE LITURGICAL YEAR

Volume A

HOMILIES FOR THE LITURGICAL YEAR

Volume A
Covering the Sundays and Feast Days of Liturgical Year A

by

GONZAGUE MOTTE O.F.M.

Translated by John Drury

FRANCISCAN HERALD PRESS
Chicago, Illinois 60609

Homilies for the Liturgical Year: Volume A, Covering the Sundays and Feast Days of the Liturgical Year A, by Gonzague Motte O.F.M., translated by John Drury from the original French, *Homélies pour une année: Homélies pour tous les dimanches et jours de fete de l'annee "A."* Mulhouse: Editions Salvator; and Paris, Tournai: Casterman, 1971, and the Italian version by Ambretta Milanoli Berti, *Omelie per un anno: Omelie per tutte le domeniche e i giorni festivi dell'anno "A,"* Torino: Marietti, 1971.

Library of Congress Cataloging in Publication Data:

Motte, Gonzague.
Homilies for the liturgical year.

Translation of Homélies pour une année.
CONTENTS: V. A. Covering the Sundays and feast days of liturgical year A.--V. B. Covering the Sundays and feast days of liturgical year B.--V. C. Covering the Sundays and feast days of liturgical year C.
1. Church year sermons. 2. Catholic Church--Sermons. 3. Sermons, French--Translations into English. 4. Sermons, American--Translations from French. I. Title.
BX1756.M686H613 251'.08 73-17144
ISBN 0-8199-0461-9 (v. C)

Nihil Obstat:
Mark Hegener O.F.M.
Censor

Imprimatur:
Msgr. Richard A. Rosemeyer. J.D.
Vicar General, Archdiocese of Chicago

"The Nihil Obstat and the Imprimatur are official declarations that a book or pamphlet is free of doctrinal error. No implication is contained therein that those who have granted the Nihil Obstat and Imprimatur agree with the contents, opinions, or statements expressed."

MADE IN THE UNITED STATES OF AMERICA

FOREWORD

When the first volume of Father Motte's homilies was published, he was interviewed on French television. During that interview the author discussed some of the reasons why the homily remains an important and ever relevant thing. Portions of that interview are given here as an introduction to the present volume.

– Interviewer: "Homily" is the rather erudite term we use for "sermon." Now today we are aware that sermons are not held in great esteem by many of the faithful. What is the problem with sermons today?

– Author: There is indeed a problem, and it is important both for those who listen to sermons and those who have the task of preparing them. Sermons do have a bad reputation, and people's discontent with them is a significant sign. It shows that people are looking for something that they are not getting. People dread sermons more than ever before. And yet, at the same time, they yearn to hear God's word more than ever before.

– Interviewer: Priests and preachers have been giving sermons for centuries, and people have been listening to them for centuries. Is there something more to be said about the Scriptures really? How is one to find something fresh and new to say today?

– Author: There is always something new and unexpected to say about God's word, for several reasons. First of all, there are reasons having to do with human knowledge and scholarship. Man's knowledge of God's word, insofar as it is studied as an ancient text, is making steady progress. Thanks to the panoply of scholarly disciplines which we subsume under the term "exegesis," we can now better understand what the text itself is saying. With the help of historical, geographical, linguistic, and literary findings, exegesis is giving us a better understanding of what is really expressed in the texts. So the homily can be new and fresh in this sense because we have a different view of the Biblical text.

Then there is also a liturgical reason. Here we begin to touch upon the mystery of the Church. For some years now, we have been reading three Scriptural passages every Sunday at Mass. When we have heard an excerpt from the Old Testament and an Epistle, we come to the reading of the Gospel with an outlook that has been shaped by the preceding readings. The Gospel now appears to be a new and fresh message, reminding us of things we have heard elsewhere.

Finally, we get to the real reason why the homily can offer something fresh and new. The word of God is not a philosophy book or an intellectual work. It is not the account of a history that is written down once and for all. It is a living word and, as such, it has a life of its own. It develops by mysterious laws of its own, it operates in a secret way that we cannot observe. God's word today is not what it was yesterday or what it will be tomorrow. Thus, to the extent that the homily expresses the work of creation being accomplished by God's word at a given moment, it is always relevant to the moment and it must be reformulated constantly.

— Interviewer: There we have the paradox of the homily, do we not? It is not a commentary on Scripture, nor is it a presentation made by the priest to some small group outside of Mass. It is something entirely different.

— Author: Yes, that is quite right. It is a difficult point to grasp, but it is important what we do.

A homily is not an exegetical commentary in the strict sense of that term, even though it presupposes exegetical knowledge and solid theology. It is not a textual explanation offered to some small group of people who get together of an evening to learn more about God's word and increase their exegetical knowledge.

The homily is situated within the assembly of believers who come to receive the food of God's word and the food of the Eucharist. So the homily is delivered in a very specific situation, where the Church exercises her prophetic role. In the midst of a particular community the Church expresses what God's word means to us today.

Therein lies the whole difficulty of the homily. The priest must be fully himself in delivering a homily, and he must be wholeheartedly committed to the message he preaches. The people will not tolerate a priest who does not believe what he is saying. Yet, at the same time, he must be completely objective. He must be willing to lose himself in a reality that is beyond him. He is there in the service of someone else, who is using him to express what God's message is saying here and now.

— Interviewer: Is your book directed to priests or to a large public that needs the nourishment of God's word?

— Author: That is very much akin to the question I ask myself when I speak on television: "To whom am I talking?" To everyone. To whom must the homily be adapted? If I am willing to face the paradox it entails, I must answer that it must be adapted to myself. In the last analysis, what matters in the homily is that the speaker has accepted God's word as it stands. While one may not always be successful, one must always seek to have oneself transformed by God's word. Then one tries to communicate this knowledge to the listener or reader, showing them how the divine message can transform us. In that sense one can say that this book is addressed to everyone (End of interview).

The arrangement of the homilies in this volume — as in Volume C — follows the arrangement of the Sundays in the Roman Lectionary. All of the ordinary Sundays of the year are grouped together in one place ahead of feast days of saints. Thus the homilies for the Sundays which fall between the feast of the Baptism of Our Lord and the first Sunday of Lent are placed after the feast of Corpus Christi. In place of the table which was offered in Volume C, page 6, the editor has prepared two calendars which are more comprehensive and will prove helpful not only for the use of this book but also in other ways. Both calendars extend to the year 1990 inclusively.

CALENDAR OF MOVEABLE FEASTS AND SUNDAYS (1975-1990)

Year	*Sunday Cycle*	*Weekday Cycle*	*Bapt. of Our Lord*	*First Sun. of Lent*	*Easter Sunday*	*Pentecost Sunday*	*Week of the Year*	*First Sun. Advent*
1975	A	I	Jan. 12	Feb. 16	Mar. 30	May 18	(VII)	Nov. 30
1976	B	II	Jan. 11	Mar. 7	Apr. 18	June 6	(X)	Nov. 28
1977	C	I	Jan. 9	Feb. 27	Apr. 10	May 29	(IX)	Nov. 27
1978	A	II	Jan. 8*	Feb. 12	Mar. 26	May 14	(VI)	Dec. 3
1979	B	I	Jan. 7*	Mar. 4	Apr. 15	June 3	(IX)	Dec. 2
1980	C	II	Jan. 13	Feb. 24	Apr. 6	May 25	(VIII)	Nov. 30
1981	A	I	Jan. 11	Mar. 8	Apr. 19	June 7	(X)	Nov. 29
1982	B	II	Jan. 10	Feb. 28	Apr. 11	May 30	(IX)	Nov. 28
1983	C	I	Jan. 9	Feb. 20	Apr. 3	May 22	(VIII)	Nov. 27
1984	A	II	Jan. 8*	Mar. 11	Apr. 22	June 10	(X)	Dec. 2
1985	B	I	Jan. 13	Feb. 24	Apr. 7	May 26	(VIII)	Dec. 1
1986	C	II	Jan. 12	Feb. 16	Mar. 30	May 18	(VII)	Nov. 30
1987	A	I	Jan. 11	Mar. 8	Apr. 19	June 7	(X)	Nov. 29
1988	B	II	Jan. 10	Feb. 21	Apr. 3	May 22	(VIII)	Nov. 27
1989	C	I	Jan. 8*	Feb. 12	Mar. 26	May 14	(VI)	Dec. 3
1990	A	II	Jan. 7*	Mar. 4	Apr. 15	June 3	(IX)	Dec. 2

*In the U. S., on this Sunday, the feast of the Epiphany of Our Lord is observed, and the feast of the Baptism of Our Lord is omitted. The week days following this Sunday are the First Week of the Year; and the Weeks of the Year follow consecutively until Ash Wednesday, the Wednesday before the first Sunday of Lent. The Weeks of the Year are resumed during the week following the feast of Pentecost, in such a way that the 34th Week of the Year is always the week before the First Sunday of Advent. The number of the Week of the Year in Pentecost Week is indicated by the Roman numeral after the date of Pentecost Sunday.

SUNDAYS OF THE YEAR FROM 1975 TO 1990

Year	*Sun. after Bapt. of Our Lord*	*Sun. before Ash Wed.*	*Sundays of the Year*	*Sun. after Corpus Christi (U.S.)*	*Sun. before Christ King*	*Sundays of the Year*
1975	Jan. 19	- Feb. 9:	II - V	June 8	- Nov. 16:	X - XXXIII
1976	Jan. 18	- Feb. 29:	II - VIII	June 27	- Nov. 14:	XIII - XXXIII
1977	Jan. 16	- Feb. 20:	II - VII	June 19	- Nov. 13:	XII - XXXIII
1978	Jan. 15*	- Feb. 5:	II - V	June 4	- Nov 19:	IX - XXXIII
1979	Jan. 14*	- Feb. 25:	II - VIII	June 24	- Nov. 18:	XII - XXXIII
1980	Jan. 20	- Feb. 17:	II - VI	June 15	- Nov. 16:	XI - XXXIII
1981	Jan. 18	- Mar. 1:	II - VIII	June 28	- Nov. 15:	XIII - XXXIII
1982	Jan. 17	- Feb. 21:	II - VII	June 20	- Nov. 14:	XII - XXXIII
1983	Jan. 16	- Feb. 13:	II - VI	June 12	- Nov. 13:	XI - XXXIII
1984	Jan. 15*	- Mar. 4:	II - IX	July 1	- Nov. 18:	XIII - XXXIII
1985	Jan. 20	- Feb. 17:	II - VI	June 16	- Nov. 17:	XI - XXXIII
1986	Jan. 19	- Feb. 9:	II - V	June 8	- Nov. 16:	X - XXXIII
1987	Jan. 18	- Mar. 1:	II - VIII	June 28	- Nov. 15:	XIII - XXXIII
1988	Jan. 17	- Feb. 14:	II - VI	June 12	- Nov. 13:	XI - XXXIII
1989	Jan. 15*	- Feb. 5:	II - V	June 4	- Nov. 19:	IX - XXXIII
1990	Jan. 14*	- Feb. 25:	II - VIII	June 24	- Nov. 18:	XII - XXXIII

*Sunday after Epiphany in the U.S.

CONTENTS

COMMON SUNDAYS OF THE YEAR

FEASTS OF SAINTS

ADVENT

I SUNDAY OF ADVENT

Is 2:1-5
Rom 13:11-14
Mt 24:37-44

A new liturgical year begins today. The Lord could not have offered us a more heartening message than the one we have just heard. We glimpse the awesome panorama by Isaiah, who tells us that the Lord will be acknowledged by all nations and that there will be an era of universal peace. We hear Matthew the Evangelist predicting the imminent coming of the Lord into the world. And we hear Paul telling us to be alert and on the watch. As we listen to all these words, we are overtaken by a vigorous hope and a deep certainty. The Lord is going to step into the picture. Indeed, he is already at work and we need only be attentive to sense his living presence.

Such is the season of Advent, and that is why we feel a real sense of interior peace when it arrives each year. It is as if some painful and distressing period of waiting, some profound nostalgia buried deep inside us, were finally going to be dispelled. Advent means "coming." As we listen to God's word, we are not completely sure what its purpose it. We do not know for sure whether it is meant to prepare us for the imminent approach of Christmas, to inform us about some transformation in the life of mankind here and now, or to represent a promise of Christ's definitive return at the end of the world. The fact is that we find all these things embodied in the Advent that is proclaimed today.

Today's Gospel does not recount a miracle, or a parable with a hidden meaning. Jesus himself talks to his apostles about his coming. He seems to indicate that he must become present to them in a different way. He is present to them now, living in their midst as he speaks. But he feels obliged to talk to them about the moment when the "Son of Man" will come.

Such is the basic announcement he makes to them. It seems that he purposely veils the circumstances and the manner of his coming in mystery. He does not offer any reasons for this mysterious return, which would seem to be to no purpose since his presence leaves no doubts in the minds of his listeners. But some things apparently can only be accomplished if he returns a second time.

In speaking about his return, Jesus first stresses the suddenness of his manifestation. He recalls the old story of the flood. No one, he says, thought anything along those lines. "People were eating and drinking, marrying and being married." The normal courses of everyday life went on, and no one could have suspected that a catastrophe was about to take place. Suddenly, "the flood came and destroyed them."

Then Jesus compares himself to a thief, who sneaks in unexpectedly. He breaks into the house when he is least expected, hoping to take advantage of the element of surprise.

These two comparisons indicate two features of the Lord's coming. The first and most evident feature is its unexpectedness. He will conduct himself as an unchallenged master. He will not have to announce himself. He will impose himself on us with irresistible authority and power. The second feature, less evident but no less real, is the universality of his manifestation. No one will be able to evade it. Just as the flood swept away everyone, so all men will be forced to confront him when he returns.

Suddenly the predicted event takes on great importance. Like a sudden worldwide earthquake, the Lord will be immediately present to each human being as an undeniable force. Just as the irresistible waters of the flood fatally enveloped every human being in the world, so the Son of Man will impose himself irresistibly on all human beings.

In a single stroke the Lord reveals to us two different sides of his coming. On the one hand, his coming will be sudden and clearly manifest to all. On the other hand, the whole world will evince little conscious awareness of this event that will be so decisive for each and every human being.

The contrast between the importance of the Lord's coming and man's lack of awareness concerning it is striking. It helps us to appreciate many things. And we might also add that it does not give us a very flattering picture of man. Man is always ready to take great pride in himself, especially today when he can make projections about what his life will be one year or ten years from now. Yet, at the same time, he is totally unconscious about the importance and the moment of a great cosmic event, Christ's coming.

We can now appreciate why the Lord urges vigilance upon us. As believers, we live in a world where it makes no sense to believe firmly in Christ's return and all its consequences. The world around us is neither for nor against his return; it simply ignores it. His return lies in the realm of the non-existent. To the world our conviction about this return is an odd aberration. To the world our faith will always be associated with some mythical reality that is now outmoded. The world may be able to accept the existence of the Church as a well organized religion which can help it with certain immediate problems that are a little beyond the world's capabilities. It will accept the Church to the extent that the Church resembles it and becomes more like it. But the deeper rationale of the Church, which is to remind us of the Lord's coming and to prepare us for it, will always be incomprehensible to the world.

So it is useless for the believer to seek reasons for believing in Jesus and his return by looking to the world or to the contemporary outlook. The world is incapable of understanding this, for all its wild and delirious dreams in other areas.

So the Lord is insistent: "Stay awake, therefore . . . you must be prepared." He realizes that we cannot be helped in this respect by the daily round of life with its professional and social obligations, or by the mentality that prevails in the human group of which we are a part. What is worse, we are drawn towards the prevailing unconsciousness and spiritual torpor in spite of ourselves. To our astonishment, we find that we ourselves suffer from it. But that is not a satisfactory reason for us to give way to resignation and to allow our conviction about the Lord's return to grow dull within us.

Paul's message in today's Epistle can be understood in the same sense. In all likelihood he knew from experience how fragile the spiritual life is in a world that constantly tries to anesthetize and deaden it. He also knew that we allow ourselves to be dominated by the powerful and comfortable spell of unconsciousness. And so he tells us: "It is now the hour for you to wake from sleep." He realized that we are still enmeshed in the darkness of night, that we only see clearly the things and people around us, and that it is difficult to persevere in convictions which are as strange as ours. He stresses his point: "Our salvation is closer . . . the day draws near."

We must let these words seep into our minds and hearts. However much we may be weighed down by our errors and failings, our neglect and our torpor, we must accept the reality of Paul's conviction even though others may say it has nothing to do with "real life." The "real" is not just that which seems evident to those around us. What is real is the sudden, shattering return of the Lord and its universal impact.

His return will transform everything. It is not just that we can believe in it and should realize that it will happen. Today we also learn that it will finally bring about what man has sought for thousands of years and has never achieved. We learn this from the majestic prophecy of Isaiah that we heard today. The nations will then emerge from their ignorance and unconsciousness. They will hear the voice of the Lord and accept him as their God. Then there will be peace. The engines of war and man's destructive plots will be turned into tools of peace that bring joy to others: "They shall beat their swords into plowshares and their spears into pruning hooks. One nation shall not raise the sword against another, nor shall they train for war again." Such words sound strange in a world where the major portion of human energy is used up in war preparations that have a refinement and efficiency never before attained in history. Depending on the strength of our faith, we can help to turn them into a reality.

During this season of Advent the Lord will manifest himself to each one of us. That is certain. Let us be vigilant and alert to grasp this moment when it comes. It will enable us to savor the truth of his love, and it will solidify our faith in his definitive coming.

II SUNDAY OF ADVENT

Is 11:1-10
Rom 15:4-9
Mt 3:1-12

In last Sunday's liturgy God's word reminded us of the imminence of Christ's return and urged us to rouse from sleep so that we would be able to welcome him when he arrived.

Today the preaching of John the Baptist and of Isaiah will tell us precisely what Christ's coming at Christmas will mean for us. Their message is a far cry from the hoary legends which Christmas has occasioned, from the atmosphere of childish festivity to which some would like to reduce Christmas because it has to do with the birth of a baby, and from any sort of facile, vaguely euphoric joy connected with a particularly beneficial divine visitation. All such things are bypassed and swallowed up in the picture that Isaiah and John the Baptist present of a mystery that is really full of strength and importance.

Using different methods and speaking in radically different idioms, both tell us who Jesus Christ is, how he will act, what results will ensue, and how we are to behave in this period of preparing for his coming.

The majestic words of Isaiah, telling us about the shoot from the stump of Jesse, still ring in our ears. We know that Jesse was the father of David, the great king of Israel, who came to play an important role in the history of his people. He is pictured as the author of the psalms, and as a figure of the Messiah. Thus the shoot of Jesse which Isaiah refers to here is David himself, first of all. Then, through David, it is Jesus Christ, who will be born into his stock. "The Spirit of the Lord shall rest upon him," says Isaiah. And he goes on to mention the qualities of this Spirit: wisdom and understanding, counsel and strength, knowledge and fear of the Lord. He could not have found more eloquent language to express the human, spiritual, divine qualities of Jesus, the "Son of David."

With deep humility John the Baptist will say: "The one who will follow me is more powerful than I. I am not even fit to carry his sandals."

Such is the person who is going to come. The prophet Isaiah depicts him endowed with all the gifts of the Spirit of God himself. John the Baptist, the holy penitent of the desert, is scarcely able to express the profound veneration he feels for him.

In the light of all this, it is not surprising that this personage should do things that are particularly decisive for human beings.

Both Isaiah and John the Baptist present him as a judge. But from their descriptions of him, this judge seems to be only remotely connected with those who preside over our courts. He seems to have a personal predilection for the weak and the humble. He is not concerned about external appearances and superficial qualities. While human beings judge the extent of their mutual guilt on the basis of criteria that can be seen and evaluated, this judge is concerned solely with the interior quality of each person.

What is more, his judgment is in fact a terrible thing, and this brings us to the crux of the whole paradox embodied in the mystery of Christmas.

Both John the Baptist and Isaiah see it in tragic terms. Isaiah tells us that "he shall strike the ruthless with the rod of his mouth." In other words, his absolute authority will impose itself on all. And Isaiah goes on to say that "with the breath of his lips he shall slay the wicked." Using a comparison that will crop up in other parts of the gospel message, John the Baptist says: "Even now the ax is laid to the root of the tree. Every tree that is not fruitful will be cut down and thrown into the fire." Then he picks up the symbol of the winnower who separates the wheat from the chaff, stores the wheat, and burns the chaff in "unquenchable fire."

We are far removed indeed from the kindly gentility of a child's birthday party. We are immersed in the tragic reality of the Lord's coming. Some commentators have felt that both Isaiah and John the Baptist were describing two successive stages of Christ's work in one happening; that they went too far in intermingling his corporeal birth with his definitive return as a judge at the end of the world. Last Sunday we saw that these two aspects of Christ's mystery were strangely bound up with each other. On the plane of exegesis or from the standpoint of an historical overview of the salvation mystery, these commentators may be right enough. But here we are concerned with accepting the mystery of Christmas and of the Lord's coming in all their richness; and on that plane it seems important that we do not minimize anything that the Lord tells us today through the mouth of his prophets.

We are compelled to admit that Christmas does entail an element of tragedy. The Lord's coming is comforting, to be sure, but it is also violent. It is the irruption of another into a world that wants to be self-sufficient. And when this other is also invested with the Spirit, when his holiness is far superior to that model of penance, the hermit John the Baptist, when the breath of his lips can slay his opponents, then we are dealing with someone to be reckoned with, someone that forces us to take sides. He demands that we make a commitment. Either we allow ourselves to be modeled after him, and that means life; or else we refuse to show such docility, and that means death in "unquenchable fire." That is the message which the Lord gives us today.

To be sure, a happy prospect awaits those who are willing to live with him and to be modelled after him. It is the prospect of universal reconciliation, announced by Isaiah in the closing section of today's reading. One can hardly imagine a more evocative description of this universal reconciliation than the fraternization of the wolf and the lamb, the leopard and the kid, the baby and the cobra. While Christmas does have a tragic aspect, it also represents the start among human beings of God's world, where all is peace and serenity. As John the Baptist puts it: "The reign of God is at hand."

Such is the mystery of Christmas which God's prophets talk about today. Christmas promises us the tragic happening of a profound perturbation caused by the presence of God's holy one in our midst. And beyond this perturbation, peace and universal reconciliation are promised to everyone.

Now we can comprehend the violence of John the Baptist's words to the Pharisees around him. And we make no mistake in applying those words to ourselves.

We can picture the mentality of those Pharisees who came to be baptzied by John the Baptist, reconstructing it from the words of John and from our own knowledge of ourselves.

John the Baptist has quite a reputation. A veritable mass movement brings countless penitents to him. Impressed by his pronouncements and his ascetic way of life, they want to shelter themselves from potential catastrophe by shaping up. One can hear their defense: "God cannot chastize me because I am a 'son of Abraham,' and because I have been baptized by John." Today we would say: "I have been baptized by the Church, I am one of the honorable people. I go to Mass. My life is guaranteed where the Lord is concerned."

The reply to us is the reply that John the Baptist made to the Pharisees. Neither membership in a community of believers nor acceptance of some rite regarded as a sort of protective magic can dispense us from effecting in our flesh and heart and mind what the Lord wishes to accomplish by inaugurating his kingdom. We cannot simply flee "from the wrath to come." We must "give some evidence that we mean to reform."

To accept Christ's coming at Christmas means to refuse to take refuge in false warranties or in magic. It means that we are willing to be purified and transformed by the fire that Christ will bring when he comes. It means that we are willing to let his Spirit be our wisdom and our strength. That is the baptism in fire and the Holy

Spirit which is announced by John the Baptist and effected by Jesus.

There we have the mystery of this potential tragedy, this divine wrath. Left to ourselves, we might well be terrified. But in today's Epistle Paul offers us two solid supports in trying to persuade us to accept the work of Christ in all its grandeur. First of all, he points to the real-life experience of the men of old as it is recorded in Scripture. God was at work in the midst of his people, Israel. He led them through atrocious tests, all of which proved to be good and necessary. That should give us comfort and encouragement. Secondly, Paul points out that God is merciful. To believe in his kindness is to realize that man is not capable of grasping the full import of the regimen that God imposes on him. We agree to submit to it because we know the love of the Lord.

Let us share each other's aspirations, as Paul tells us. Let us learn how to accept one another. In that way we will become capable of accepting the Lord who is coming.

III SUNDAY OF ADVENT

Is 35:1-6a,10
Jas 5:7-10
Mt 11:2-11

John the Baptist—the hermit, the preacher, the loyal precursor—is in prison. It is an odd reward, indeed, from the Lord for all his faithful service. John had become intolerable to the king and his entourage. People find it pretty hard to accept someone who reproaches them for their mistakes and bad habits. But when that someone acts in accordance with his words, then his listeners are forced either to change their way of life or else to get rid of him. The latter fate awaits John the Baptist.

For the moment he is in prison. Today's Gospel shows him sending some of his disciples to Jesus to ask him if he is or is not the awaited Messiah. Commentators have generally interpreted this mission as an indication of John's own anguish and doubt. As they see it, John is taken aback by the behavior of the one whom he designated as the Messiah, as the one who would take away the sins of the world. In prison John faces a crisis of despair and sends some disciples to Jesus for reassurance. On reflection, however, this hypothesis is unsatisfying and makes little sense. As we saw last week, John the Baptist is a hermit, an ascetic. He is familiar with loneliness and suffering. He has put all his faith in the Lord. He has abandoned himself to the Lord in all things, and he knows what such abandonment entails. Why should be suddenly need some direct testimony or proof, which might not be convincing anyway?

Upon closer examination of today's text and of John's whole life, it would seem that the journey of his disciples to Jesus has a much more positive sense. In every set of circumstances John the Baptist has shown up as the precursor. His importance resides wholly in the fact that it is he who announces the coming of the Lord. He has been thrown into prison, and he can readily imagine the fate that awaits him. But still he has disciples around him. How can he logically allow these generous souls to remain attached to him, now that his role is about to come to an end? Hence he is compelled to complete his task and to send his disciples to Jesus. That would seem to be the real meaning of the trip he sends them on. John sends his friends to Jesus so that Jesus may reveal himself to them. John had already made clear that he himself was not the Messiah. Quite naturally, then, his disciples are led to ask Jesus: "Are you 'He who is to come' or do we look for another?"

Shortly before, John the Baptist had said: "That is my joy, and it is complete. He must increase while I must decrease. The One who comes from above is above all" (Jn 3:29-31). Isn't the sending of his disciples to Jesus a perfect illustration of these sentiments? John wishes to decrease to the point where he is left alone once again.

The line of behavior is coherent, and it is also very beautiful. In so acting, John is truly the precursor; and he follows the demands of his role through to their ultimate, cruel consequences. Jesus says as much when he talks to the crowd around him: "History has not known a man born of woman greater than John the Baptist." In other words, a man could not go further in fidelity to the Lord and obedience to his mission.

John's sending of his disciples to Jesus and his quest for personal solitude are admirable traits. Saint James would seem to be alluding to this sort of attitude when he says in today's Epistle: "As your models in suffering, hardship, and patience . . . take the prophets who spoke in the name of the Lord."

We often have the feeling that salvation is slow in coming, that the Lord is leaving us in the lurch instead of carrying out his work. We are sorely tempted to hurry along the whole process on our own, to bring our seeking and struggling to an end without waiting for the Lord to manifest himself. Advent, which promises the coming of our God, involves patience. It is not a negative, inactive, sterile patience. It is a patience exercised in fidelity to what has already been given. And that fidelity must be consistent, carrying through the first promising signs to the very end no matter what risks that might entail. Yes, John the Baptist is "a prophet indeed, and something more!" He is the messenger so identified with his role that he loses himself completly in it. That is the first message we are given today.

Jesus then responds to those sent by John the Baptist. He seems to be playing John's game when he sends them back with this reply: "The blind recover their sight, cripples walk, lepers are cured. . ." It seems to be an echo of the words Isaiah uttered in today's first reading. Jesus does not answer "yes" or "no" to John's messengers. He simply invites them to take a look and to discover the truth for themselves. He does not want to impose himself on them, to constrain them to acceptance of himself. He wants to help them to read the signs given by the prophets, and then to draw their own conclusions. Those who can see, who have been given the capacity for it, will be convinced. Those who see nothing cannot be transformed. Then Jesus ends with these surprising words: "Blest is the man who finds no stumbling block in me." He is suggesting that the Lord could be so incomprehensible and untouchable that a man's resultant stupefaction might lead him to reject God.

We must admit that the statement is quite mysterious. But if we relate it to Isaiah's prophecy, we can glimpse the summons to watchfulness that it embodies. Isaiah says: "Here is your God, he comes with vindication; with divine recompense he comes to save you." The vindication in question is the vindication the Lord will effect when he comes. It is the establishment of his justice, the purification of evil, the triumph of goodness. Only he is capable of doing it. Only he does it, in the way and manner that seems right to him. He does not do it the way we human beings—with our impatience, our inconsistencies, our limited knowledge—might like or imagine.

This may well be one of the most difficult and subtle things for a generous-hearted believer to accept. The fact is that his faith always puts him in a position of inferiority. He suffers daily, because fidelity to the Lord often seems to entail a rejection of success, of human plans, of life itself. Even as the world often seems to persecute his faith, so the believer feels persecuted within himself. With the best intentions in the world, he will be tempted to vindicate himself, to hasten the coming of the kingdom in his own way. He will continually discover that the Lord does not operate the way he would like. He will want to take back the initiative on his own. But it is God who brings vindication and salvation; all man has to do is to be faithful to the very end. That is what the prophets did, St. James tells us. They suffered unjust persecution, but they left the task of restoring justice up to God.

We discover another dimension of Advent today. The coming of the Lord will be a day of joy: "Those whom the Lord has ransomed . . . will meet with joy and gladness, sorrow and mourning will flee." All that is part of the kingdom that the Lord is fashioning for us. But even if our faith and our virtue were as strong and as coherent as the faith and virtue of John the Baptist, they would not be enough to effect this. We do not know what the kingdom will be like or how it will be brought about. The only possible attitude for us is one of patience and hope. Anything else is liable to make the Lord a stumbling block for us.

But if we give this message a good reception, if we follow the example of John the Baptist, who was willing to run the ultimate risk, and of the prophets, whose patient hope was never disappointed, then this Advent will be joyous. For we will soon see "the splendor of our God."

In one way or another we all are blind or lame or leprous or deaf or even dead to real life. We all are rich men incapable of understanding and accepting the good news. Today let us renew our hope in the Lord's return. Let us strip off all our presumption and ask him to give us the patience and perseverance we need to carry out all that he expects of us. This patience and perseverance will enable us to recognize and acknowledge him, and it will usher us into his kingdom.

IV SUNDAY OF ADVENT

Is 7:10-14
Rom 1:1-7
Mt 1:18-24

In a few days we will celebrate the feast of Christmas. We have prepared ourselves for it by listening to the word of God each Sunday and trying to probe into its deeper meaning, without fearing to let ourselves be shaken and transformed by it. Today is our last get-together before the day of our Lord's coming. To help us with our final preparations the Church offers us a model, Saint Joseph. In his own way Matthew tells us about the virginal conception of Jesus: how he was begotten and incorporated into the Hebrew people even though he was the son of God. That is how the plan of God was carried out, the plan that we heard described in today's selection from the prophecies of Isaiah.

First of all, Matthew evokes the mystery of the Annunciation. Luke describes it in greater detail. Matthew is content to recount the principal elements: Mary, Joseph's fiancée, becomes pregnant through the work of the Holy Spirit. Matthew goes into greater detail on the reactions of Joseph and on the role that he is to play. He is so specific about this matter that his account might well be called "the Annunciation to Joseph." Like Mary, his fiancée, he will have a mission that is revealed to him by the Lord; and this mission will be a decisive one in the history of salvation. He will be commissioned to take Mary into his home and to give a name to the child that she will bring into the world. He will be entrusted with the task of incorporating Mary's child into the progeny of David by adopting him and giving him the name indicated by the angel.

Let us try to grasp the nature of the spiritual adventure which Joseph lived through. If we do, we will soon see how it may benefit our own preparation for Christmas.

The most prevalent interpretation of Joseph's adventure might be dubbed "the story of the cuckold." Since Joseph is an upright and honest man, so this interpretation goes, he does not want to crush his wife under the weight of an odious public trial. He wants to give her the freedom that she seems to desire, since she is expecting a child that is not by him. At the last minute an angel intervenes to prevent catastrophe. He informs Joseph about the supernatural origin of the child's conception, and he gives the young man a specific and major mission. Joseph is to incorporate the coming child into the people of Israel. He will be the child's official father because he will take him in, give him a name, and raise him.

That is how many commentators interpret the conjugal test to which Joseph is put. He survives it, thanks to the angel's message. And in so doing we get a glimpse of the quality of his soul, of his disinterestedness and his obedience. We also learn of the privileged role that Joseph is to play vis-a-vis Mary and Jesus.

On deeper reflection, however, this interpretation makes little sense. The deceived husband, miraculously consoled and encouraged by an angel, does not fit in well with what we know about Joseph.

Joseph is called "an upright man." Yet we are then told that he wants to put Mary away in secret. Wherein lies his uprightness and his sense of justice in that case? If he thinks Mary is really guilty, then he should be willing to denounce her publicly if he is a true follower of the law. By not doing so, he proves that his justice and uprightness are not what they should be. On the other hand, if he thinks Mary is innocent, then he would be unjust to put her away secretly. His justice goes overboard.

The real problem is not to know whether Joseph believes Mary to be innocent or guilty. The real question is whether Joseph does or does not know the secret of Mary's virginal conception of Jesus. Does he know that Mary was visited by the angel Gabriel, and that the Holy Spirit overshadowed her so that she could become the mother of God's Son?

If we ponder the angel's message to Joseph more closely and place it in the general context of Matthew's whole Gospel, we can then paraphrase the words of the angel as follows: "Joseph, son of David, do not be afraid to take Mary as your wife . . . You know very well that the one begotten in her is the work of the Holy Spirit. She will bear a son and you will give him the name Jesus."

Everything indicates that Joseph knew about the supernatural origin of the child Mary was expecting. Hence the whole story makes sense, and there is no need to engage in fancy acrobatics to tie the whole story together.

Joseph's uprightness does not reside in his plan to put Mary away in secret. The fact is that Joseph refuses to pass himself off as the child's father because he knows that the child is the Son of God. He does not want to usurp a role that God has not entrusted to him. His plan to repudiate Mary is a sign of his tactfulness, of his obedience to the will of God. God apparently had not entrusted him with any mission vis-a-vis Mary and her child. God is at work in this whole matter, and Joseph wants to tiptoe out of the picture so as not to interfere in a project that goes far beyond him.

It is at this point that God intervenes, sending an angel to Joseph in a dream. In one stroke we clearly see Joseph's personal uprightness and the role that has been entrusted to him by God. We clearly appreciate his personal integrity and his importance in salvation history.

His position is so decisive that it can be compared with that of John the Baptist, whom we have accompanied on the two preceding Sundays. The precursor proclaimed and pinpointed the Messiah. He echoed the prophets, Isaiah and Elijah in particular. Joseph welcomes the Messiah and Lord. He is the son of David who adopts the Son of God, the just man who welcomes Emmanuel into his lineage.

Joseph can also be compared to Mary, his fiancée. Mary conceives and gives birth to the child. Joseph makes the child a son of David and incorporates him into the human race, thus fulfilling the promise made to David and recalled by Paul in today's Epistle.

Because of his spiritual qualities and of the mission for which he was chosen by God, Joseph is singled out as one who can help us to make our final preparations for the feast of Christmas.

Joseph's destiny would seem to be quite different from our own, but in fact the elements that constitute his uprightness are the same as ours. We can summarize them very succinctly: Joseph knows, accepts, and serves.

Joseph knows about Mary's virginal conception of Jesus. He knows that the Son of God is born, thanks to her "fiat." The same message is revealed to us, because God's word comes to shed further light on the Spirit's workings within us. We, too, know it. We know that in a few days the Lord will manifest himself. Do we have Joseph's respect and faith for Christ's coming?

Joseph accepts and welcomes the living Jesus. We, too, are supposed to accept and welcome him. The Lord is truly living for us in his Church. Thanks to the Church, he communes with us in his word and his sacraments. It is no more difficult for us to believe in that communion than it was for Joseph to believe that the child expected by his fiancée is the Son of the Most High. Do we imitate Joseph's tender acceptance of the Lord?

Joseph serves the living Jesus Christ. Are we not obliged to serve him too, by seeking to bring about the universal peace and reconciliation which believers in the gospel are meant to flesh out? And does not this work bring us close to Joseph, whose life certainly was not simplified by the presence of Jesus in his home? Are we willing to let ourselves be disturbed by others and to live in peace with them in the name of Christ?

Now we can better appreciate the role and importance of Joseph, the just man. In our own way, and in accordance with our own specific vocation, we all are supposed to display an uprightness akin to his. Let us ask him to help us, so that we may be capable of welcoming Christmas and serving the living Christ as he did.

CHRISTMAS SEASON

December 25
CHRISTMAS
Midnight Mass

Is 9:1-6
Ti 2:11-14
Lk 2:1-14

"Upon those who dwelt in the land of gloom a light has shone." So Isaiah tells us in today's first reading. And that is what happened to the shepherds who were sleeping near their flocks in the countryside around Bethlehem. It was night, and "there were shepherds in that region, living in the fields and keeping night watch by turns over their flocks." It was dark all around them. Nothing distinguished that night from any other night. A lot of people were in Bethlehem at the time, because all the descendants of David had come to enroll for the ceusus ordered by Caesar Augustus. Suddenly "the glory of the Lord shone around them." At first they were afraid, but then the angel reassured them. He had "tidings of great joy to be shared by the whole people . . . A savior has been born to you."

Every year we hear the same message repeated at Midnight Mass. Yet we never really get used to it. Each time the words seem to have a new and distinctive sense. Each time, in the intimate secrecy of this night on which our Savior was born, we feel an indescribable hope awakening within us. We feel that something more joyous and solid is now beginning once again. Tomorrow cannot possibly be just like today. But then the loud voice of common sense and reasonableness interrupts our musing. You know very well, it says, that everything will go back to being the same after the holidays and festivities are over. You will be the same weak miscreant you have always been. Life and its many problems will quickly gain the upper hand. You will see around you as much tragedy, poverty, and sickness as before—if not more. So what is the fuss about a supposed savior? Isn't your hope a delusion?

The fact is that Christmas would be nothing more than a stirring legend incapable of giving us any real hope, if it were merely the birthday of a child—even if that child were the most beautiful, intelligent, and marvelous child imaginable. A human child may be born in dramatic surroundings of poverty and abandonment. But however great a genius he may be, what real interest would that have for us today?

The fact is that we are not dealing with an ordinary birth. Luke has just reported the precise and immediate historical circumstances of that birth. Isaiah has told us who will be capable of appreciating it. And Paul has just told us who will be capable of accepting and welcoming it.

We suddenly discover that this happy, moving story about a nocturnal birth in Bethlehem has taken on striking dimensions.

Isaiah says: "A child is born to us, a son is given us." Then he tells us for whom this birth will be a source of great joy: "The people who walked in darkness . . . those who dwelt in gloom." All those who are enslaved or menaced by enemies and all those afflicted with suffering and poverty will now rejoice. It is as if this light in the night is perceptible only to those who can no longer see or hope for anything. And the prophet concludes: "Both now and forever, the zeal of the Lord of hosts will do this."

Right off we are sorely tempted to look for mollifying explanations. That is poetic language, we say. He is using dramatic images to help us appreciate the grandeur of God vis-a-vis the meanness of man. But we have been listening to the word of God during Advent, so we sense that we are dealing here with a spiritual message of incredible depth.

Until Christ came, until his birth took place, man could not possibly know at first hand God's love. Yet man needs this love so urgently and desperately that, in its absence, man suffers from a desperate yearning and a sense of panic whose source he cannot pinpoint. So true is this that to remain true to the word of God in the absence of his Son is to accept the hard fact of living in a state of darkness. In our present state as wayfarers in a world that seeks to be sufficient unto itself, non-possession of God's love inevitably reduces us to darkness and to solitude. At the same time, however, we believers trust in the word of God. We know that his love is zealous, which means that it will be revealed only to those who refuse to look for alibis or other ways to escape the intolerable burden of darkness and solitude. Only to such people is the Lord's light revealed on this night of Christmas: to the lonely, the broken, the restless. In short, it is only to the poor that God the Father gives his Son. He is a gift to all those who have had the patience and trust to wander through the darkness, seeking only the light promised by God's word; to all those who have persevered in their fidelity while God's word seemed to grow more distant and out of reach.

That is how Isaiah describes those for whom Christmas is something more than a moving legend which is part and parcel of the cultural patrimony of Christian nations. The birth in Bethlehem is a comforting and vivifying light for us only insofar as we have taken the zealous love of God into account in our personal choices and decisions.

It is another way of telling us the same things that we heard during Advent, when we were preparing for Christ's coming.

But here we can also discover a future-oriented message: the promise of a kingdom of peace and light. That is what Paul speaks about in the Epistle: "The grace of God has appeared, offering salvation to all men."

If we read his words hastily, we may see nothing more than pleasant promises. But on closer inspection we see that they represent a demanding project for anyone who takes them seriously.

This child Jesus, just born of Mary in a manger at Bethlehem, is not the delightful, inoffensive babe that our laziness would make him out to be. He comes "to cleanse for himself a people of his own." In other words, he is going to set up for himself a community of human beings who will be transformed according to his own plans—who will heed the Apostle's call "to reject godless ways and worldly desires, and live temperately, justly, and devoutly in this age as we await our blessed hope, the appearing of the glory . . . of our savior Christ Jesus."

Thus these human beings will be set apart, turned away from their spontaneous desires, and motivated by a wisdom of a very special character. So special will it be that it will appear quite aberrant to other human beings. It will not look forward to earthly success or wellbeing. It will look forward to a manifestation of the Lord. The world, it would seem, is incapable of satisfying those who are motivated by this special wisdom.

The tragic element in the feast of Christmas, which we pondered during Advent, could not be expressed more clearly. It is indeed a new world that begins with the nocturnal birth of this Child in Bethlehem. Christmas is the fulfillment of a hope and a profound desire, the hope of a whole people yearning for the coming of the Messiah and the desire of every believer today to see the luminous manifestation of his Lord.

Christmas is the birth of a new world—not the spontaneous generation of something that did not exist up to now but the transformation of our world this night by the arrival of a Being who will break up and destroy everything to create "a people of his own." If we collaborate in this new and necessary birth, then we will find that the yoke is sweet and the burden is light. If we do not, then our life will be miserable. For a moment we may find pleasure and contentment in the resources it offers us, but in the end we will sink into a dark despair far more terrible than the uprooting caused by the Child of Bethlehem.

Finally, Christmas is the expectation of another coming which will mark the end of our transformation. While Christmas meets our hope in one respect, it also summons us to await something else. It prohibits us from locking ourselves up within the present world. It stimulates us to abandon ourselves to the Spirit of the Lord, so that he may complete his work of renewal.

Let us stop and linger before the Christmas crib during these festive days. God's word has helped us discover the dizzying, incomparable richness of the Nativity mystery. As we gaze upon the crib, let us ask the Lord to make us more simple, to teach us how to see his vivifying love and how to admire such profound tenderness. Then let us offer ourselves to him who has clearly given himself wholly to us.

December 25
CHRISTMAS
Day Mass

Is 52:7-10
Heb 1:1-6
Jn 1:1-18

In the full light of Christmas day we hear John's Gospel and the Epistle to the Hebrews proclaiming the mystery in all its grandeur: "The Word became flesh and made his dwelling among us."

In the dark hours of night a short time ago we celebrated the birth of Jesus, the Son of God become Man. The Baby came into the world in the most modest and quiet way. He was laid in a manger because his parents could find no room at the inn. A few shepherds, mysteriously notified by God's angels, came to worship him.

With the dawning of Christmas day itself, all that seems far away. The words we have just heard in today's readings bear no trace of the serene family intimacy and peace that were reflected in the accounts of Jesus' birth.

The magnificent opening passage of Saint John's Gospel gets right down to the fundamental message. In an awesome fresco he ushers us into the mystery of the intimate encounter, the communion, between God and humanity. When we listen to his words, however, we do not feel that we are listening to the dry or rigid exposition of a theologian. We feel that we are listening to something vital, strong, and necessary. It is the realization of a meeting that was announced long ago and for which there was a time of preparation ever since. It is as if two streams, originating far away from each other at different sources, moved towards each other gradually until they joined to form a single river.

That is the first impression we get from our readings today. We are dealing with an encounter akin to the fusion of two living beings who had been waiting for each other expectantly and who had been destined from the start to form one.

In his Gospel, John tells us that "the Word became flesh." We know that this Word is God's speech. But we want to focus carefully on this term, because we know that God's speech is not like man's speech. When a human being speaks, he uses a stock of agreed upon sounds to communicate with his peers. But God has no peer or equal. When God speaks, he can only express himself to himself. His speech is the Word, and the Word "was in God's presence" and "was God."

In the course of its history Israel gradually discovered what God's speech was. God spoke to this nation from very ancient times. It was a real part of its existence from the time of Abraham and the patriarchs, the days of Moses, the kings, and the prophets, right down to the days of the sapiential authors. As time went on, the Israelite people perceived that God's speech was quite different from the word or speech of human beings. God does not just reveal a law or a rule of life. His word also acts; it is a dynamic reality. God's speech creates, as if it were endowed with some intrinsic capability of its own. And it will be effective down to the end of time.

As the spiritual life and experience of the Israelite nation grew deeper, it gradually came to personalize God's speech. It is God's word that creates, that gives meaning to man's history, that compels human beings to make a personal commitment with regard to it. If man accepts God's word, then he can live. If he rejects it, he is doomed to destruction.

Approximately nineteen centuries elapsed between the time that God spoke to Abraham and the Word was made flesh. God had promised Abraham that his progeny would be numerous and powerful. Nineteen centuries passed. And during those centuries the Israelite people progressively discovered the existence, importance, and necessity of "The Word." Then suddenly one day an Evangelist writes the words we have just heard. Everything that the Israelites had learned, everything that their sages had proclaimed, everything that they all had longed for, is picked up again here and transformed. All their yearnings for a Messiah-Lord, a universal Savior, and a personal and sovereign Word were really yearning for the presence of God himself, who would fuse his life with that of man. "The Word became flesh."

Another current runs through man at the same time. While God is coming towards him, man is moving towards God. The promises made to Abraham and made more explicit for David took on increasing urgency when the nation underwent severe trials and lost all trace of human power. More and more the Israelites longed to receive and to give birth to the Savior. When would they get the child that was to be born of some young woman, according to Isaiah's prophecy some seven hundred years earlier? The whole house and family of David had been preparing itself for this event. Now, suddenly, this long period of waiting is at an end; the yearning is fulfilled.

In the Son, through whom God speaks to us "in this, the final age," there is a meeting and fusion of the human descendant of David and the Word: "the reflection of the Father's glory, the exact representation of the Father's being." That is the mystery of the Incarnation revealed to us by the message God gives us today.

We would think that the people would have reacted with great enthusiasm and joy at the proclamation of such an important mystery, which fulfilled a basic and serious expectation. A deep longing, felt for many centuries, had finally been satisfied. Yet today, more than 1900 years later, the Jewish people have not yet recognized Him. It would even seem that the Lord did not want to be recognized in any spectacular fashion. He was born in a stable off in a corner of the world. His herald, entrusted with the task of preparing the way for his arrival, was an ascetic in the desert. John the Baptist's task was merely "to testify to the light, for he himself was not the light." Yet when the Lord came, "the world did not know who he was . . . His own did not accept him."

In the selection from Isaiah that we just heard, the prophet announces that exultant joy surrounding this coming. But at the same time he seems to be telling us that very few will recognize it and tell others about it. They are the "watchmen" of whom Isaiah speaks: "Hearken! your watchmen raise a cry, together they shout for joy." They see the Lord and raise a cry, inviting the whole nation to rejoice. But the nation itself does not see Him. However important and dazzling his coming will appear to believers. it will go unnoticed and unacknowledged by the vast majority. "To his own he came"; we all are his own because we have been fashioned and created by Him, and then regenerated in the waters of baptism. But "his own did not accept him."

Perhaps the problem is that the Lord's coming is so discreet and, at the same time, so ordinary. I am almost tempted to say "so natural." After all, hasn't man been created for this communion? Doesn't the Word exist wholly for this reunion, this felt communion of shared love? Isn't Christmas the revelation of him who is, who always has been, who always will be? So why should human beings get excited today? Isn't God always with them? Yes, God is always with them. But the tragedy is that human beings ignore him or are unaware of him. That is the source of their doubts, their torments, and their disastrous failings. Failing to know themselves truly, they fail to recognize their Lord. They are no longer capable of detecting the signs of his presence, they remain deaf to the cries of the "watchmen." And while it is true that the Jewish people have not always recognized the coming of their Messiah-Lord, can we say that the baptized who profess faith in him have really accepted and welcomed him?

We are confronted with a paradoxical question. Is it possible that the Word, through whom "all things came into being," made them only too well? Is it possible that creation is a bit too rich in power and beauty? Is it possible that man is a bit too impressed with his intelligence and his potentialities. All that seduces him to the point where he allows himself to be totally absorbed by the surface appearance of creatures and things. He is so satisfied with all this that he seems to remain outside the precincts of the authentic reality. The image of God that he bears within him and the reflected glory of the

Almighty in creation overwhelm him, so man remains closed up within these narrow boundaries. He no longer realizes that he is content with the reflection of an image, and that this illusion will be fatal to him. Enlightened by the mystery of Christmas, we can get beyond mere appearances and find the authentic reality. If we do, then we will be able to echo the words of John the Evangelist: "Of his fullness we have all had a share."

Sunday in the Octave of Christmas
FEAST OF THE HOLY FAMILY

Sir 3:2-6,12-14
Col 3:12-21
Mt 2:13-15,19-23

Christmas was just celebrated. A few days ago a couple, named Mary and Joseph, and a Child became a family. Right away the Church proposes that we celebrate the community formed by these three beings who are united by blood and the Holy Spirit. It offers them as a model for all family life today and for all societal life. That seems to be the clear lesson of the message that God offers us today.

And yet the choice of text for the Gospel is quite astonishing. It concerns the well known story of the flight into Egypt. Astrologers arrived from the east to worship the baby Jesus and to offer him their presents. They have just headed back towards home. In all likelihood one or two years have gone by since the birth of Jesus. His parents managed to find some lodging in Bethlehem, and that is where the astrologers found the family. In a dream, shortly after the departure of the astrologers, Joseph is ordered to depart for Egypt because the Child's life is in danger. He sets out right away in the middle of the night with Mary and the Child.

Tradition has often painted pictures of this scene. Mary is seated on a donkey with the Baby in her arms while Joseph leads the animal by the bridle. We have seen this scene painted on the walls of our cathedrals, pictured on traditional masterpieces, sculptured in stone.

It was a risky adventure to undertake—setting out alone at night for Egypt. No caravan would leave Bethlehem at that hour for Egypt—a journey of five or six days through the desert to reach an unknown country. Of course Joseph could count on the fact that he would be helped by the Jewish communities in Alexandria or Hierapolis when he arrived at his destination. But he might well worry about what would happen to him and his family once he settled down in Egypt. And then there would be the whole problem of returning to Israel and establishing himself there. To judge from the narrative, they had not made any firm decision about where to reside once they came back to Israel. Political reasons would lead them to Nazareth. There we have a brief summary of the Gospel story.

That is the adventure of Joseph, Mary, and Jesus which took place some time after the Child's birth and which the Church offers us today as a theme for meditation on our own family life today. It is a story of three persons, but the figure who commands our attention here is the father. It is Joseph who gets the orders, carries them out, and ultimately decides to establish himself in Nazareth. But while he holds the largest place in the story, it is not the most important place. The one who is the source of it all, the one who gvies the orders, is God himself. And the one for whom all these things are organized is Jesus. Hence everything derives from God. Joseph gets God's orders and makes sure that they are carried out for the welfare of the Child. The Child and his Mother do not step into the foreground of the story. We can assume that they followed what Joseph told them to do.

We probably do well to focus on Joseph here. He is the pivotal figure in the story—not the most important figure, as we noted above, but the figure whose role is most clearly highlighted in this first adventure that befalls the Holy Family.

Joseph is the father. He is the head whom the others obey. All that is true. But the authority exercised by him presupposes certain important preconditions.

Joseph shows up as a man who knows how to listen. In a dream he receives the message of an angel who speaks in God's name. There is no real value in trying to discuss the reality of this angel or the way in which Joseph perceived him. That does not really matter. What matters is the fact that Joseph knew God was asking something of him. The ability to hear and understand what God is saying: that is the first and foremost trait of Joseph, the father.

Next, Joseph obeys. Joseph hears the message: "*Get up, take* the child and his mother, and *flee* to Egypt. *Stay* there until I tell you otherwise." And Joseph "*got up* and *took* the child and his mother and *left* that night for Egypt." Carrying out the rest of God's command, he will remain there until God steps in again to bid him return home.

The authority of Joseph, the father of this family, is that of an intermediary. He receives God's orders and transmits them to the members of his family. This authority is a service. The goal it envisions is not self-satisfaction. One must realize that this sudden departure greatly complicates Joseph's life. His aim is to serve the Child Jesus by preserving him from a particular danger.

As far as Mary and Jesus are concerned, logic requires that they obey him strictly. Joseph is serving them. He is the intermediary between them and the Almighty. How could they not consider his orders to be absolute commands?

Such is the relationship between the members of this family which shows up in this story. We said above that the Church is presenting it to us here as the model for all societal life. But how are we to take it in that sense, since the event in question is quite singular and most likely will not happen to us? What is more, it is very rare for fathers of families or leaders of groups to have special revelations. such as the one Joseph had in today's story.

It is Paul who makes the concrete application of this story in today's Epistle, where he offers us a series of instructions about our societal and group life. We are to show kindness, humility, meekness, and patience. We are to forgive one another. Above all, we are to practice love, which binds the other virtues together and makes them perfect.

However, none of these instructions are offered gratuitously. They all rest on the example given by God himself. It would appear that when Paul wants to set guidelines for interpersonal and group relations between human beings, he appeals first to our knowledge of God and our concrete personal relations with him. If a person has experienced the pardon and tenderness of God the Father, then he will bear faithful witness to this relationship and flesh it out in his dealings with human beings.

Paul also puts great stress on our concrete acquaintance with the word of the Lord. Knowing all the richness of this word and giving praise and glory to God, we will live in an atmosphere that is the direct opposite of seeking self-satisfaction.

If we comprehended and accepted all that, how easy it would make our societal life! We would not go looking for merely "clever" solutions to our conflicts. We would not shut ourselves up in juridical categories, however necessary they may be at times. Instead we would learn the Lord's responses. Then we would try to apply them with all the love that one can show when one seeks only to serve the Lord and to avoid trying to dominate anyone else.

That is how we can interpret and appreciate the precious instructions which Paul offers us in the area of conjugal relationships and parent-child relationships.

Paul says that the wife is to be subject to her husband. These words do not sit well with modern minds. Indeed Paul has been slandered a lot because of them. But if we are careful not to isolate them from his instructions to husbands, urging them to love their wives and not to be bitter towards them, then we will find the harmony of their conplementary roles once again. This harmony is brought out very well in the story of the flight to Egypt. If either one of the two spouses fails to fulfill his or her proper role as it is indicated in today's reading, then we get disharmony and end up with a travesty of God's word.

The same holds true for relations between children and their parents. Children should pay heed in all cases, but their parents should not aggravate them. They should make an effort to express the truth always, God's truth rather than their own version of it. Otherwise we get domination by the young over their elders, which is the source of many disorders.

At the end of our reflection here, we all are directed back to ourselves. It would be absurd to put the other members of our family on trial, to use today's divine message against them. That would be the exact opposite of what the Lord expects from us. Whoever we may be, whatever our responsibilities are, we all are obliged to fill a role entrusted to us by the Lord. How do we carry it out? How well do we try to prepare and transform ourselves so that we may be able to carry it out well? These are the questions posed to us by the attitude of Joseph, who listens, understands, and then performs.

January 1
SOLEMNITY OF MARY MOTHER OF GOD

Nm 6:22-27
Gal 4:4-7
Lk 2:16-21

One week ago the birth of Jesus took place in the intimate atmosphere of a night in Bethlehem. At that time we heard the angels breaking the joyous news to the shepherds who were watching their flocks in the vicinity and urging them to go and pay their homage to their new-born Savior. So that the shepherds might recognize Jesus more easily, they offered them a specific sign: "In a manger you will find an infant wrapped in swaddling clothes." The shepherds get up immediately and head for the place indicated.

At this point we get the start of the gospel scene we have just read. The shepherds find a man and a woman, Joseph and Mary, and "the baby lying in the manger." Delighted to find that the angel's message is confirmed by their own personal investigation, the shepherds go out to speak this message to others. They themselves become messengers of the good news about Jesus, the Baby who has been born in Bethlehem and who will be a source of joy for many in Israel. And these shepherds are also the first human beings to proclaim that the young woman, Mary, is the Mother of God. Needless to say, they do not proclaim it in the accents of an erudite theologian. Their words well up from the living faith of their people, a faith nourished by the Bible and suffused with hope in the coming of the Messiah and Lord.

And everyone is astonished. Who could have imagined such a thing! And Mary herself "treasured all these things and reflected on them in her heart."

Thus the divine maternity of Mary is announced to us as well. Mary herself certainly knew everything that the shepherds had to say. They could not tell her anything new, for she had been accosted by an angel at the Annunciation and told: "The Holy Spirit will come upon you and the power of the Most High will overshadow you; hence, the holy offspring to be born will be called Son of God" (Lk 1:35). From that point on, Mary knows what is to happen and she prepares herself. Today the happening is made public by a band of shepherds who have been informed in some mysterious way by God's messengers. Mary is the mother of Jesus, and Jesus is the Son of the Most High.

What an unfathomable mystery! Mary is the mother of God. She is simultaneously the mother of her God and a faithful believer in his Son. She is simultaneously the child and the mother of God. That is the point which is brought out clearly in the gospel message.

By agreeing to be the mother of God at the Annunciation, Mary will voluntarily become a mother in the full sense of that word. She will work out the difficult balance of being a real mother without being overprotective, of being a real child of God without being absolutely servile. Failure to maintain the proper balance would not be good for the upbringing of her son.

Right around the time of Jesus' birth, the aged Simeon warns her that her role will be an extremely difficult one. She will have to maintain an almost impossible and crucifying balance between maternal love and filial docility. As Simeon predicts: "You yourself shall be pierced with a sword." It is not just that Mary will suffer the pangs of Jesus himself during his passion—the point that most commentators have deduced from Simeon's words. In addition, her own soul will be pierced and probed and divided by a sword. Apparently her two-edged relationship to Jesus—as mother and as child—will force her to harmonize contrary things; and it will be a painful process. Pierced with a sword, Mary will be totally a mother and totally a child of God. She will find peace and harmony only in unconditional, unwavering docility to the will of the Almighty. It is with good reason that we call her "Holy Mary, Mother of God." This maternity was her essential function, and it inevitably became the means of her sanctification.

Her whole life bears witness to that fact. Here we need only touch upon a few of the important moments in that life.

At the Annunciation Mary consciously and willingly accepts this maternity. When Jesus is presented in the temple, Simeon utters a startling prophetic statement about her maternity—which had already been acknowledged and proclaimed by the shepherds.

So Mary goes on to nurture and rear her son. Like all mothers, whose function does not end with the birth of their children, Mary will raise him with the help of her spouse Joseph. The child is circumcised to show clearly that he was "born under the law," as Paul puts it. And because they are motivated by the same central concern, his parents will not overlook any of the duties relating to his status as their child. They present him in the temple. They have him go on the traditional pilgrimages to the temple in Jerusalem, as all Hebrew boys of that era did. In the course of one such pilgrimage there takes place the adventure which we know so well but which seems so unlikely. Unknown to his parents, Jesus stays behind in Jerusalem. His distressed parents look for him everywhere. When they find him, Mary speaks to him as any mother in a similar situation would: "Son, why have you done this to us? You see that your father and I have been searching for you in sorrow." Here we have the mother reacting as she ought. Then her son replies, reminding her that he must be concerned with his Father's business. Mary does not understand his words, but she accepts his words as a dutiful daughter of God. With perfect docility she "kept all these things in memory" (Lk 2:51).

Later, at the wedding feast in Cana, she will approach her son with the daring and intimacy that only a loving mother can show to her now adult son. But her son will react as one who bears responsibility for the kingdom, and the mother will give way once again to the faithful daughter of God.

Soon afterwards, Jesus will start to gain attention and grow in popularity. Inevitably he will have detractors, who accuse him of casting out demons in the name of the devil himself. It is the first serious difficulty faced by Jesus. Mary hastens to him and sends word that she is there: "Your mother and your brothers and sisters are outside asking for you." Jesus' response is: "Whoever does the will of God is brother and sister and mother to me" (Mk 3:31-35). The apparent opposition between the son and his mother can only be resolved in their common fidelity to the word of God. There the two of them, purifying their personal impulses, will come together again in spiritual communion.

Finally, at the foot of the cross, Jesus is about to return to his Father. At one stroke he seems to repudiate his mother while at the same time exalting her maternal function to its loftiest grandeur. He entrusts the disciple John to his mother, and his mother to John—thus giving her another son. He detaches himself radically from her, yet without repudiating her. Here we have the creation and realization of a new maternity that is universal in scope. The mother of God inevitably was to become the mother of mankind. Constantly driven to go beyond the individuality of her son, Jesus, she finds it once again by becoming the mother of the whole Christ. But this could only come about insofar as she managed to harmonize her two roles, that of Christ's mother and that of God's child. Exclusive concentration on one of those roles would have ruled this out.

On this level of holiness, where Mary becomes the mother of all, her destiny comes very close to that of every woman who becomes a mother—and indeed to that of every believer.

Here we have one of the great paradoxes of this feast. Mary is the virgin mother of God. It is a mystery that seems to be strictly reserved to her, and it certainly was at the start. But gradually, as her specific function opens out and takes on universal dimensions, Mary becomes the first to show us what authentic maternal love is. She loves so much that she refuses to suffocate her child in an anxiety-ridden tenderness, in an overprotectiveness where the mother receives more than her child does. Throughout her son's life, from the Annunciation to his death on Calvary, Mary is the mother who never reneges, who always gets beyond herself even when she does not understand. She will endure the labors of motherhood to their furthest extreme, but she will never cease to nurture the most loving tenderness in her heart. It is through her harmonizing of these two opposing currents that the virgin Mary becomes the model for all mothers. Here we have love in all its purity.

As the year starts, the Church providentially offers us this model of love in all its fullness. The Church offers us Mary, whom some people venerate under the title, "Our Lady of Gracious Love." The message is a precious one for us, because it reminds us that Jesus has entrusted us to her. The quality of the love she lavished on Jesus is not reserved for him alone. It is ours to share. This is the first and most important bit of consolation that we get in the course of this coming year.

Moreover, the Virgin Mary helps us to establish the proper kind of relationships with those nearest to us. Today we are greatly concerned not to weigh down the liberty of others or infringe upon their fidelity to God's grace. In this context Mary teaches us how to achieve the difficult balance between a normal sense of attachment and the necessary detachment. Such balance is necessary for any kind of love that seeks to be faithful to the word of God.

SUNDAY AFTER CHRISTMAS OCTAVE

Sir 24:1-4,12-16
Eph 1:3-6,15-18
Jn 1:1-18

Once again the Church offers us the prologue of John's Gospel which we read on Christmas day. We read it again, along with the two Scriptural passages that precede it. But this time the mystery of Christmas, seemingly deepened by the absence of all surface imagery, appears to us in all its universal scope and depth. Going far beyond a mere evocation of Jesus' birth in history, the words we hear today seem to be impregnated with the whole history of the world.

Today the divine message lingers on the coming of the Lord Jesus, successively described as "Wisdom" and "the Word"; on God's predilection for man and man's reason for being in the Creator's eyes; and finally, on the way in which this destiny, inscribed in the very nature of beings, is brought to fulfillment through the presence of the Lord and through faith in him.

It is an impressive fresco. We cannot help but examine it and try to discover all the wealth it contains.

Sirach's "Wisdom" and John's "Word" existed always. They existed before time and creation. All things were made through them. When we speak of "all things," we can ponder the whole universe that science has begun to discover. There are countless constellations, and something new is revealed to us every day. Our planetary system and our earth are an infinitesimal portion of that immense whole. The distance from the earth to the moon, which required such great effort to be crossed, is insignificant in terms of the wider firmament. Its boundaries escape us, and we grow dizzy when we try to picture it for ourselves. And then there is the world of the infinitesimally small, which is equally beyond our imagination. The precise nature of its construction and its interconnections defies the investigations of even the most expert minds. And then there is the whole wondrous world of animals and plants—not to mention man, whose body is a prodigy of inventiveness, whose mind and spirit dazzles us.

Before all that, the Word existed. All things were created through Him. It is He who came to strike root "in the portion of the Lord." It is He whom the offspring of Jacob should have acknowledged, because He was their reason for being. He existed throughout those many generations so that Wisdom might dwell "in the assembly of the Most High" and sing her praises "before her own people."

Yet this event, so basic and important for the history of the world and the further evolution of creation, went unsuspected by human beings—even though they were endowed with the intelligence and perspicacity to perceive it. As the first stage of his people's history came to a close, the Lord sent a precursor named John the Baptist. He was not the Light which he knew and spoke about. That Light was believed only by a small handful of disciples. His own people—the Jewish people first of all, and the rest of humanity afterwards—were not able to truly recognize and acknowledge him. They did not go en masse to join the one who had come to gather them together and to lead them to the ultimate satisfying fulfillment of their destiny, a destiny that was difficult to achieve. That is the Wisdom which came into our midst with such an important mission and went unrecognized.

But some people did recognize Him. Some did accept Him. And they now enjoy satisfaction. Paul tells us the story from way back, starting before the creation of the world. He informs us that the creation of man was not a fortuitous occurrence at the end of some casual evolutionary process—as some biologists today would have us believe.

Paul tells us that the Father chose us from before the creation of the world. Even then he knew what he was doing. Even if man is the result of an evolutionary process, even if creation did not take place in an instant but rather took millions or billions of years, even if it is not at an end today, the fact is that man's existence ties in with a plan on the part of God. All of us have been chosen and destined by him to be his children. All of us, by virtue of our human nature itself, have been created to form an integral part of Christ and to live with the Father in filial intimacy. All this does not take place for us in such a way that we are independent of each other. Rather, it is part of the reconciliation of the whole universe into the peace of Christ.

If we want to grasp the sense and purpose of man's evolution, we cannot ignore its origin and its goal, which are recalled to us today by God's word; Now one might think that these perspectives are too distant to be concrete for us. One might feel that our day-to-day life, absorbed and confined by often vexing problems, prevents us from raising our vision to such abstract heights. But if we do not raise our vision to these heights, then our day-to-day life becomes absurd. It is limited to the purchase of a new automobile, to the preparation of a good meal, to the enjoyment of watching a television spectacular. If we do not raise our vision to those heights, then it becomes almost impossible to see any happy prospects for the individual. No sort of effort seems worthwhile, and man is degraded to the level of a producing and consuming automaton.

But suppose, on the other hand, that we do know the goal for which we were created. Suppose we know that the one for whom we were made is someone who set up his dwelling place in our midst, who spoke and acted, who informed us how we might be able to join up with him in a life-giving way and thus attain the goal that will satisfy our deepest and most urgent yearnings. If that is true, then what we have heard today becomes extraordinarily concrete and important. Christmas is all that. Its roots lie buried in the very wellsprings of life, and it leads us towards the ultimate heights of our destiny.

Paul completes the message which John gives in his

prologue. He tells us that he has "seen his glory." He, and we too, have discovered his reality, his mysterious presence that is both cosmic in its dimensions and discreet in its appearance. But this presence does not impose itself on us. Only those who have faith can detect it and follow its lead. Paul tells us that this involves an awareness or recognition of the true identity of the person named Jesus. We must be wise enough to discern the eternal Son of the Father, the incarnate Word, in the son of Mary. We must be able to see that it is Wisdom striking root among his people. This is the first impulse of faith which Paul presents today. But as soon as we recognize Jesus, the Son of God, then we must go on to accept him as such. If we do, then his work moves on towards completion: the evolution of humanity proceeds.

But faith is not a stable acquisition, which produces its effect and bears its fruits instantaneously. It is a seed that must germinate and flower in order to produce its unexpected and inexhaustible fruits. That is why Paul does more than simply express his wonder and admiration over those believers who have recognized Christ and have begun to work out their real destiny in fidelity to the Lord. He also prays that they will receive wisdom and insight "to know him clearly." They still need to undergo transformation, a transformation that results from opening up their hearts. Until the final, ultimate transformation takes place, until they get beyond the final stage of bodily death, the believers must continually renew their fidelity, their recognition of the Lord, and their submission to him.

That is what the Church has to offer us today, as it prolongs our contemplation of the Christmas mystery. Today we are in an even better position to realize that this mystery is one which concerns anyone and everyone—whether we have been convinced of the divine reality of Mary's son for a long time or are still unable to accept this message as true. Christmas concerns all human beings. It is not simply the feast of Christ's birth. It is also the feast of our own rebirth. Whether we are among those who believe that they have already been born to a real, active spiritual life or are among those who deny the reality of this mystery, we all are stimulated today to a thoroughgoing process of self-renewal through closer fidelity to our real nature.

In the Eucharistic sacrifice the Lord really offers us the means to transform ourselves and to be united more intimately with him. Let us open our minds and hearts so that his presence may seep into us, transform us, and make us authentic children of God.

January 6
EPIPHANY

Is 60:1-9
Eph 3:2-3a,5-6
Mt 2:1-12

We know that this somewhat curious word "epiphany" means "manifestation." What we celebrate today is the fact that our Lord, Jesus Christ, has come and made himself known. He is the presence of the Most High among men, and he wanted all of us to know about it. It was his wish that we all be able to approach him and receive him. Today we celebrate his desire to manifest himself to us.

This is the common message of today's three readings. In today's Epistle Paul briefly sums up what we celebrate today: "the mystery of Christ . . . now revealed by the Spirit." If we follow the journey of the astrologers step by step, as it is recounted by Matthew, we will find rich food for thought in the Lord's manifestation.

We know that Jesus was born in Bethlehem of Judea. Matthew notes this fact and adds that it was during the reign of Herod, so that the full import of the event may be appreciated.

Some astrologers show up unexpectedly from the east. Their arrival in Jerusalem must have caused a sensation. We can picture these mysterious strangers making inquiries about the birth of the "king of the Jews" and telling people that they had "observed his star at its rising." Needless to say, we would like to know what that mysterious star signified and to what astronomical observation it corresponded. Answers to such questions would give us intellectual comfort, but this is not the place for us to linger over them. The important point for us here is that these men were alerted by some sign which was compelling enough to make them set out in search of this king of the Jews. And their respect for him was such that they got together a rich store of presents to give him.

Thus God manifested himself in singular fashion to

these men who have just arrived in Jerusalem. It was an unexpected manifestation, scarcely believable and certainly alarming. "King Herod became greatly disturbed, and with him all Jerusalem." Such a cosmic manifestation would certainly trouble them because the Jews of that day regarded the stars as the loci of relatively unknown and constraining forces. The words of the newly arrived astrologers necessarily suggested that some catastrophe might be imminent.

That explains Herod's haste in summoning "all of the chief priests and scribes of the people," that is, all the doctrinal and exegetic scholars residing in Jerusalem. The foreign astrologers, who had been perspicacious enough to detect such a troubling sign, had to be satisfied as quickly as possible.

Having examined the Scriptures, the wise men of Jerusalem noticed Micah's prediction about the future glory of Bethlehem: "From you shall come a ruler who is to shepherd my people Israel." The astrologers have their answer, they start out again, and the star reappears to them.

Note that in the story we find a second manifestation of God. The first was the star, but its message was incomplete. The astrologers had to have recourse to the Scriptural knowledge of the people of Israel. The institutional hierarchy of the Israelite people, which was in charge of the storehouse of Scripture, had recourse to God's message in the prophets so that the message of the star would be complete and make sense.

The second way in which the Lord intervenes in history is embodied in the existence of his people, who were chosen to preserve and transmit his divine word. Subsequent events will show that this does not necessarily mean that his people will possess the openness of spirit required to recognize and accept unexpected signs. Indeed the people will be opposed to Christ, who is the authentic presence of God; and they will not be wise enough to see that the Scriptures which they preserve and know so well are also a living word for them. Be that as it may, in the case of the astrologers it is an instrument which God uses in order to manifest himself.

For the astrologers, the convergence of signs is what guarantees the truth. The star alone was insufficient, but it led them to the guardians of the divine word which confirmed and completed the star's message.

In like manner the Lord manifests himself to each of us in two ways, and we cannot focus on one way at the expense of the other. We discover him through the intimate personal communication of prayer and personal experiences. But we also discover him through the divine message uttered by the Church. Only the Church can offer us a proper commentary on it, no matter what one's personal character or spiritual strength may be. If we find a contradiction between these two messages spoken to us by the Lord, then either we have listened badly or we have deluded ourselves about the origin of the message. In an age such as ours, it is an important reminder for us. The fact is that we cannot go to Christ independently of the Church, that an intellectual knowledge of the whole content of divine revelation is not enough. We must possess the openness of heart that will enable us to perceive and comprehend the unexpected and always extraordinary appeals of the Lord.

As the astrologers set out again, "they were overjoyed to see the star." Thanks to this sign, they recognize the Child when they meet him. Then they offer him presents, which express their respect and their submission to the Lord.

The star, God's word, and the people's explanation of it have led the astrologers to the Child in Bethlehem. That is the set of events which Matthew narrates to highlight Christ's manifestation.

And there is a sequel to this chapter in the gospel message. Although Herod had asked the astrologers to come back and tell him where the child was, they are warned in a dream not to go back by way of Jerusalem; so they go home by a different route. Herod had not seen the star, and he would not have been able to recognize the Child because he lacked the inner enlightenment of the astrologers. But we do know that Herod wanted to eliminate this young rival, and soon he would massacre innocent babes. What the account here stresses, however, is the docility of the astrologers in obeying the message of the dream unquestioningly and the protection God lavishes on the Child. Here again we see God intervening in two ways, both directly and indirectly through men. Both methods must exist and converge in order to ensure the divine origin of the impulse.

Perusing this story of the astrologers and their journey to Jerusalem, we have received an important message for ourselves. There is the certainty that God intervenes when he chooses and in the way he chooses. But over and above that we can find reasons for rejoicing, we can strengthen our hope, and we can learn the preconditions for being able to perceive God's manifestations.

In prophesying about the glory of Jerusalem, Isaiah stresses one fact: "Darkness covers the earth, and thick clouds cover the peoples." In his letter to the Ephesians, Paul talks about the mystery "unknown to men in former ages." If we are to perceive the Lord's manifestation, the first precondition is that we realize that we are now in darkness. We have to learn and appreciate something else, but we cannot discover it solely by a well-rounded scholarly knowledge of the Scriptures. The astrologers from the east perceived the light of a star and were willing to be enlightened by someone else. We could say that they combined great curiosity with a deep humility.

From Herod and the inhabitants of Jerusalem we learn that we must be willing to accept everything that comes from the Lord. Their uneasiness made them incapable of discovering or interpreting the signs.

Finally, it is the message pronounced by the Church that enables us to verify the truth of personal signs; and it is the inner knowledge of our own personal experience which turns our knowledge of God's word into a living reality.

The story of the astrologers from the east is always relevant and pertinent. That is what we learn from our meditation today. Realizing that the Lord manifests himself to us unceasingly, let us be attentive and docile so that none of these manifestations escapes us. His light is something we need.

SUNDAY AFTER EPIPHANY BAPTISM OF JESUS

Is 42:1,4.6-7
Acts 10:34-38
Mt 3:13-17

Today we celebrate the first public manifestation of Jesus as an adult. Since Christmas we have followed Jesus through some of the events in his life. We have seen him being brought to the temple by his parents. We have seen him escaping Herod's persecution and fleeing to Egypt. We have seen his parents return with him to Nazareth. From there on we have only the story of Jesus being lost in Jerusalem at the age of twelve.

Now Jesus is around thirty years of age. The accounts of his life, which will give us a very intimate knowledge of him from here on, have been regrettably circumspect up to now. But all of these accounts are unanimous in depicting this baptism as the beginning of his "public life."

By pondering today's readings in the light of what we know about John the Baptist's baptism from elsewhere, we can come to appreciate the importance of the ceremony which Jesus chose to go through. It is the starting point for his public life. Hence it enables us to glimpse how Jesus conceives and intends to live his life from here on.

From the opening words of today's Gospel it would seem that Jesus, desiring to be baptized in the Jordan by John the Baptist, makes the journey from Galilee. John the Baptist tries to dissuade him from this, because he has some knowledge of Jesus' exceptional character. But Jesus insists, indicating that his decision is irrevocable, and then gives his reason: "We must do this if we would fulfill all of God's demands."

So Jesus wants to be baptized by John in order to fulfill all of God's demands. To understand this remark, we must realize that baptism by complete immersion in water was a very well known rite among the Jews of Christ's time. It was given to every alien who came to adopt the Hebrew religion, and some people considered it to be as important as circumcision. Baptism also had another meaning for many pious and zealous communities of Israelites—the Essenes, for example. It was the rite that marked the end of a long series of purification exercises and complete personal commitment to a life of greater fidelity to God. The baptism given by John the Baptist can be related to both of these precedents. It effected a person's affiliation with the true posterity of Abraham. Insofar as it was offered to the whole Jewish people, it entailed a person's admission of sinfulness and repentance for sin. It signified the definitive conversion of the recipient, who thus prepared himself to accept the Messiah who was to come.

Thus John's baptism was given to people who were aware of their sins, acknowledged them, and repented. In it they received the Lord's pardon; at the same time they expressed their decision to be faithful to God from then on.

We can now appreciate why John the Baptist was somewhat reluctant when Jesus presented himself for baptism. But it also enables us to get a clearer insight into Christ's outlook and approach.

What seems clear is that Jesus chooses purposely to put himself on the side of sinners. He chooses solidarity with man in all his spiritual frailty, in his repentance, his pardon, and his rehabilitation.

Jesus' way of acting highlights his desire to be in solidarity with man and reveals his whole approach to life. He will never impose himself on human beings. Designated by the Father to direct and transform man's destiny, he will do it from within. He will give impetus to a certain movement while fully respecting each man's liberty and refusing to apply constraints of any sort.

His approach is described in today's passage from the prophet Isaiah: "Not crying out, not shouting, not making his voice heard in the street." Jesus wants to be intimately associated with man in his poverty and distress. He will stimulate the revitalization of humanity by persevering faithfully in this approach. As Isaiah puts it: "He shall bring forth justice . . . A bruised reed he shall not break, and a smoldering wick he shall not quench, until he establishes justice on the earth."

Never in the future will Jesus change this basic attitude. Never will we see him dominating people. Never will he try to impose his personality or his project on others by appealing to his prestigious knowledge or to the spectacular heroism of his life. In fact, when he does perform miracles or reveal his true identity, he will usually enjoin silence on those involved. When he becomes a great popular success, almost in spite of himself, he will run away to avoid being crowned as a temporal ruler. On the other hand, the leaders of the day will lay violent hands on him when they can because they cannot tolerate his desire to "bring forth justice." They will end up plotting to destroy him. In Jesus' decision to join in fellowship with sinners and to receive baptism we can already glimpse the shadow of a cross on Calvary. Jesus himself will later talk about it as his real baptism, of which this one is only a forerunner.

This is the first and primary message of Jesus' baptism, or rather, of the desire for baptism that he displays here. But it has a sequel, which must be appreciated if we are not to distort the meaning of this scene.

Matthew tells us: "Jesus . . . came directly out of the water. Suddenly the sky opened. . . ." Apparently the Father was going to respond to Jesus' voluntary humiliation. Apparently it was necessary for Jesus to publicly affirm his solidarity with sinners so that the Father might bear witness, through his words and through his sending of the Spirit, that Jesus of Nazareth is his well beloved Son.

It is after his death on the cross that Jesus is resurrected and endowed with the imperishable life that awaits all those who believe in him. That is what is prefigured here in the sending of the Spirit and the words of the Father. We shall hear these words again at the time of the Transfiguration, another event which clearly prefigures the resurrection.

Thus everything is put plainly in Jesus' baptism, the event which inaugurates his public life. His only desire is to establish ties with the world of sinners and to embrace all those who desire conversion. This goal will lead him to the cross. The Father will come to him in the depths of his humiliation, turning the crucified Jesus into Christ and Lord. So Paul tells us many times.

As we come to the end of our meditation, we might well feel uneasy. What does that have to say to us? Well, here we can come to learn how we may encounter the Lord Jesus and how we may be able to be resurrected with him—the goals our faith strives to attain.

Jesus chooses solidarity with man in all his poverty and frailty. It is there that he awaits us. It is vain for us to vaunt our own importance before him, to seek to be worthy of his protection or his love. It is in the very depths of our own bad conscience, recognized as such, that he will meet us. It is there he will teach us to have recourse to him in order to find the road that leads to rehabilitation. By travelling with him through the path of destruction which is the inevitable consequence of our sins, we will be able to "come out" with him and to receive the Spirit that makes us sons.

The same holds true for the Church, and for all believers who sense their mission to make Jesus present to the world. They will not accomplish this mission by displaying dignified or virtuous external appearances. Like Jesus before John the Baptist, they must accept solidarity with the frailty of all human beings. Such solidarity will force them to intensify their own desire for purification and their own process of conversion.

In his baptism by John the Baptist. Jesus shows us what he wants to be, what the Father will make of him, and what road we must take in order to encounter him and communicate him to others. May the example of his humility stimulate us to accept this road—the road he later described in the beatitudes.

LENT

FIRST SUNDAY OF LENT

Gn 2:7-9;3:1-7
Rom 5:12-19
Mt 4:1-11

Last week some of you came to receive ashes, intending thereby to inaugurate the penitential season of Lent. There is no doubt that the word "penance" sounds bad to the ears of our contemporaries. It calls up images of spectacular privations and heroic mortifications. Today is the right day to get beyond these distorted images and to rediscover what authentic penance is. We can do so by trying to understand and appreciate the divine message we have heard today. It will help us to give the proper orientation to our whole Lent.

We have just heard accounts of two temptations, probably the two most famous temptations in history. The story from Genesis recounts the episode in which Adam and Eve confront the forbidden fruit. As the story of the "forbidden apple," it has become an integral part of our popular folklore. The story of Jesus' temptation in the desert is one which we read on the first Sunday of Lent each year. It is less popular, but it is also well known.

The first story recounts the success of the tempter, the second recounts his failure. And between these two readings today we have a more theological meditation by Paul, who sees in these two episodes the origin of our spiritual conflicts and who tries to help us choose aright.

Now if today's divine message enlightens us on the nature of our Lent, then we do well to see how the temptations show up, how the tempted parties reacted, and what results followed. The experience of Adam and Eve and the experience of Jesus reveal to us the elements that will constitute our own spiritual conflicts.

All three parties—Adam and Eve in the garden, Jesus in the desert—were enticed by the devil in some way that dovetailed with the conditions which surrounded them.

What is more, their temptations pushed them towards greater domination of, and closer proximity with, the whole creation which God had given to man so that he might subdue and complete it. Adam and Eve were in a paradise, as Genesis narrates quite vividly. They could make use of everything, except the fruit of one tree. The latter, however, was the most precious and valuable fruit of all. Why should there be this exception. Was it not an annoyance, as the tempter suggested? Why should they not have all the trees in the garden? And this particular one would give them even greater powers, enabling them to break through the limitations placed on their domination.

Jesus had just spent forty days fasting in the desert. He was hungry. Why not use his powers to satisfy his most pressing physical needs? Jesus is the Son of God. Why should he not experience the concrete protection of the Almighty and make use of his promises? Jesus has come to conquer the whole world for God. Why should he not do it all at once—the easy way? In the temptations each individual is approached in his or her own context and enticed to seek a more satisfying way of reaching human fulfillment.

What is most striking is the seeming good sense and logic of the temptations. It is clear that God's command does seem absurd to Adam and Eve, and that the tempter's line of argument is quite intelligent. There is no tinge of utopianism in his remarks. They sound right and appealing. The same holds true for the temptations of Jesus. They seem to be so full of good sense that they are hardly debatable.

Finally, there is a third feature in all of these temptations. They all tend to ensure autonomy and personal power to man. They all seek to "deliver" him from his dependence on God, this dependence being presented as an abusive thing unworthy of a creature seeking personal fulfillment as a human being. This holds true for the temptation in the garden of Eden and for the temptations in the desert.

Thus the temptations are similar in their method. In a manner replete with good sense, they propose to bring quick and easy improvement to a situation that has been rendered absurd by the incomprehensible arbitrariness of an authoritarian God.

Now the parties react, and it is at this point that the two stories differ. The woman pays heed to the suggestions of the tempter. She perceives their inner logicalness and is seduced by their superficial appeal. She is fascinated by the benefits she can derive from heeding them, and these benefits are far from being illusory. Jesus, on the other hand, seems to step outside the whole conflict. Over against each suggestion made by the tempter he sets the word of God. He refuses to get involved in a logic that leaves out divine revelation. This compels him to step back some distance from the proposals made to him and to compare them, not with his own personal inclinations and desires, but with the word of God. He allows the latter to pass judgment on the value of the proposals.

Then the two stories tell us the results that ensue. Here again we find consistency.

First of all, Adam and Eve, who let themselves be convinced by the reasonableness of the tempter's suggestion, get what they had been promised. "The eyes of both of them were opened," as the tempter had told them. Now they realize that they are naked and feel a need to clothe themselves. They have advanced in knowledge, as they were promised. Indeed they have gained godlike knowledge of good and evil, as they were promised. They have gotten everything they were promised. At the same time, however, they are now locked into what they have acquired. They are imprisoned in created things, in matter and time, even though their minds can achieve brilliant things in that sphere. They have everything they were promised, but they have nothing else. Hence they are shackled in an implacable bondage. They can operate within it, but they cannot free themselves from it. Instead of living to enjoy the fruits of the garden in complete liberty, they are preoccupied with making clothes: "They sewed fig leaves together and made loincloths for themselves." That in fact is how we spend the greater part of our time and energy today. It is a tradition that goes way back.

Jesus was led into the desert by the Spirit so that he might be tempted. When he was tempted, he did not decide to reason logically. Instead he let God's word judge the suggestions of the tempter. He gets very different results.

We find it somewhat embarrassing to describe the results, however. Matthew simply says: "At that the devil left him, and angels came and waited on him." We do grasp that Jesus, by not succumbing to the tempter's rational logic, is ushered into another world. In contrast to Adam and Eve, he is not imprisoned in time and the material world. Having been led into the desert by the Spirit in the first place, he remains faithful to the wishes of the Spirit by having recourse to God's word. Unlike Adam and Eve, he gives the impression that he enjoys liberty and fulfillment; but it is the liberty and plenitude of God, not of earth. Hence it can only be described in the mysterious and vague terms which the evangelist employs. Jesus will have everything he needs for his earthly life—angels will wait on him. At the same time, however, his acceptance of dependence on God will give him the liberty that is properly possessed by those who will never die; i.e., by those who are willing to be animated unendingly by the creator Spirit.

In our meditation we have discovered the persuasive power of temptations, the effects they produce if we give in to them, and the way we should handle them if we want to live in accordance with the Spirit. We must realize that the conflicts experienced by Adam, Eve, and Jesus are conflicts that we will experience more keenly during

Lent than during any other time of the year. And Paul, in today's Epistle, stresses the persistent nature of this antagonism.

We are in a better position than Adam and Eve because we have Jesus' example and his Spirit to help us. We are not in as good a position as Jesus because we are not in the desert. In concrete life things are never so clear. The conflicts surrounding our patterns of conduct are always full of ambiguity, the possible options are always an intermingled complex of good and evil. Our lenten penance will be complete and definitive only insofar as we have constant recourse to God's word, which transcends all logic and effects true harmony.

SECOND SUNDAY OF LENT

Gn 12:1-4a
2 Tm 1:8b-10
Mt 17:1-9

We have just heard two stories that seem odd, to say the least. The first deals with Abraham. God comes to him and tells him to give up everything—family, home, and regular routine—and to head out, at the age of seventy-five, for a land on the other side of the desert. If Abraham agrees to do this, then he will be the forefather of a great nation. What is more, God will bless those who bless Abraham and curse those who curse Abraham. So Abraham sets out. When Abraham arrives at his destination, he offers a sacrifice to God and God appears to him. Here we have the story of a man who is approached directly by God and who sets off on an adventure in his old age on the mere strength of God's word.

Then we have the story narrated in today's Gospel. Accompanied by three men whose names are familiar to us (Peter, James, and John), Jesus ascends a high mountain. There he becomes unrecognizable to them. He is bathed in light and converses with two men who have been dead for centuries. A phantom cloud covers the group and a mysterious voice speaks to the three dumbfounded witnesses. Then they come back down and Jesus enjoins silence on them.

Who would dare to make up such stories today? And who would dare to add the element of faith to them? Yet we are not dealing here with myths or legends. For Abraham in the first case, and for Peter, James, and John in the second case, that is the way things really happened. They did not invent anything. They were not the victims of some personal or collective illusion. They actually experienced what we have just heard.

It was a singular experience that these four men had, and it is important for us to grasp what happened to them. All four saw and heard things. All four were the object of confidential messages and promises. What was the effect on them?

The first thing that strikes us as we read these stories is the odd character of what takes place. It is so strange that it seems almost impossible to describe it in words. When the evangelist describes the transfigured Christ, he gropes for the most striking and illuminating terms. But he seems completely unsatisfied with the words he uses, as if his expressions were completely inferior to the reality. In the story of Abraham the author is even more laconic. Instead of risking an inept description, he simply says that God appeared to him; he does not try to describe him. In mentioning Jesus' conversation with Moses and Elijah, the author speaks of it in a matter-of-fact way. But Moses and Elijah have been dead for centuries. How did the apostles manage to recognize them? How did the two figures get there? Time no longer exists for Jesus or Peter or James or John. They are in a perduring present where succession and disappearance no longer affect things and beings. It is something we cannot really imagine. But it is true. Those men lived through the experience.

And here we come to what may well be the most incredible part of the whole experience. The apostles remained themselves throughout the whole happening. They found themselves in the presence of another world where time no longer exists, where matter is completely transfigured, and where the human is not operative. Yet they also remained themselves, with their human responses and reactions to the event and the impression it made on them. First of all, they felt a happiness that was complete and indescribable. They wanted to stay with Jesus, Moses, and Elijah and to set up booths for their encampment there. But later, when they hear a mysterious voice speaking to them, they are seized with a terrible fear and want to crawl for cover.

Not only did they remain human beings during the whole episode, they also felt that they themselves had received some sort of personal summons. They felt obliged to take seriously what was said to them. They realized that the event was not meant for them alone, that they had been invited to it as representatives of all the others.

Finally, there is another critical point. If the event experienced by Abraham had been an ecstatic frenzy, he would not have set out on such an uncertain journey; he would have thought better of the idea the next morning. And Jesus would not have had to enjoin silence on the three apostles if he had not felt that they were anxious to tell others about it.

These are the points we might well note about the experience reported in today's readings. Abraham and the three apostles remained human beings and reacted as such. But at the same time they were projected beyond matter and time into a world that lies far beyond their normal existence and that cannot be described by human words. What does all that mean?

Paul offers us an answer in today's Epistle. He talks about the grace of God which summons and sustains himself and Timothy, "the grace held out to us in Christ Jesus before the world began but now made manifest through the appearance of our Savior." Even before we existed, this gift of grace was already living for us. It was given to us in Jesus Christ, who was already in existence even though his appearance on the scene of human history would come much later.

In Paul's words we discover an important truth: our world, the world which we can touch and see and measure, is inhabited and sustained by an inaccessible and perduring and necessary reality which is the source of its existence and vitality. That latter reality has been made manifest to us in the human being Jesus Christ. Three of his chosen disciples have just experienced it. While remaining ordinary human beings, they have been brought into the presence of the living Lord.

Here the Transfiguration assumes its full importance and becomes astonishingly concrete. It is the fleeting and unexpected appearance of the fundamental and perduring reality of our universe. The invisible and the unbelievable are truer than the visible and the tangible. If we want to borrow a comparison from the world of nature, we could say that the Transfiguration is comparable to a sudden volcanic eruption in the midst of a flowering meadow.

Our meditation on the experiences of Abraham and the three apostles, aided by Paul's remarks in today's Epistle, has helped us to grasp the full importance of Jesus' Transfiguration. We needed to share in this vision during our own time of Lent.

For the apostles, the sense and import of this adventure is clear. Jesus had just told them about his upcoming passion and death on the cross, and he did not want their view of this happening to be distorted by a false conception of reality. He wanted to prepare them in advance to face the drama of Calvary and to grasp the true meaning of his death. So atop a mountain he lets them see who he really is and what they themselves will become when they follow him through death to resurrection.

The message for us is that which Paul gives us in today's Epistle: "Bear your share of the hardship which the gospel entails." Once again we link up with the message of last Sunday's readings. The stories about the temptation of Adam and Eve and the temptation of Jesus taught us that sin is an attempt to settle down more securely in what we have and are, and to enjoy these things more completely. Such an approach, however, closes us up in this decrepit world; everything becomes distorted and absurd. Penance, on the other hand, is loyal confidence in God's word which passes judgment on our temptations and builds up our fidelity to the Lord.

Inevitably this loyal confidence entails an uprooting. Paul tells us this and encourages us to presevere: "Bear your share of the hardship which the gospel entails." It entails uprooting because it means dependence on, and fidelity to, someone unknown. This unknown someone cannot be imagined or pictured *a priori.* He will reveal himself only in our concrete experience. The risk of discouragement is great. We will often feel that we are being urged beyond our human capabilities and that full satisfaction keeps eluding our grasp.

Today the Lord reveals the origin and end of it all. He tells us where the true and ultimate reality lies, thereby helping us to get through the world of appearances. The Transfiguration is a flash of pure light in the dark night of faith; it is the source of strength which forestalls any possible feeling of discouragement.

We all would do well to reread the account of the Transfiguration in the days ahead, letting ourselves be enveloped by the presence of the Lord.

THIRD SUNDAY OF LENT

Ex 17:3-7
Rom 5:1-2,5-8
Jn 4:5-42

Jesus is travelling through Samaria and he arrives at a village named Shechem. He has made a tiring journey and it is now close to noon. The sun is at its hottest right now. It is time for the usual midday siesta. The village proper is a short distance away. Jesus himself is alone by a well to which the village dwellers come for water. He has sent his apostles ahead to pick up supplies and he is calmly awaiting their return.

A woman comes to draw some water from the well, and a conversation starts up between her and Jesus. It starts off simply enough. Jesus is thirsty after his journey over the last few hours, but he has nothing with which to draw water from the well. So he addresses the woman: "Give me a drink."

The remark seems simple enough, but it surprises the woman. She reminds him that a Jew does not talk to a Samaritan. These joint descendants of Abraham had allowed a wall of enmity and hatred to be built up between them. They accused each other of being unfaithful to God, and each group condemned any and all contact with members of the other group. But Jesus is bold enough to speak to a Samaritan woman and to ask a service of her. To the woman Jesus now appears to be rather odd. He, a Jew, takes the liberty of breaking down the barrier between them. He speaks to a member of a despised group and tries to make himself understood.

But that is only the beginning. The conversation, which starts as a surprise, rapidly becomes completely incredible. Jesus' remarks soon seem to go far beyond the bounds of elementary common sense. Two remarks, separated by two ironic questions from the woman, will carry the conversation into unheard-of depths.

First Jesus tells the woman: "If only you recognized God's gift and who it is that is asking you for a drink, you would have asked him instead, and he would have given you living water." Quite sensibly, the woman asks him how he is going to do that since he lacks a bucket. Who does this young Jew think he is? Is he greater than the great men of old? Is he greater than their venerable ancestor, Jacob?

Jesus then goes further. The water in this particular well cannot slake a person's thirst once and for all. Its satisfaction is temporary. But he himself will give people another kind of water that will slake man's thirst once and for all. If a man drinks this water, "the water I give shall become a fountain within him, leaping up to provide eternal life." The woman senses that this water will relieve her of her daily trip to the well, so she promptly asks for some. In all likelihood she is no longer sure what the whole conversation is about. She may sense that this young Jew, who has the air of a prophet, can offer her something important. But what exactly?

How could she be sure? Jesus' words are off the beaten track. Despite the fact that John the Evangelist recounts the conversation in a pleasant fashion so that an air of simplicity and grandeur surrounds it, the fact remains that Jesus' words are disturbing to say the least. His promise goes beyond the laws governing the physical world, and we cannot find anything comparable to it in the normal round of human experience.

Jesus uses the well water as a figure and symbol of another kind of water, the water that he will give. His is the real thing, which will never disappoint people. It is the living water that will never run out. But what is it exactly? Is it real? Is it a figurative way of announcing some supernatural reality and, if so, what supernatural reality?

In today's Epistle we find a message that may help us to comprehend Christ's intriguing words. Five different times Paul refers to a gift that the Lord has given us. It is a grace that we have received, a love that has been poured into our hearts. As Paul explains it, it is the Lord who takes the initiative and heaps his favor on man.

His initiative is gratuitous and undeserved: "While we were still sinners, Christ died for us." This gratuitous initiative fills man with a hope and a forceful energy that can never disappoint us. And "we now stand" in this ever fruitful grace.

Jesus promises to give each human being a mysterious kind of water that will become a wellspring of life within him. Paul recalls the gift of the Spirit, the love that is poured out on us and that fills us beyond all our expectations. Is it not clear that the water mentioned by Jesus is an image of the Spirit of wisdom which Paul discusses and which is given to each person profusely?

That is the gift which God gives us. That is the reality embodied in every human being who is baptized and thereby garbed in Jesus Christ. How is it possible that we seem to be so poorly acquainted with it? For if it is real and true, then we would expect to see and feel it quite readily. How is it that we seem to have such a poor acquaintance with our own reality?

Today's reading from the book of Exodus answers these questions. The adventure of the Israelites in the desert is very important, in my opinion, if we are to understand ourselves and appreciate our own blindness.

The Hebrew people have crossed the Red Sea and are now in the Sinai desert. It is a place of insecurity. Nothing grows there, no edible animals live there, a person suffers greatly from thirst. It is a place where the Lord seems to be absent, where the feeling of abandonment is felt more poignantly than elsewhere. The desert is the place of "testing." The Hebrew people are thirsty. They cannot endure any more. The test is too hard. Their anger rises against the Lord, who has led them into this critical situation; and they vent this anger on Moses, their leader and prophet. It is only logical because the Lord seems to have led them into the desert only to watch them die there of thirst.

Moses prays. The Lord answers him: "Strike the rock, and the water will flow from it for the people to drink." It does flow in abundance.

Several important points strike us at this juncture. The people longed for water, but it could not be seen anywhere. That is why they were angry. God reveals his presence and pinpoints where water is—in the last place one would expect to find it. We would logically figure that they might have dug a well somewhere, or that they might find it in some secluded valley a short distance away. But no, the water comes from a rock. In response to Moses' prayer God speaks and acts and gives him what he seeks, but He does it in his own way. He gives him water in a spot where we would not expect to find it.

We all are looking for the sources of life-giving water. We all desire the gift of the Spirit, the love that has been "poured out." We look for these things where we feel we are most likely to find them—in the things we like to do most or in the nicest parts of our being and character. But perhaps they are to be found where we least expect them. Like the water in the desert, they may be located in the rocklike recesses of our hard, rebellious hearts. Perhaps we should let the Lord strike our hearts as Moses struck the rock in the desert, thereby revealing the treasures of love which God himself has stored there.

Last Sunday we celebrated the Transfiguration. For a moment Jesus showed himself to us in all his perduring reality, stripping away the temporary mask of the earthly man and revealing himself as the resurrected man.

Today Jesus speaks to the Samaritan woman in tones that are both charming and mysterious, revealing to us who and what we really are. With the help of today's other two readings, we have come to appreciate the import of his words. Now we know ourselves as the beings which God intended us to be, and we can readily follow Jesus' conversation with the Samaritan woman. We realize that a God who shares his Spirit with all the effervescence of an inexhaustible font of water is not to be found in one specific place or another, does not depend on magic rites or the influence of some person. Such a God gives each person full knowledge of himself because He "is Spirit, and those who worship him must worship him in Spirit and truth."

So we are once again immersed in the spirit of Lent, the season which we entered a couple of weeks ago. At the Easter Vigil service, a certain number of catechumens will receive baptism. We can readily see that today's message is related to them in a special way. Most of us have already received baptism. But the gray pall of daily routine and spiritual stagnation may well have petrified our hearts anew, turning them into rocks in the desert. The source of living water remains present, but it cannot flow out; we have clogged up all the outlets. Yet it remains a bubbling source of invigorating and life-giving water.

Today's gracious gift is the revelation of who and what we truly are. We are invited to be persuaded of that reality, and then to be bold enough to have recourse to it.

FOURTH SUNDAY OF LENT

1 Sm 16:1b,6-7,10-13a
Eph 5:8-14
Jn 9:1-41

We have just listened to a long story recounted in Saint John's Gospel: Jesus' cure of the man who had been blind from birth. We also know that John reports very few of Jesus' miracles—only seven, in fact. They are carefully chosen and narrated at length in order to spell out some specific message of importance regarding the person or activity of Jesus. Hence this account of the cure of a blind man and the reactions to it is very precious. It has many things to tell us and, insofar as it is situated here in Lent close to the upcoming paschal events, it has many concrete applications.

One figure holds center stage in this story. He provokes and intrigues people by his actions. He steps in to explain the sense and meaning of things. The figure is Christ. Everyone else will react as best he or she can in the face of the unexpected happening. So let us try to follow the story step by step.

Jesus is leaving the Temple in the company of his disciples. At the entrance they come upon a beggar, a man who has been blind from birth. The apostles are intrigued by the man. They ask Jesus whether his blindness is due to his own personal sin or to that of his parents. Jesus replies that the man is there for a reason, and he gives the key to everything that will ensue: The man was born blind "to let God's works show forth in him." Then he talks about the one whom God has sent and who must perform his task while he still has time in the world.

Then we have a curious scene. Jesus spits on the ground, makes mud, anoints the eyes of the blind man, and sends him off to wash his eyes in the pool of Siloam —that is, the pool of "the one who has been sent."

Jesus' words and actions may seem bizarre, but we can be sure that they are not accidental or haphazard. First of all, we recall the story of man's creation in Genesis, where God forms man out of clay (Gn 2:7). Jesus, who had just said that the beggar was blind so that God could manifest his glory through his intermediary, presents himself as the emissary who is carying on the work of creation that was begun long ago but is not yet completed. From his very first words here, Jesus presents himself as the envoy of the Creator. He re-enacts the same gestures to cure a human being whose infirmity is symbolic of a deeper lack.

The gospel account then dwells at length on the reactions of other people. Bewilderment and confusion overtake them, for they all knew the blind man. He has been blind since birth, he has begged daily at the entrance of the Temple, but now suddenly he can see. Is it really he? Stunned by the transformation, his neighbors cannot agree. The matter is so serious that the man is brought to the authorities. Their judgment will clear up everything or, at the very least, it will ease everyone's mind. The authorities question him. He repeats the story he had already told others. Everyone is perplexed. The person who healed him could not be from God because he did the healing on the Sabbath; he did not observe the Law. The parents of the blind man are summoned. They recognize and acknowledge their son, but they will not volunteer any further information. The blind man is recalled. He sticks to his story. With a mixture of boldness and irony he continues to maintain that the one who healed him simply must come from God. The authorities can hardly put up with such a man, so they finally kick him out.

Throughout all this hubbub of activity and discussion, argument and counter-argument, everyone has been speaking of Jesus but no one has bothered to call him to the scene. He remains unknown and mysterious to everyone. The cured man displayed a great deal of courage before the authorities, but he confined his remarks to what he knew at first hand. He could not come to any more solid conclusion than the others could.

At this point Jesus comes looking for him. Once again it is Jesus who takes the initiative. It would seem that human beings cannot advance in their knowledge if they are left to themselves. The work entailed in making further progress is too onerous for them; they do not have the courage to undertake it on their own. So Jesus returns to the man who has been cured of his blindness and lets him know who he is. The blind man prostrates himself before him: "I do believe, Lord."

The story of the blind man ends here. He had an infirmity, he experienced Jesus' power, and he then believed in his word. But Jesus' further statements complement the opening words of the story and give universal scope to it. He speaks in paradoxical terms, but the overall context makes the meaning clear to us: "I came into this world to divide it, to make the sightless see and the seeing blind." Rather than a calm process of evolution, some great transformation and re-ordering of things is to take place.

Some human beings do not see, they know it, and they feel that they cannot be healed. The blind beggar in the gospel story is their symbolic representative. Jesus restored the integral use of his human faculties to the blind man in the story. He does the same for any human being who is aware of his personal ignorance and his own inner darkness; he brings such a person the inner light that is true knowledge. He enables him to discern and know what truly is and to disregard mere superficial appearances.

But there are other human beings who think they see. They are not aware of any blindness. What they already know is enough for them; they desire nothing else. They are closed up in their present knowledge and awareness, they will not go any further. Gradually they become impervious to everything that the Lord might want them to discover some day.

Here we seem to hear echoes of God's words to the

prophet Samuel: "Not as man sees does God see, because man sees the appearance but the Lord looks into the heart." And the story goes on to show that God must intervene before Samuel is able to discover David, the man selected to govern the nation. Quite logically, then, Jesus now concludes with these words: " 'But we see,' you say, and your sin remains." How could he possibly cure the blindness of someone who thinks he sees and knows everything, who refrains from seeking his aid or even refuses it outright?

We have meditated on this story at great length because it seemed worthwhile to follow it step by step. In it the person of Jesus and his work—or more specifically, his mission—took center stage and assumed great importance. Jesus reveals himself to us through his statements, his actions, and the personal experience of the man who was cured in the pool of Siloam.

From the very start of the story Jesus shows up as the emissary of the omnipotent Creator. He is entrusted with the task of carrying on creation. To be more exact, he is charged with the task of carrying creation to a new stage, of bringing it over a threshold which lies beyond the power and capacity of the creature itself. It is as if creation in general, and mankind in particular, were inevitably intended for a destiny which their limitations prevented them from discovering and achieving without the intervention of God himself. But in this process of intervention, the activity of the Lord would still be subject to man's liberty. Insofar as man chooses to shut himself up within himself, to focus wholly on his own satisfaction, he ends up an accursed creature and the Lord will not be able to do anything for him.

The account does not simply depict Jesus as the one sent by the Father to effect this transformation in man. It also spells out how Jesus will do it. Other gospel accounts will develop complementary aspects of the same theme. The account under consideration here depicts Jesus bringing light to man. Jesus enables man to get beyond the level of surface appearances and to perceive the real heart of reality. By nature man's view is limited; his faculties of perception lack the necessary sharpness. The blind man of today's Gospel symbolizes a humanity blind to itself, its Lord, and its true destiny, and forced to have recourse to "the light" in order to achieve its "uprightness": i.e., its fulfillment.

Is that not the aim that will be achieved in the paschal feasts? Is that not the goal for which Lent has been preparing us? That is certainly what Paul tells us, the baptized, in today's Epistle. As he points out, the baptized have benefited from Christ's light. Hence their way of life should dovetail with this light. They should reject the works of darkness and carry out the works of light. But Paul, and we too, realize full well that the finest outbursts of generosity can succumb to slumber. So he offers us a timely reminder in this time of Lent: "Awake, O sleeper, arise from the dead, and Christ will give you light."

FIFTH SUNDAY OF LENT

Ez 37:12-14
Rom 8:8-11
Jn 11:1-45

Last Sunday we listened to John's account of one of Jesus' miracles; the cure of the man who had been blind from birth. We tried to meditate on that account together, and we learned from it that Christ is the one who brings us light.

Today we hear the story of an even more well-known miracle: the resurrection of Lazarus. With the help of the other two readings, we shall try to discover the most important points that the Lord wishes to reveal to us today.

Lazarus, who lives in Bethany, is seriously ill. Bethany lies on the eastern slope of the Mount of Olives. Jesus has just been informed of Lazarus' illness. Contrary to all expectation, he does not make any effort to hasten to see his friend. He is content to make a simple statement: "This sickness is not to end in death; rather it is for God's glory." We heard a similar statement regarding the blind man at the entrance of the Temple in last week's Gospel, and so we have an inkling that this is no ordinary event. Once again we are going to be the beneficiaries of an important revelation.

Two days later Jesus leaves the place where he has been staying and sets out for Bethany. By the time he gets there, Lazarus has been in the tomb for four days already. Jesus meets his two sisters, Martha and Mary, and urges them to have trust in him: "I am the resurrection and the life . . . whoever is alive and believes in me will never die." He has them bring him to the tomb of Lazarus and orders the stone removed from the entrance. Then he speaks in a loud voice: "Lazarus, come out!" The dead man walks out, still wrapped in linen strips and his shroud. That is a brief summary of the miracle that Jesus wrought in today's narrative.

It is important for us to take careful note of Jesus' demeanor throughout this episode. If we do this, we will be able to grasp what is at stake in the resurrection of Lazarus.

From the very start of the story it is quite evident that Jesus lets Lazarus die. Indeed he carefully avoids going to visit his dying friend and deliberately puts off his trip to Bethany until Lazarus has been dead four days. Jesus himself explains why. As he sees it, it is important that people know that Lazarus is really dead. If there were any doubt on that score, the point he intended to make would be of little value. Jesus says: "This sickness . . . is for God's glory, that through it the Son of God may be glorified." And later he adds: "Lazarus is dead. For your sakes I am glad I was not there." The mysterious glory in question is spelled out for Martha: "I am the resurrection and the life: whoever believes in me, though he should die, will come to life; and whoever is alive and believes in me will never die." Jesus really possesses the power to communicate immortality. In the prayer which precedes Lazarus' resurrection, he thanks his Father for it: "Father, I thank you for having heard me." So Jesus knows he possesses this power even before Lazarus comes forth from his tomb.

But even though all the glory of Jesus Christ is clearly evident, and even though he is thoroughly convinced that he possesses the power to restore Lazarus to life, it seems that Jesus' human tenderness remains very sensitive and vulnerable—so much so that he seems bereft of the very capabilities he claims to have. Three times the evangelist alludes to Jesus' human feelings. Jesus is "moved by the deepest emotions." He "began to weep" and was "troubled in spirit." A great deal of affection is evident in his dealings with Martha and Mary. Even as he offers them encouragement, his very presence clearly manifests his solidarity with them in their time of trial. So evident is this to the onlookers that they ask quite logically: "Why could he not have done something to stop this man from dying?"

It is as if a battle were raging inside Jesus. Or perhaps it would be better to say that two different feelings were at work. He has an absolute faith in the power that the Father has given him. But it in no way diminishes his solidarity with human beings, his suffering at the death of a dear friend.

Moreover, it is clear that the resurrection of Lazarus will not fulfill the promise given to Martha: "Whoever believes in me . . . will never die." When Lazarus comes forth from the tomb, he is still garbed in the accouterments of death. When Jesus rises from the dead, he will be completely free from death and its trappings. Lazarus, we know, will soon die again. And we also know that he has really died once already. So we can say that Jesus did not give Lazarus the imperishable life which he promised to Martha for all those who believe in him. He wanted to show that he was capable of granting it by giving a dazzling performance. He wanted everyone to believe him, and that is why he prays to his Father as he does.

What he really shows people is his mastery over death. He shows them that death has no power against him, that it cannot stand against him. His tears at the scene may not have been over the death of his friend, but rather over the suffering it caused his family and friends. Lazarus was truly dead, and Jesus exerted his power over death. He commands death as he chooses. As far as eternal life is concerned, that is for those who will believe in him when he has risen from the dead.

In all likelihood the resurrection of Lazarus prefigures and announces Jesus' own resurrection. But his own resurrection will be so different that it would be wiser not to focus too much on that particular point.

When we speak of Jesus as the master over death, we link up with the passage in Ezechiel which we heard today. It is a prophecy, and at the same time a promise which God makes to his people. God will open the tombs: "Then you shall know that I am the Lord." People will come to recognize the Lord by experiencing his mastery over death. It is in this sense that Jesus prays to his

Father. He wants the resurrection of Lazarus to spark our faith.

Ezechiel goes on to promise the Spirit of the Lord. His Spirit will revivify his people and restore them to their true home. That brings us back to Paul's words to the Romans in today's Epistle. They are very important because they will enable us to apply the Gospel message to our concrete, everyday life.

Our present state seems to be dominated by two contradictory forces: the death of the body and the life of the Spirit. In fact Paul makes an astonishing statement: "The body is indeed dead." Remember that he is addressing believers who have already been buried and resurrected with Christ in baptism. What is clear to Paul is that the baptized person has already agreed to die to the flesh in order to live by the Spirit. This Spirit within him is the life of the resurrected one which God gives us. The ambiguity of our condition results from two facts. On the one hand, the Spirit tends to give us a life and a way of acting that befits one who has been resurrected. On the other hand the flesh, though dead already, continues to demand that we serve it. It closes man up in its world as if it were the only lasting and satisfying world. The believer will always be tempted to give way to the flesh, to succumb to its power of death, to prefer it over the uncertain, disquieting power of the Spirit which comes to us unknown from God.

In the resurrection of Lazarus Jesus presents himself as the master over death, the one who destroys death and its power. If a person trusts in the Lord and possesses the Spirit of the risen one, then death loses all its destructive power over him.

If this be true, then the direct and practical consequences are quite considerable. And they are also quite evident, are they not? The basic temptation facing us is the inclination to regard what is dead as living, to invest too much interest in the body, to allow it to become more and more important in a world of human beings who have not yet been resurrected into the kingdom. Our great temptation is our hunger to exist for ourselves and for others. With such an outlook, we find that death takes on the aspect of a powerful enemy because it is an obstacle to our personal fulfillment, our continuing existence, and our full development. But if we believe, with Saint Paul, that "all died," then our death will already seem to be a reality of the bygone past. Jesus, the master of death. has already liberated us from it. He has resurrected us with himself through the sharing of his Spirit. If we express the matter that way, then we are very close to the words of Saint Paul himself.

The same point will be brought home on another occasion when we deal with the beatitudes. The whole Christian idiom dealing with death to self does not refer to self-defeat or self-destruction. It tells us that we must come to know and accept what is truly real, that we must choose what is certain and substantial over that which is already destroyed—even though surface appearances may give us the very opposite impression.

In this Mass we will repeat the sacrifice of Christ. May our participation in his mystery of death and resurrection increase our faith in him and help us to live in accordance with his life-giving Spirit.

PALM SUNDAY

Is 50:4-7
Phil 2:6-11
Mt 26:14-27,66

The lengthy account of Christ's passion, which we know so well, has just unfolded the incredible story of Jesus' last hours on this earth. We have accompanied Jesus from Judas' sordid bargain with the high priests to his own burial in a tomb. We have witnessed his last evening with his apostles, his agony in Gethsemane, the desertion of his friends, his condemnation by the high priest and Pilate, his crucifixion, and his death after three hours of agony. With its poignant simplicity and its highly evocative images, the story always leaves us deeply moved. We want to appreciate it fully so as not to add to the infamy it details.

To help us appreciate it properly, the Church provides us with two other valuable readings: a prophecy of Isaiah, and a spiritual exposition by Saint Paul. Let us try to grasp the message of these two readings first. Then we will see how they were fulfilled in the passion of Jesus, and we will have a better grasp of its import.

The prophet Isaiah offers us the portrait of a man who hears and heeds the word of his God. Rather than presenting a psychological portrait of such a person or an intellectual study of what that means, Isaiah focuses on the servant. He describes what goes on in his soul and the external consequences that inevitably follow.

Every morning the servant awakens to God's word. It instructs him so that he becomes capable of speaking "to the weary." But the servant is content to let himself be instructed. He does not seek anything else. He does not sneak away or rebel. He heeds and accepts the lessons taught by God's word, and he has full confidence in it. For this reason he becomes the prey of other people who seek power or possessions. They cannot tolerate the servant who allows himself to be motivated by God's word.

Following the logic of his option, the servant refuses to protect himself. He exposes himself to the blows and outrages perpetrated by others. In short, the servant refuses to "exist." He refuses to regard himself as someone important, so he accepts their apparent domination. At the same time, however, he refuses to let the presence of God's word in him to be whittled away. He refuses to let anything else but God's word make an impact on him. He puts up with insults, outrages, and all sorts of aggression, but he does not allow his fidelity to be undermined. While he shows complete docility, he will not allow these attacks from outside to infringe upon the power of God's word. And so he can truly say: "I have set my face like flint."

There we have the servant depicted by Isaiah. He accepts God's word and all the consequences it may entail. He puts up with all the persecutions which may result from his option, but he will not tolerate any infringement on the presence of God's word.

In his letter to the Philippians Paul picks up the same theme. But his treatment of it is even more concrete because the events predicted by Isaiah some 700 years earlier have now found fulfillment in the person of Jesus. Hence Paul describes the behavior of Christ.

As Paul describes it, Jesus too refuses to win by the use of force. He chooses to accept humiliation and self-privation. He becomes like man in every respect, "obediently accepting even death, death on a cross." Out of obedience he accepts the worst humiliation and degradation. Note that the "obedience" described by Paul has much the same consequences as the "hearing" of God's word described by Isaiah. When we realize that our word "obedience" comes from a Latin word *obedire,* and that the root meaning of the latter is "hearing" also (*ob-audire*), we are struck by the similarity of the messages transmitted to us by Isaiah and Paul. We cannot hear God's word without heeding it and allowing it to grow within us. We cannot obey without knowing the thinking of another and conforming to it. To realize that hearing and obeying are two words which express the same basic reality is to draw a step closer to true wisdom.

While Paul begins by picking up the description of Isaiah, he goes much further. He shows us the sense and meaning of this hearing, this obedience, this abasement: "Because of this, God highly exalted him." Because of this self-abasement, he will be recognized and honored by all creatures. They will confer the supreme title on him, the name that surpasses every name. They will see their Lord in him. But here again it will not follow the human way of doing things. Jesus was dispossessed and humiliated. When he is recognized as the Lord, he will be dispossessed once again "to the glory of God the Father." His abasement and humiliation had freed him from any and every possible satisfaction, and his recognition as Lord will not bring any self-satisfaction to him either. It will be offered for the glory of God and the salvation of others.

That is the message we were given just before we read the passion account in Saint Matthew's Gospel. In the light of this message we can examine the gospel narrative and find the most important points highlighted by the evangelist to show that Jesus is the one who fulfills the prophecies.

First of all, we note the conscious awareness of Jesus. He is cognizant of everything that is happening and he desires it. He knows who is going to betray him and when the betrayal will take place. He knows that he is supposed to offer himself up completely for others, and he does this in the Eucharist. He refuses to be defended when he is arrested in the garden. He says the only words that need be said to bring on condemnation, and he knows what he is doing. Everything, including the price to be paid for man's ransom, was spelled out beforehand; and Jesus willed it all. He says: "The Son of Man is to be handed over to the power of evil men." He knows what all that means, and he decides that it is to be done. He is not the unconscious victims of events that get beyond him. He is one who voluntarily fulfills God's word.

The prophet Isaiah spoke of outrages, but we cannot help but be struck by the plethora of sadistic actions taken against Jesus—for no good reason. He is condemned by the high priest. Right away people begin to spit in his face and beat him. Why? Pilate's soldiers do the same right after the grotesque judgment is passed. Why? Then there are the taunts, which grow even more brutal while he is hanging on the cross. Why? Finally, there is the excessive suspicion of the priests, who send soldiers to guard the tomb of a dead man. Why? These monstrous cruelties go far beyond what was necessary. One would think that those involved would have tried to tone them down. Why did they display such cruel and senseless barbarity? It appears to be an outpouring of vengeance designed to expiate something that is totally intolerable. Is it not man's reaction to God's word?

There is a third point which is very important. We must note it if we want to grasp the whole thrust of the account. Saint Matthew puts great stress on the whole cosmic dimension of Jesus' death. As we read his account, we sense a violent tremor that is universal in scope. Darkness covers the landscape, the veil of the temple is rent, rocks split asunder, tombs open up, and the dead rise. Remember what Jesus said to the Pharisees when they tried to still the shouts of the crowd upon his triumphal entry into Jerusalem: "If they were to keep silence, I tell you the very stones would cry out" (Lk 19:40). Now, at the moment of Jesus' death, a violent tremor shakes all of creation and fills the spectators with terror. It is after that violent upheaval of the cosmos that the whole theme of rehabilitation, described by Paul in today's Epistle, can begin to unfold.

And we also have the observation of one foreign spectator at the crucifixion. A Roman centurion, charged with the task of making sure that the sentence is carried out, is quick to respond to what he has witnessed: "Clearly this was the Son of God." His words foreshadow Paul's prediction that every tongue will proclaim that "Jesus Christ is Lord." Overwhelmed by the execution, the behavior of Jesus, and the universal upheaval, he has a revelation of who and what Christ is.

And so we have come to see the message that God has given us this Palm Sunday. Its concrete import for us is readily apparent.

With the death of Jesus, something new began in the world. It marked the turning point of our history, the great opening up to another world. The tearing of the veil of the Temple clearly symbolizes all this.

But this opening up, this transformation of man, is not effected by the dominating sway of some powerful king or some undisputed leader. It is the work of a suffering servant who went to the limits of self-surrender, who refused any and all domination, who did not pat himself on the back, who obliterated any yearning for continued existence. By so doing, he inaugurates this new mode of being which Saint Paul will call "the new man."

If that is the path chosen by Christ and followed to the very end, then we know to what extent we truly resemble him. When we hear and obey, then we diminish and begin to live. When we defend ourselves within or against others, then we no longer are listening or heeding; we are then on the pathway that leads to real, definitive death. Real death does not exist for Christ. For him death is a transition, a Passover.

HOLY THURSDAY

Ex 12:1-8,11-14
1 Cor 11:23-26
Jn 13:1-15

The Mass of Holy Thursday is the first ceremony in the cycle of paschal feasts. We all know the importance of this evening party, which inaugurates the great events that mark the end of Jesus' life. In order to help us comprehend the content and importance of this festive evening, the Church has presented two stories to us. And situated between them is a reminder of what the Eucharist is and an indication of its dynamic power.

The first story comes from the book of Exodus. It recounts the inauguration of the first Hebrew Passover. While the Jewish people are still enslaved in Egypt, they are visited by their God; He delivers them from the hands of the Egyptians. The second story deals with the evening of Holy Thursday, presenting the wondrous and awesome scene of Jesus washing the feet of his disciples. In so doing, he bears witness to his love for them and gives them a concrete example of it. In between these two stories we hear Paul's account of the institution of the Eucharist.

On the surface we would seem to be dealing with three very different messages that apparently have very little to do with each other. But if we ponder these texts and correlate their messages, we will find a marvelous fresco unfolding before our eyes.

The fact is that two principal themes show up in the reading from the book of Exodus. It deals with a meal and a passage. In his letter, Paul recalls the meal instituted by Christ. And in today's Gospel Saint John tells the story of Christ washing the feet of his disciples, focusing on Jesus' passover. If we take a close look at these three accounts, we will see that the events are intimately linked with each other.

In great detail the book of Exodus reports the orders which God gives to Moses and his brother Aaron. These orders are to be carried out by the whole Hebrew people, and the penalty for disregarding them will be death. They center around a meal.

Each family must select a young lamb or kid, kill it at a designated time, cook it in a certain way, smear its blood on the door posts and lintel, and then eat it rather hurriedly as if they were travellers on a journey. In the words of Exodus: "You shall eat like those who are in flight." That is the meal, and it is to be repeated with the same rites annually. It is to be the great meal of Passover.

To us who are far removed in time from that event, and whose outlook has been shaped by an age-old Christian culture, the story seems quite nice but at the same time a bit bizarre. In the Israelite tradition, however, it is the most important rite of all, and it symbolizes the promises made by God and the fidelity of his people to him. Indeed it is the rite that Jesus is celebrating this Thursday evening with his disciples.

Paul tells us what took place that evening between Jesus and his friends, just before he was arrested. Once again it has to do with a meal: "This is my body, which is for you." Jesus then takes a cup and says: "This cup is the new covenant in my blood." Of his own volition Jesus transforms bread and wine, turning them into his body and blood. He gives himself to his apostles, exhorting them to repeat the same words and gestures later on. Such is the meal which Jesus shares with his disciples.

The first meal, the one which the Jewish people ate just before they were liberated from Egypt, was a figure of the meal Jesus ate with his disciples. But in the latter case the paschal lamb is Christ himself, who had been pointed out by John the Baptist as "the Lamb of God who takes away the sin of the world" (Jn 1:29).

In Paul's epistle, as in the book of Exodus, the food is designated by God himself. The eating of it is to be repeated as a sign of the covenant and a symbol of the people's fidelity. But the differences between the two meals are considerable. The food is now the Lord himself. The covenant is no longer the same. Now there is a new covenant, and Paul spells out its novel aspect: "Every time . . . you eat this bread and drink this cup, you proclaim the death of the Lord until he comes." Apparently the presence of the Lord in the Eucharist means that those who consume it are obliged to be dedicated to the proclamation of a disappearance and a return.

In reality this meal is the life-giving impregnation of humanity by the living God. The Lord becomes such an integral part of humanity that now he shares one life with mankind. This life will develop and grow step by step, reaching its definitive fulfillment when Christ returns at the end of time. All that was announced in God's first covenant with the Jewish people and fulfilled in the person of Christ. Now we shall examine just how it was fulfilled in the concrete.

At the start we noted that the stories also had to do with a passover. The book of Exodus tells us: "It is the Passover of the Lord." And God himself says: "I will go through Egypt." The feast of Passover is the day when the Lord passes through, and his passover is necessary and important for his people. At this point they are captives in Egypt. The Lord's passover will mean their deliverance from Egypt. The text of Exodus is quite clear on this matter. When the Lord passes over Egypt, he will sow death in every family of Egypt. The first-born child in every house in Egypt will be killed—except those in the houses of the Hebrews who have smeared their door posts and lintel with the blood of the lamb.

Thus the Lord's passover is a passover that demolishes and slays those who are opposed to his plans. And it is also a passover which spares, protects, saves, and vivifies those who are loyal to Him. That is the great happening which remains a basic memory for the Israelite nation: in his passover, God delivered them from bondage in Egypt.

Today's Gospel is also suffused with a passover, the passover of Jesus. Several times John tells us that the hour had come for Jesus to pass over from this world to his Father. Jesus had come from God to dwell among men; now he is returning to God. John notes the last moments of this new passover by God, in the person of Jesus, by telling us the story of the washing of the apostles' feet. Framed in the context of such a solemn moment, it takes on great importance. In passing over, the God of Exodus slew the Egyptians and freed his people. In passing over, God in Jesus Christ washed the feet of sinful men; that is precisely what the apostles, including Judas, were.

What a difference there is between the two passovers! Yet the more we consider the matter, the more we see that the difference lies in the manner rather than in the reality. Jesus himself explains why he washed the feet of his apostles: "If I washed your feet—I who am Teacher and Lord—then you must wash each other's feet. What I just did was to give you an example." Washing people's feet was a duty for slaves and servants. It was so intolerable an obligation that Peter reacted strongly and refused at first to let Jesus wash his feet. But Peter, like we, will be obliged to do the same in turn.

In Jesus it is God who passes over and washes men's feet. In Jesus it is God who continues to demolish, just as he demolished the first-born of Egypt. But now he demolishes those who believe in him. If they wish to be his disciples, they are now urged to strip themselves of pride and of their fierce desire to live for themselves. They must now live in a totally different and unheard-of way—as the servants and slaves of others. They must live a life of love rather than a life of self-contentment.

Reading the message of Jesus today, one may find him more alluring than the God who passed over Egypt in the Exodus. But the fact is that Jesus, too, proposes a death, a death brought about by a conversion to love. The distinction between human beings is no longer between those who have the blood of the lamb on their doorposts and those who do not. It is now between those who choose to have a share in Christ's passage and those who do not. God passes over in Christ, but he also causes all human beings to pass through purification in order to arrive at love.

Here the passover of God, announced in the Exodus, finds its fulfillment in Christ.

At this point the meal and the passover are one and the same reality. The reception of Christ's body and blood gives the believer the light and the energy he needs to kill his hunger for a self-centered existence and to open up to the love which the Lord Jesus never ceases to impart to him.

We shall now participate in the Eucharistic meal. Let us welcome the Lord and allow him to transform us. It is our Passover to the kingdom of God, where peace and joy pervade everything. It will become a reality to the extent that we surrender to the power of Christ.

EASTER SEASON

Easter Vigil:
Gn 1:1-2:2
Rom 6:3-11
Mt 28:1-10

EASTER

Easter Sunday:
Acts 10:34a,37-43
1 Cor 5:6b-8
Mt 28:1-10

We all know what it means to suffer the death of a loved one, to lose someone we held very dear. We all have lost someone whose existence seemed very necessary to us because the ties of mutual affection kept growing deeper all the time. It may have been our father or mother, a spouse or a child, a deeply loved friend or a highly respected teacher.

We took part in this person's funeral service, and we were deeply shaken. We may even have felt that our faith could not possibly survive this test, because we were torn up inside. Since we could not bear the suffering, we may have returned to the graveside a few days later in order to get closer to the presence and memory of the deceased person.

That is what took place with the two women in today's Gospel. "As the first day of the week was dawning, Mary Magdalene came with the other Mary to inspect the tomb." Jesus was their friend, their teacher, their Lord. Envious of his influence, the authorities had passed him off as an agitator and a blasphemer and seen to it that he was condemned to death. So he died, ignominiously crucified before a snarling mob of people. The two women had been present at all that. Displaying their usual reserve, the gospel accounts do not say anything about their inner anguish; but we can readily imagine it.

The crucifixion had taken place on Friday. Saturday was the Sabbath day, and they were forbidden to go out. But the two women rushed to the tomb as soon as Sunday dawned. They fully realize the guards have been posted, but it does not frighten them. When a person has lost his most precious and indispensable friend, he no longer has anything to fear; he can take any risk. But the two women have a stupefying experience, and we can picture what it must have been like for them. Suppose we were to go to the tomb of a close friend as they did. Suddenly the earth shakes beneath our feet and an angel rolls away the stone that is blocking the entrance to the tomb. The angel is radiant and resplendent, impossible to describe, but he is really there. The guards, overcome with fear, fall to the ground in a faint.

That is what these two women saw when they arrived at the tomb on Easter morning. They were ordinary women who loved Jesus of Nazareth. They themselves had helped to bury him. Now they come to the tomb and an angel says: "I know you are looking for Jesus the crucified, but he is not here. He has been raised, exactly as he promised. . . . Then go quickly and tell his disciples."

Then, as if to persuade them that the news is true, Jesus himself comes to meet them. They recognize him right away. It is a strange happening, indeed. It is not surprising that the disciples find it somewhat difficult to believe the story that the women tell them. It is not surprising that Thomas wants to see and touch Christ's wounds. It is, in fact, unbelievable for the most part. Even when we are suffering from excruciating grief over the death of a loved one, we are not really prepared to find them alive again three days later amid such spectacular circumstances.

And yet this story is true. That is what happened on the morning of Easter. Jesus, who died on the cross on Friday and was buried shortly afterwards, came back to life and appeared to his friends on Sunday morning.

A radical overturning of our whole human history has just taken place. We appreciate this fact insofar as we advert to our own personal experience of death. We realize that the consequences of this Easter event are enormous and incalculable.

The Scriptural passages we have just heard are inspired commentaries on the event. They provide us with some insight into it. We discover that a new kind of existence begins here for man. It is an existence that cannot come to an end, an existence that is immortal and untouchable. It is as if some sort of implacable, underground vitality had just surfaced from the innermost depths of humanity and would gradually flood everything, imposing itself on man's existence irresistibly.

Today's message tells us that. It says that the risen Lord destroys death. Instead of annihilating man, death now becomes the instrument for man's transformation and fulfillment. What is more, this resurrection means victory over sin.

But it is just a little too simple to say that Jesus' resurrection destroys death. We are forced to admit that today, almost two thousand years after his resurrection, people still die just as they did then. Biological death has not been eliminated. It is the most normal and natural thing in the world. It is our attitude towards death that is abnormal now. We are readily inclined to regard it as an absurd and desperate ending. It makes us afraid because it projects us into the unknown; it drives us to despair because it separates us from those who are dear to us. When Scripture tells us that death has been destroyed, it means that death's malignant and unsupportable power has been destroyed, it means that the malignant and intolerable power we attribute to it does not really exist. Rising today, Jesus proves that. And he also serves as the model of the life which follows our passage through death.

In terms of our human experience, of course, we cannot possibly imagine what that means; nor can we give satisfactory descriptions of the life that will follow this passover. And since it all escapes our observation and our predictive power, we are greatly tempted to conclude that it does not exist. This is often the end result of a scientific outlook, which so reduces our knowledge to the measurable that it concludes that nothing exists above or beyond its own observations.

But there are many moments in life when our heeding of the Lord seems to lead us into some sort of impasse. There seems to be no way out. Then the Lord comes along and creates an opening where we could never have imagined one.

Do you recall the story recounted in the book of Exodus? The Hebrews had been freed from Egypt by the Lord and were on their way to the promised land. They arrive at the Red Sea with the armies of the Pharaoh right behind them. There seem to be only two options open to them: to drown in the sea or to let the Egyptian armies massacre them. It is all over; they have lost. But no, God provides an unexpected solution which saves them from certain catastrophe. So it is in our life. Certain solutions escape our notice, and we are readily inclined to think that God's word only leads to absurdities. Such is the case today in connection with life beyond death, with man's passage from this world to another. Its existence is proved today by Jesus.

If the risen Jesus destroys death, then he also exerts dominion over sin. Many times during Lent we have discovered what sin is. It is not so much moral culpability resulting from the failure to follow some regulation. Rather, it has shown up as our complicity in our incapacity to achieve our inevitable destiny. In short, it is a refusal to move beyond this world, a desire to stay firmly entrenched in the ongoing flow of worldly power and worldly security. Despite the repeated failure of these things over the centuries, they still continue to beguile human beings.

Jesus' resurrection defuses the seductive power of earthly success by proving that authentic life is not to be found in holding on to this earth but in faithfully following the Spirit. The first course is subject to the inevitable law of destruction. The second course fashions the new man, who lives in the justice and love of our heavenly Father.

It is in this sense that Jesus' resurrection destroys the power of sin. It does so, even though man clings tenaciously to his illusions and is not easily roused from his unconsciousness. The conquest of sin is a reality as of that Easter morning when the ground shook, when the Son of Mary rose from his tomb to life and appeared to the two enraptured women.

Christ's resurrection is the strange and power-laden event that destroys death and overcomes sin. That is what God's word has just told us. And this event is not some remote, inaccessible reality. It is in us, it is real day-to-day life for us. That is the whole meaning of our baptism, which associates us intimately with Jesus' death and gives us a share in his resurrection. The association and participation is so clearcut to the believer that his whole life on earth is a lengthy process of mutation in which death is already an accomplished fact and the life of the new man wells up gradually from the depths of his being until it floods him entirely.

We can readily understand why the Church has each Christian renew his or her baptismal promises during the Easter season. We must act in accordance with the energy of the risen Christ, which is thus communicated and renewed in us. If we do, then the joy of Easter will be our most solid source of comfort.

SECOND SUNDAY OF EASTER

Acts 2:42-47
1 Pt 1:3-9
Jn 20:19-31

In the course of today's Mass, the priest prays that God will revive our faith in the resurrection of Jesus; and today's readings have been selected by the Church to help us have faith. As John says in his Gospel: "Jesus performed many other signs as well, signs not recorded here . . . but these have been recorded to help you believe that Jesus is the Messiah, the Son of God." So we shall try to grasp what God tells us today about faith.

The very way in which Jesus and his disciples meet on Easter evening is a lesson in itself. The apostles are fearful of the Jews. They have been deeply upset by the events of the last few days. In all likelihood they are afraid that the hostility which rose against Jesus will be directed in turn against them. So they have bolted the doors in the place where they are gathered. The same day, to be sure, some people brought reports that Jesus, alive, had appeared to them. But how can one believe them? The apostles are paralyzed by fear; their hopes have crumbled. Although people found the tomb empty, no attempt has been made to find out what happened to Jesus' body.

Suddenly "Jesus came and stood before them. . . . He showed them his hands and his side. At the sight of the Lord, the disciples rejoiced." It is Jesus who takes the initiative. Alive, he appears to them. He, Jesus of Nazareth, who was crucified, died, and was buried, is really alive. The apostles do not ask for any explanation; they know it is he. Later they will tell Thomas: "We have seen the Lord!" They know it is true. It is not a collective illusion or a phantom apparition.

The apostles know that Jesus is alive. They have seen and recognized Him. In the course of time all human beings, like them, will be invited to recognize and acknowledge him through the sacraments of reconciliation entrusted to them by the Lord. That is what we are told in today's selection from the letter of Peter: "Praised be the God and Father of our Lord Jesus Christ, he who in his great mercy gave us new birth . . . from the resurrection of Jesus Christ." As we know, this regeneration—in which we experience the living presence of the resurrected Christ—is effected by the sacrament of baptism and renewed each time we receive the sacrament of penance.

For the apostles visited by Jesus on Easter evening, and for every believer living in the world since then, faith is the work of the Lord. It is he who sparks it. It is he who gives it solidity and permanence.

In taking this initiative, the Lord accomplishes his plan. We discover this plan to the extent that faith seeps deeper and deeper into us. As today's Epistle says: "Although you have never seen him, you love him, and without seeing you now believe in him, and rejoice with inexpressible joy touched with glory, because you are achieving faith's goal, your salvation."

Communicated by the Lord, faith is an energy that enables us to live above and beyond biological death and that gives us dominion over a powerful enemy known as "the world." Jesus once told his disciples: "Take courage! I have overcome the world" (Jn 16:33). It is important to realize that this term has two different meanings in the gospel stories. Sometimes it refers to all of creation, or to the whole human family, which God loves and wishes to save. At other times it refers to a powerful force that hates and opposes God and his Christ. Obviously it is the latter sense that is meant here. Faith is victorious over "the world," over a powerful force that tries to bring the Lord's work to nought. How it seeks to do this is something that we must grasp clearly.

We get a first glimmer of the world's *modus operandi* in Thomas' reaction to the news reported by the other apostles. Since the resurrection of Jesus is an unlikely and troublesome thing, there is a strong temptation to reject it. Following this lead, Thomas limits his real world and his cognitive possibilities to criteria based on concrete personal experience and his own powers of reflection. He will deny anything and everything that he cannot touch, feel, measure, or understand. That is the spirit of the world, leading him back to his own self and refusing to accept anything it cannot contain.

Faith always entails risk, precisely insofar as it does not impose itself on us by virtue of our personal experience or a reasoning process. It is difficult for us all, as it was for Thomas. It teaches us things that hardly seem likely. It presupposes a constant overcoming of ourselves, because it is a progressive growth and movement towards someone who will always be an unknown, who will always be surprising to us.

Not only is faith a risk, it is also a struggle and a battle. There is nothing comfortable about it. It will create and fashion us anew, but only at the price of our destruction. The world over which faith is victorious is not some abstract or remote reality. It is we ourselves—with our fears and anxieties, our vain thoughts and jealousies, our attachments and lusts. And since we are all pretty much alike, we justify each other, we assuage each other's consciences about disobeying God's word, we encourage each other in saying no to faith. The "world" is also the collective mentality of society. It pervades us so much that we come to feel we would be denying our own ideas, or dissociating ourselves from others, or destroying something necessary and precious, if we were to think or live differently from our group.

Fortunately, Jesus has foreseen our predicament: "If you find that the world hates you, know it has hated me before you" (Jn 15:18). The "world" is that portion of our selves which is impervious to everything that surpasses its experience and its rational knowledge. It is also the collective mentality which refuses to undergo destruction for the sake of resurrection, which compels us to exclude faith. This being so, it is inevitable that a part of our selves should hate our faith, and that the same opposition should come from others too, including believers. That is the paradox we must understand if we do not want to be surprised by the inner repercussions of our attachment to the Lord, if we want to be faithful to this attachment.

Faith destroys us. To put it better, it is our acceptance of the destruction which God effects in us in order to conform us to the image of the risen Christ. Hence it must be intolerable to us at times. What is more, we live in a relationship with other believers, who are also being destroyed and refashioned by their faith. Hence it is inevitable that they will sometimes feel a tinge of vertigo, that they will be tempted to say no to faith and to see others as responsible for their inner torments. Quite logically, then, the work of establishing relationships of deep and solid peace will be most difficult in communities of believers; yet it is there that they are most necessary, because they become a sign of man's total acceptance of the work of renewal being carried on by the risen Christ.

That is how we are to interpret today's account of the life of the primitive community in Jerusalem. Their oneness in praising God, breaking bread, and sharing their goods is the sign of their acceptance of the resurrection. It might take us too long to show, on the basis of that account, that true human relationships and real interpersonal communication can only be effected between men and women who have accepted the Lord's resurrection and its consequences for their personal lives. It is such an important point that we shall return to it soon. Right now it is enough to indicate that these relationships are rooted in faith in the resurrection of Jesus.

Today we are forewarned and encouraged at the same time. Faith is difficult because it hurls us into the realm of the unlikely and improbable. It is painful because it snatches the world away from us. But it is also strong in the power of the Spirit, and victorious in Christ's victory over the world and death.

In today's Gospel Jesus tells us three times over: "Peace be with you." Living in the world and the Church today, with all their troubles and violence and injustice, let us bask in the peace of the risen Christ. We ourselves will be artisans of peace to the extent that faith has overcome the world in ourselves.

THIRD SUNDAY OF EASTER

Acts 2:14,22-28
1 Pt 1:17-21
Lk 24:13-35

We almost feel a tinge of envy as we listen to the story of the two men who were on their way to Emmaus that Sunday after Christ's death. Yet they themselves were quite sad and discouraged when they left Jerusalem. It was evening, and nightfall would soon arrive. They had to travel about seven miles to the west of Jerusalem. In all likelihood they stayed on in Jerusalem as long as they could. But finally it was time to leave; they had no choice. So they started on their journey, discussing and arguing about all that had happened in Jerusalem in recent days and also about the rumors that had started to circulate that very morning.

A stranger joins them enroute. They must have looked very sad because he asks them why they look so downhearted. The two travellers are astonished at the stranger's ignorance, for all Jerusalem is in an uproar. They tell him about the events in question: "All those things that had to do with Jesus of Nazareth, a prophet powerful in word and deed in the eyes of God and all the people; how our chief priests and leaders delivered him up to be condemned to death, and crucified him. We were hoping that he was the one who would set Israel free. Besides all this, today, the third day since these things happened, some women of our group have just brought us some astonishing news. They were at the tomb before dawn and failed to find his body, but returned with the tale that they had seen a vision of angels who declared he was alive. Some of our number went to the tomb and found it to be just as the women said; but him they did not see."

Their words say it all, in calm and sorrowful tones. They had nourished a profound hope; now there was nothing left. They had been disciples, but they had not been important disciples. They were not among the twelve that Jesus had invited to share the passover meal on the preceding Thursday. They were not among those whom Jesus had singled out and trained to be the founders of the future Church. They were part of the larger following who firmly believed in Jesus, attended him hopefully, and helped him as best they could. We get the feeling that they kept up with the news and remained in close contact with the twelve apostles. Now they are deeply disappointed, and with good reason.

But what happened to them is hardly very singular. It was true then, and it has remained true right up to our own day. Many people put their hope in the Lord or in the Church, only to be disappointed by the turn of events. Christ was supposed to give them hope and peace. The Church is supposed to provide them with certainty and truly convincing examples. None of that happens. The Lord is not recognized and acknowledged by all men of good will, and the Church is disappointing inasmuch as the conduct of some of its members is downright scandalous. Things definitely do not work out as expected, and our hope is often disappointed.

Then the mysterious traveller speaks to them. They did not yet recognize him: "They were restrained from recognizing him." After all, how can we recognize or even see someone when sadness covers us like a pall? We become a blob of sorrow, completely blind to everything and everyone outside. That is what had happened to these two men.

Their travelling companion reproaches them gently: "How slow you are to believe all that the prophets have announced!" It is indeed true that the Spirit is prompt to give its adherence, but the flesh and the heart are slow to undergo conversion. It is not easy for them to acquire reactions that are automatically in harmony with God's revelation. So the stranger explains the Scriptures to them: "Beginning, then, with Moses and all the prophets, he interpreted for them every passage of Scripture which referred to him." It must have been a lively and detailed account of the Hebrew people's whole history: their many wanderings, their alternating periods of fidelity and betrayal, the long string of divine interventions in the course of succeeding generations. For when dramatic or blessed events occurred, God sent prophets to enlighten their beclouded faith and to promise that a savior would come one day to re-establish peace and harmony over everything. We can readily imagine that the stranger reminded them of the passages dealing with the suffering servant, and of the psalms, even as Peter reminded the Jews who were attracted by the noise of the Spirit's appearance on Pentecost. In short, in his powerful evocation of twelve centuries of history the stranger showed them that the Messiah had to suffer in order to "enter into his glory."

In the course of this meditation, which brought them back into the company of their great ancestors in the faith—all the prophets and wise men who sang the praises of the omnipotent God—they could begin to glimpse that things were not as desperate as they had seemed. Perhaps things were in order after all, even though it was not the order they would have established on their own. Their faith in Jesus of Nazareth began to bloom once again. Perhaps it was not impossible that he was the Savior after all! Their faith may not have been rational. It may have operated outside a certain brand of human logic, the logic in which they had been imprisoned and which had led them to deep sadness. But at least their faith no longer seemed absurd. In fact it was entirely consistent with a view or preview of the world that derived from God and that had been announced gradually by prophets and wise men over the course of twelve hundred years.

But it was getting late now. Darkness was falling. The stranger wishes to withdraw, but they urge him to stay with them. It is good being with him. His words warm them up, set them on fire.

So the stranger remains with them, and a troubling scene takes place. They sit down to eat. The stranger takes bread, blesses it, breaks it, and gives it to them:

"With that their eyes were opened and they recognized him; whereupon he vanished from their sight."

We recognize the gestures at once, of course. We immediately recall the words that Jesus spoke on Holy Thursday when he instituted the Eucharist for his twelve apostles. On the evening of Easter he does the same thing again for these two disciples. But remember that these two men were not present on Holy Thursday, so they did not recognize him because he reiterated the same words and gestures. It was something else that enabled them to recognize him. Today's reading from Peter's letter suggests that it was: "You were delivered . . . by Christ's blood . . . the blood of a spotless, unblemished lamb."

Their eyes, which had been closed up to then and could not recognize him, were opened by their reception of the bread which the Lord had transformed. They were suddenly capable of an extra dose of discernment or perspicacity. Not only was their discernment better, they also rediscovered a modicum of energy that seemed to have slipped away from them. They immediately make the return trip to Jerusalem, anxious to report the good news to the other disciples. Once back in Jerusalem they learn that Simon Peter has seen him too.

The story of these travellers is important for us. Their distress is ours to some extent, and their sadness is not unknown to us. By the end of the story sadness and distress have given way to new-found hope and joy. In the meantime they had listened to God's word and gradually come to a different outlook. They had expanded their knowledge and come to realize that there was another way to approach and evaluate reality. Then they receive Food which transformed them: they now saw and immediately acted upon their new vision. If one is to believe in the crucified, vanquished, risen Christ, one must be willing to step outside his own logic, to immerse himself in God's plan, and to let himself be revitalized by it. Then it becomes very simple.

When we pondered the story of the apostle Thomas

last Sunday, we saw that faith entails a permanent risk because it projects us into the realm of the non-rational and the surprising. Thus it is almost unbearable, because there is an interior backlash to the transformations it effects. Today we learn that our faith in the risen Christ can be non-rational without being absurd, improbable without being off-base. Man need only be willing to be guided by the Lord. Then all his cognitive faculties are integrated into a broader reality and bolstered by a support he could never have imagined. Last Sunday our struggle against the world seemed to be a tragic one, and it is in a real sense. Viewing it in the light of the transformation wrought in the two travellers by the Breaking of Bread, however, we see it as the painful but tolerable price we must pay if we want to participate personally in the life of the risen Christ. As today's second reading puts it: "It is through him that you are believers in God, the God who raised him from the dead and gave him glory. Your faith and hope, then, are centered in God."

FOURTH SUNDAY OF EASTER

Acts 2:14a,36-41
1 Pt 2:20b-25
Jn 10:1-10

Since Easter God's word to us has been wholly oriented around our faith in the resurrection of Jesus Christ. We have made an effort to be docile and attentive to God's word, and we have thus discovered the principal features of our faith and their repercussions in each of us.

Today's message is designed to help us progress further in our attachment to the Lord. The passage from Acts show us three thousand people expressing a desire to be baptized after listening to Peter. The Epistle and Gospel seek to convince us that if the Lord's resurrection is an historical reality, then it is a necessary part of man's destiny and demands a concrete attitude from each and every individual.

Saint John recounts a parable, a comparison made by Jesus. Parables are rare in his Gospel, so we can assume that he attaches particular importance to it. This parable is addressed to the Pharisees; it is an important message aimed at them. Note also that it is not a story, as many of the gospel parables are. Instead it is a series of statements that are replete with good sense. We shall be able to draw a lesson from them.

We are invited to consider the life of a sheepfold. Even though we probably have no experiential knowledge about raising sheep, we can easily picture the scene Jesus portrays and grasp the point of his remarks.

The sheepfold has only one gate. If a person does not enter by this gate, if he climbs in some other way, then he is an evildoer. The true shepherd, on the other hand, enters by the gate; it is not opened to anyone else. The true shepherd speaks to his sheep, and they recognize his voice. He leads them out and they follow him readily, which would not be the case if he were a stranger.

That is the comparison drawn by Jesus. Remember that it is addressed to the Pharisees. They are men who claim to guide others in the name of the Lord. Moreover, they are very jealous of Jesus, who is wiping out their spiritual authority. A serious conflict of influence exists between them and him. Yet they do not seem to grasp the rather obvious allusions of the parable. Jesus must explain them to his listeners.

To do that, he is content to elucidate one term of the comparison. Where does he, Jesus, fit in? Once that point is clear, everything else can be explained by a simple process of deduction.

Here he is not the legitimate shepherd, as John will indicate that he is elsewhere in his Gospel. He says here: "I am the sheepgate." It is by passing through the gate that the sheep enter, leave, and find their food. And he goes on: "Whoever enters through me will be safe. He will go in and out, and find pasture."

Thus, in a single stroke, he elevates the debate to a different level. We would have expected him to set himself over against the Pharisees on a parallel line: i.e., they are the evildoers who climb over the walls whereas he is the true shepherd who comes through the gate. But no, he is the gate, and he does not exclude anyone from salvation: "I came that they might have life and have it to the full." He does not exclude even the Pharisees, who spurn him.

His exclusive role in communicating salvation could not possibly be stated more clearly. All the others, who came before him, are brigands and thieves. And he insists: "The thief comes only to steal and slaughter and destroy."

That is the first part of today's message. It is directed to those who see him as a competitor who will have to be knocked down to size some day. Jesus tells them that he is the only gateway to whatever salvation is possible and that all must be willing to pass through him. No one enjoys the privilege of being dispensed from this requirement—not even those who seem to enjoy spiritual authority or competence in the community of believers.

It is an important and critical teaching. Are we truly convinced that there is no other guide or teacher or passageway for man except Christ? Christians who would dare to proclaim that today would almost feel embarrassed. They would have the impression that they were giving themselves special privileges or prerogatives vis-a-vis other human beings. They are almost ashamed of their faith in Jesus Christ in their desire for a misconstrued ecumenism or an off-balance form of tolerance, and in the atmosphere of general confusion that surrounds values. Don't we say that all religions are of equal value; that all doctrines and churches are legitimate so long as they are sincere? There is no doubt that this kind of universal accommodation is quite convenient for everyone concerned. It justifies the behavior of the believer who lets others go their own way. It justifies others, dispensing them from further search.

The Lord is quite clear in what he says to us today. There are not several gateways to salvation. One cannot choose between several possible passageways. There is only one truth: himself. Any and all others exist and have value only insofar as they lead to him and derive from him. Christ is the one and only "sheepgate," for sure. But what are the characteristics of this unique "sheepgate"? How are we to recognize it, so that we can be faithful to him? Today's other two readings answer these questions.

The answer can be summed up in two words: choose, persevere. In today's reading from Acts, Peter says: "Save yourself from this generation which has gone astray." And he also says: "You must reform and be baptized, each one of you, in the name of Jesus Christ."

As Peter sees it, the mentality of the world and faith in Christ are incompatible. They radically differ in their knowledge of man, and they propose radically different programs.

The world offers happiness and self-fulfillment to man in a process of improvement that is achieved through increasing his knowledge, developing his potential capacities, and advancing his technical skills. Efficiency and profitability are the principles underlying his conduct.

Jesus and his apostles, and after them the Church, present baptism: that is, a new birth achieved by being immersed in Christ's death in order to rise with him. That does not signify a rejection or demeaning of human values. But it does not signify their exaltation either. They are both useful and inadequate, necessary and fragile. They should be developed, but not served slavishly. They must be subordinated to something else. In the first place, they are necessarily marked by time and therefore bear the seed of their own death. Secondly, they are limited to the dimensions of humanity, and therefore are open to, and drawn towards, the divine.

Choosing to be baptized is accepting to die with Christ in order to be created anew with him and through him. It presupposes choosing, of course. But it also assumes that one will persevere to the end, and Peter tells us what that means exactly: "If you put up with suffering for doing what is right, this is acceptable in God's eyes. It was for this you were called, since Christ suffered for you."

There we have the central message in today's reading from the first letter of Peter. It tells us what it means in the concrete to live as a baptized person who has chosen to pursue the consequences of his baptism to the very end, to pass through the "sheepgate" that is Christ.

There is no doubt that we must do what is good. Peter does not distinguish between several different types of good. We can readily grasp what he means: do everything you should do, and everything you can do, in any area whatsoever. But then, "put up with suffering for doing what is right." There is where we give expression to the logic of baptism, to the reality of death present in every human being and every human work. We run counter to the logic of baptism and the demand of the "sheepgate" when we cling tenaciously to the profit derived from our efforts, to pride in some work that was particularly difficult or generous-hearted, to the esteem we win from others or the honors that accrue to us, to comfortable entrenchment in what we have done or achieved.

That is the lesson which Peter draws from the example of Jesus, the just man who was completely loving and who died on the cross. That is what the word "persevere" means in the idiom of the gospel. We must persevere in love and in doing good, spurning any lure of profit. If we do, then we will gradually discover that what we are doing is something given to us by the Lord in order to serve all; that he expects us to be willing to become resurrected beings in turn by continually accepting death, which is the price we must pay for resurrection.

As we know, the sacrifice of the Mass is a participation in Christ's death and resurrection. Let us associate ourselves with the mystery that is renewed there, so that the Lord may effect in us the renewal for which we long.

FIFTH SUNDAY OF EASTER

Acts 6:1-7
1 Pt 2:4-9
Jn 14:1-12

On the first few Sundays of the Easter season the Church has persuaded us of the reality of the Lord's resurrection. Last Sunday we came to see, in a more concrete and precise way, what our personal integration into that mystery entailed. Today the message is reiterated in an even more profound way. But instead of showing us its applications to our individual lives, it points up the applications of the mystery to our life in the community of believers.

The words of Jesus we hear today are part of the colloquy he held with his apostles on the evening of Holy Thursday. He had just instituted the Eucharist and made them the first priests of his Church. During the course of the few hours that precede his arrest in the garden of Gethsemane, he will hold his last conversation with them and bequeathe to them his spiritual testament. We hear a few fragments of that conversation today.

Right away Jesus tells them about his imminent departure. In his Father's house there are many mansions. Jesus is returning there to prepare a place for them. Later he will come back to look for his apostles and to conduct them there, so that they may all be reunited with him in his Father's house. Jesus concludes: "You know the way that leads where I go." The apostles seem to have a hard time understanding him. Thomas voices their perplexity: "Lord . . . we do not know where you are going. How can we know the way?" Whereupon Jesus utters the central phrase in his whole discourse here. It is the well known statement in which he tells us the role we are to give him in our personal lives: "I am the way, and the truth, and the life." Mysterious language it is indeed. How can a man claim to be a road to be followed? How can a man equate himself with truth? How can a man propose himself as the source of life-giving energy? His language is definitely queer, and he himself uses the rest of his colloquy to comment further on his statement.

"I am the way," he says. And he goes on to explain: "No one comes to the Father but through me." Last Sunday we heard him say: "I am the sheepgate." At that time we learned that Jesus was presenting himself as the one and only passageway leading into the kingdom.

"I am the truth," he says. And he goes on to explain: "If you really knew me, you would know my Father also." He is the perfect expression of the Father because, as he puts it, "I am in the Father and the Father is in me." If one has come to know him, if one has observed his actions and grasped his outlook, if one has savored the quality of his wisdom, then one has also come to know the Father in the same ways.

"I am the life," he says. And he explains: "From this point on you know him; you have seen him." The point seems to be that one experiences the presence of the Father to the extent that he accepts and welcomes Christ.

All this reiterates the same message we heard last week, when Jesus depicted himself as the sheepgate. If man is to be sure of his destiny, then he simply must know Christ, share in his work, and be docile to his message. Moreover, in today's discourse Jesus lays claim to an exclusive role. He is the only way, the only truth, the only life. This way of expressing the matter can well pose considerable problems for us with respect to other religions. It is even possible that we cannot yet tie in this teaching satisfactorily with a real respect for the value of other religions. But our inability to reconcile different truths should not prompt us to call these truths into question. Instead it should stimulate us to gain an ever deeper understanding of them. That is the way to bring them into overall harmony.

In any case, today's Epistle goes even further in affirming the necessary role of Christ in our attainment of our destiny.

The Epistle picks up the message of the Gospel and expresses it in terms of another image, that of the "cornerstone." Jesus is the cornerstone, "an approved stone, and precious. He who puts his faith in it shall not be shaken." Then the author goes on to indicate that the fate of each individual depends on his acceptance or rejection of this stone, for the construction and solidity of an edifice depends on the cornerstone.

For those who do not believe, it is "an obstacle and a stumbling stone." Those who reject the Lord will inevitably be destroyed. Those who accept him, on the other hand, will pass "from darkness into his marvelous light." They will become "a chosen race, a royal priesthood, a holy nation, a people he claims for his own," to proclaim his glorious works. Such is the destiny of those who choose Christ as the way, the truth, and the life, as the "cornerstone" of their existence.

We must acknowledge the fact that such language has a curious ring today. It appears to echo an intolerable triumphalism that was rightly condemned by Vatican II. Not only is it psychologically intolerable, it also seems to be quite unreasonable. "A chosen race, a royal priesthood, a holy nation": it seems foolish and ridiculous to apply such terms to a Church whose influence, importance, and effective force is steadily diminishing in no small measure. How can one dare apply these epithets to a Christian community which is an infinitesimal minority in the world—viewed suspiciously by many, very unsure of itself, and ever tempted to adapt its faith and its behavior to the standards of the prevailing materialism?

This language can indeed be criticized if we take it as a description of the Church as the latter appears to an outside observer. But it is not so astonishing if it is an expression of our faith and our hope in the Church. The Church could hardly have had more allure when the first letter of Peter was written—back in the days of Roman rule.

Every baptized person and every community of believers—whatever their failings may be—is on the road to resurrection in Christ and possesses the Spirit. The Spirit is working on them to bring about their transformation. For this reason they deserve infinite respect from us. The epithets of today's Epistle may seem strange to us because we do not regard the Church with the eyes of faith. To the eyes of faith, change does not necessarily mean progress and the firm maintenance of certain attitudes does not necessarily mean fidelity. The eyes of faith are wise enough to glimpse God's Spirit at work—destroying the old man and fashioning the new man.

But the viewpoint of faith is not to be identified with mere idealism. It is a concrete reality, where the most lofty mystical forces are incarnated in concrete, specific human questions.

If we have faith in the spiritual reality of the Church, that does not prevent us from realizing that its concrete incarnation is often less than glorious. With a few notable exceptions, the Church is a community of sinners who are as vain, as wicked, as self-centered, and as materialistic as their contemporaries. That fact is well attested in today's selection from Acts: The disciples "who spoke Greek complained that their widows were being neglected in the daily distribution of food, as compared with the widows of those who spoke Hebrew." Side remarks such as these tell us much about the human pettiness and partisanship that was already evident in the primitive Church. We are all too readily inclined to picture that early Christian community as a paragon of perfect charity.

The problems were so great that the twelve apostles were compelled to get together and examine matters. They came to realize that they could not keep tabs on everything, that their priesthood obliged them to give priority to the preaching of God's word. They solved the problem by enlisting the help of deacons.

This suggests to us that the normal life of a believing community will inevitably entail some pettiness and conflict. The latter will always astonish us, and they may even be quite scandalous at times. But there is a way to deal with them. If we accept them in the context of faith and rely on the help of the Spirit, they can become a means of purification. They can help us to make further progress in evangelical charity insofar as we agree to review our conduct together and to be docile to the Spirit.

Once again today we learn the importance of our personal adherence to Christ, who is the way, the truth, and the life. We learn that this adherence is verified in our membership in the Church, where fraternal charity is difficult but also fruitful. May our ready acceptance of these lessons mirror the life of the early Church, where "the word of God continued to spread."

SIXTH SUNDAY OF EASTER

Acts 8:5-8,14-17
1 Pt 3:15-18
Jn 14:15-21

Once again we hear parts of Jesus' colloquy with his apostles during the Last Supper. Today he tells us more concretely how his presence will continue even though he is soon to depart. Jesus proclaims the coming of "another Paraclete." Then he stipulates the conditions which the apostles must fulfill in order to receive this Paraclete, and spells out the repercussions of his coming. It is a message of considerable importance for us. With the help of today's other two readings, it will prepare us for the feast of Pentecost and stipulate the conditions underlying spiritual progress.

Jesus promises to send the "Paraclete." The word is not current in our language. It is a transliteration of a Greek word, *parakleton,* which basically means "called to the aid of." We could translate it as "helper" or "advocate." Jesus speaks of "another" Paraclete." He himself was the first paraclete, as it were. The one who will be sent to the apostles will help them to know the Lord Jesus better. He will reveal and defend Christ in the heart of the believer. He will intensify the loving communion between Jesus and his faithful followers, and between the believers themselves. In the carrying on of Jesus work, in the expansion of the kingdom, and in the maintenance of the individual's fidelity, the Paraclete will show up as the light and strength which the Father sends to human beings and which they cannot do without.

Hence it is not surprising that Jesus tries to impress upon us the importance of his Spirit's presence. And we can see why he spells out the conditions we must meet in order to receive the Spirit.

From the account in Acts we learn that the first condition for receiving the Spirit is acknowledgment of Jesus Christ. Philip enters Samaria and talks about Jesus. Huge crowds gather to listen to him, and they see the signs that accompany his words: possessed people are exorcised, sick people are cured. The "good news" is indeed being proclaimed to them.

Knowledge of Christ's power in operation for the people of Samaria is just as necessary for the apostles who are listening to his colloquy: "I will not leave you orphaned. . . . A little while now and the world will see me no more; but you see me as one who has life, and you will have life." Soon Jesus will be arrested, condemned, and put to death on the cross. Then the world will see him no longer. He will have finished his first earthly passage and men of mortal flesh will not be able to see him any more. One will have to possess a certain kind of life in order to be able to see him still—the life of the risen Jesus which will be shared with his apostles. At the same time that Jesus promises the Spirit will come after his own departure, he also gives them a sign which will enable them to believe in this promise: his apostles will be able to see him even after he has died and disappeared from the world. Knowledge and sight of the risen Christ is the sign that will enable them to believe in the coming of the Spirit.

This first fact, important as it may be for the apostles, will not suffice. Jesus imposes another condition that is intimately tied up with the previous one: You will receive the Spirit "if you love me and obey the command I give you." Fidelity to his command is a prerequisite for his own plea to the Father regarding the sending of the Spirit. This is an important point, and it is confirmed by today's other two readings. It is because the people of Samaria have accepted God's word that Peter and John go to lay their hands on them and communicate the Spirit to them. The author of today's Epistle goes even further in writing to the faithful. They must be fully faithful to the holiness of Christ. They must worship him in their hearts and pattern themselves after his conduct. If need be, they must be willing to follow him in making the supreme sacrifice: "Christ died for sins once for all, the just man for the sake of the unjust." If a person wants to receive the Spirit of Jesus, then clearly he must first know and love Jesus. From this knowledge there must spring a thoroughgoing obedience to Christ's command, no matter how risky or tragic the consequences may be. We must remember that Jesus "was given life in the realm of the spirit" only after he "was put to death insofar as fleshly existence goes."

It seems very harsh, but it is logical. Does a person really long for the Spirit of God if his fidelity to God contains reservations, if he tries to have his cake and eat it too by relying both on wordly security and surrender to the Lord? The two are incompatible. If a person does not realize this and accept the consequences, then he is incapable of receiving the Spirit. As Jesus puts it: "No man can serve two masters" (Mt 6:24).

There is one final precondition which flows from the two mentioned above (i.e., knowledge and obedience). One must no longer be of the world; one must be baptized. A person must be willing to be immersed in Christ's death in order to rise with him and share his very life.

Jesus talks about the Spirit of truth, "whom the world cannot accept since it neither sees him nor recognizes him." Insofar as we belong to this world, we are incapable of seeing and knowing the Spirit. That explains a lot of our blind spots and imperviousness. We are incapable of receiving the Spirit to the extent that our baptism has not yet wrought all its effects in us, to the extent that we are still motivated by the spirit of the world. When we feel that the Spirit is absent or far away, we tend to react against the Lord or to blame all sorts of psychological or sociological determinisms. It might be better for us to step back a bit and take a hard look at the situation. Without denying the existence of such determinisms, we may discover that there are others as well. We may see that the spiritual power of our baptism is not as powerful as the forces of the world and the flesh.

There we have the three conditions which Jesus spells out to his apostles on Holy Thursday. And the other two readings indicate that they must be met by anyone who wishes to receive the Spirit.

But there is another condition after all, and it does not depend on the person who desires the Spirit. It is no less mysterious, and it is just as important. The Spirit is not given by the Father willy-nilly. Jesus tells his apostles: "I will ask the Father and he will give you another Paraclete." The account in Acts says that Peter and John "went down to these people and prayed that they might receive the Holy Spirit." It would appear that the Spirit can be communicated to human beings only through the prayer of someone else who is already imbued with Him. It is Jesus who obtains the Spirit for his apostles. It is Peter and John who obtain the Spirit for the people of Samaria.

We also know that in the Gospel Jesus says that his Father will not refuse the Spirit to someone who asks him for it. Thus the prayer is always heard, but still it must be formulated.

There is no sense asking why it should be that way. We cannot dispute the ways of God, but we can take note of their consequences. Pentecost is coming soon. The Church and each one of us will receive the Lord's Spirit only if we request the Spirit for each other. The prayer of all the baptized is indispensable to the spiritual vitality of the Church. We can understand why the apostles attributed such an important place to prayer in their work of preaching the gospel and communicating the Spirit. We can understand why the Church has always encouraged the contemplative life among men and women, for it is their faithful prayer that obtains spiritual strength for all believers. In short: together with the proclamation of God's word and the sacraments, prayer and intercession have a basic and essential function in the Church. Without this prayer and mediation, the world would remain deprived of the power it must get from Christ's Spirit.

With the help of the Spirit and his power, we can realize the goal described by Jesus in today's Gospel: "He who loves me will be loved by my Father. I too will love him and reveal myself to him." Perfect harmony will become a reality; we will participate in the love of the Father, Son, and Holy Spirit.

Let us pray for one another. Let us ask the Lord to make himself better known to each one of us, to give us the courage we need to be loyal, and to endow us lavishly with the Spirit that renews the face of the earth.

ASCENSION OF JESUS

Acts 1:1-11
Eph 1:17-23
Mt 28:16-20

Today the Lord Jesus, who was resurrected from the dead forty days ago, appears to his apostles for the last time. He will not return again until the end of earthly history. That is what we celebrate today: the glorious ascent of Jesus to his Father. Today's Scriptural texts will help us to look at different aspects of this mystery and to see how they concern our day-to-day life.

The first thing that shows up clearly is that the Ascension marks the end of one story. It marks the end of Christ's physical presence among men. Jesus, the incarnate Word, departs from mankind on this earth.

The story began about thirty-three years earlier when the angel Gabriel appeared to the virgin named Mary, telling her that the Holy Spirit would overshadow her and that she would beget the Son of God. Then came his birth in the stable near Bethlehem, the adoration of the shepherds, the visit of the astrologers, and the flight into Egypt to escape persecution by Herod. Shortly afterwards, the family settled in Nazareth and Jesus led a secluded life for some thirty years. Except for his adventure in Jerusalem at the age of twelve, we know nothing about this period.

Around the age of thirty, Jesus begins to step into the public spotlight. For three years he wanders up and down Palestine, recruiting desciples, selecting apostles, proclaiming a message, and performing astounding miracles. Finally he is arrested, condemned to death, and crucified. But that is not the end, for it is then that everything acquires real sense and meaning.

Jesus is buried right after his death. Three days later he bursts forth, living the life of a resurrected person. Although he is already glorified and living in the intimacy of his Father, Jesus shows himself to his apostles and completes their training as the founders of his Church.

Through his resurrection Jesus proves that he is the first human being to reach the full term of his development. Passing through the final barrier, he becomes the last man to "die." He destroys all the oppressive power of death and turns it into a passageway to complete fulfillment. And thus he shows us how the creation of man is to reach its fulfillment.

All that we know. That is the message we have heard as we celebrated the paschal feasts over the course of the last forty days. Today that story reaches its denouement. Jesus of Nazareth ascends to his Father and shares in God's glory. He is "high above every principality, power, virtue, and domination, and every name that can be given in this age or in the age to come." The feast of the Ascension celebrates the end of his corporeal presence here and the beginning of his glorified presence with the Father.

There is nothing for us to do today except to be persuaded of all that. We must believe in this life story of Jesus Christ and in all its consequences. And then we must ask ourselves: How can our faith become a more vital and determining factor in the conduct of our lives?

We certainly do believe in the resurrection and ascension of Jesus. But how are we to make progress in this belief, and what results will ensue? Perhaps we can answer these questions by looking at what happened to the apostles when Jesus ascended into heaven.

We just heard the opening section of the book of the Acts. Luke, the author, makes the transition from his Gospel to this book by reporting Jesus' last meal with his apostles before his ascent into heaven. We read about the Lord's last words and the reactions they evoked in those who would be the pillars of his Church.

After talking about the kingdom, Jesus tells the apostles that they will soon be baptized in the Holy Spirit. So they ask him: "Lord, are you going to restore the rule to Israel now?" The question astonishes us. We can hardly believe that they are still wedded to a temporal brand of Messianism. But they are. They cannot fathom what a spiritual kingdom might be. If Jesus' kingdom is a reality with any solidity to it, then it should be able to improve man's lot or restore order to his life on this earth. And since that would mean delivering them from the Roman invader, they do not see why Jesus should hesitate to do just that. Then people would certainly believe in him!

We can almost hear the cries of reformers in every age, the complaint of all those who identify the kingdom with their system or party and thus champion some brand of temporal Messianism. The question of the apostles is clearly our own. Like them, we are incapable of conceiving a spiritual kingdom. We always need concrete performances in the material domain. For many, human progress or the satisfaction of their political aspirations is the sign of the progress of the kingdom.

But Jesus' response to them is that the progress of the kingdom is a mystery known only to the Father. And he goes on: "You will receive power when the Holy Spirit comes down on you; then you are to be my witnesses . . . even to the ends of the earth." What a paradox! Like us, the apostles are given a mission which they can carry out only because they receive God's Spirit. Jesus' promise crushes them more surely than any word of reproach might have done. They have value and importance in the world and for mankind only by virtue of God's Spirit. If they merely want to be human beings like any other human beings, they have no usefulness at all.

At the same time, by virtue of their personal incapacity, they become indispensable. Therein lies their glory and their honor. For, it is through them that the Spirit continues to fashion mankind. That is what Jesus tells them: "Full authority has been given to me both in heaven and on earth; go, therefore, and make disciples of all nations, baptize them . . . teach them . . . and know that I am with you always. . . ."

There we have the experience of the apostles—the witnesses to his departure, the trustees of his message, the pioneers of his work. Their faith lies above and beyond human knowledge, their activity lies above and beyond their capabilities. They are useful and important only to the extent that they act above and beyond themselves. It is then that they are indispensable, because they have chosen to be resurrected creatures and instruments for the re-creation of others.

How does this concern us? It would seem that the experience is peculiar to the apostles alone. But in fact it is important to us in at least three respects.

First, it helps us to appreciate the difficulties faced by bishops, and their delegates—priests, in their life today. They share the anguish that broods over the world today. God's word has become such a stranger that they hardly know how to proclaim it. And hence they do not know what people expect from them as clearly as they did in the past.

Secondly, it tells us what we might legitimately ask of them. It is not that they be good community directors or recreation leaders. It is that they give us the life of the Spirit, with all the destruction and re-creation it entails. It is that they give us the peace of Christ, which is not the same as the world's brand of peace. The latter is an absence of conflict based on a balance of satisfied interests. The peace of Christ is rooted in faith in his resurrection, a faith that enables us to hope for everything even in the midst of the most cruel trials.

Thirdly, the experience of the apostles enables us to measure the strength and vitality of our faith. The lure of temporal Messianism is stronger today than it ever was, for we live in troubled times. Our faith must liberate itself from such Messianism. It will be strong and vital when it no longer needs to be reassured by any sort of efficacy, when it finds its energy in itself.

There is nothing else for us to do but repeat the prayer of Paul in today's Epistle: "May the God of our Lord Jesus Christ, the Father of glory, grant you a spirit of wisdom and insight to know him clearly. May he enlighten your inermost vision that you may know the great hope to which he has called you."

SEVENTH SUNDAY OF EASTER

Acts 1:12-14
1 Pt 4:13-16
Jn 17:1-11a

Last Thursday we celebrated Jesus' last appearance to his apostles. They saw him depart, and an angel explained that he would return some day in like manner. But they were not to stand there waiting for him, and so they took the short trip back to Jerusalem. "Together they devoted themselves to constant prayer," as if they were waiting for something. They did not know exactly what was going to happen, but they were prepared for whatever the Lord chose to do.

We are in somewhat the same frame of mind this Sunday. We stand between Ascension and Pentecost. Nothing special is happening. No special event is recorded in today's Scriptural message. The texts point more towards meditation and inwardness, as if they were meant for people who were coming out of one trying experience and approaching another one. That indeed does seem to be the situation of the apostles right now, as they leave Christ's ascension behind them and prepare for Pentecost.

Does it not mirror our situation as well? We perpetually stand between the Lord's two comings. The first ended with his ascension, the second will take place at the end of the world. This does not mean that he has abandoned us. It does signify that he has changed the manner of his presence and that his work goes on in a different way. This is evident from the prayer he addresses to the Father in today's Gospel.

Jesus is on his way back to his Father. He asks him for the help he needs to carry off the next phase in accordance with the Father's will. In the gospel narrative we often see Jesus withdrawing to a hillside to pray, sometimes for the whole night. Rarely are we informed of his colloquy with his Father. But John the Evangelist was present at the Last Supper when Jesus uttered this particular prayer, and it seemed so important that John reports it to us.

Jesus asks the Father to "give glory" to him because "the hour has come." We know he is talking about the hour of his own passover from this world to the home of his Father where he had been "before the world began."

To us such a request seems quite odd. The whole notion of asking God to "give glory" to someone seems to smack of haughtiness and pride. But in the Bible, and especially in the mind of John the Evangelist, the "glory" of a being is the vitality and solidity it possesses. In asking to be glorified, Jesus is acknowledging that one's whole value, importance, and potential comes from the Father; and also that he will need an extra dose of strength for his passover. So he asks the Father for it.

Right away, however, it is made clear that Jesus does not want anything for himself or for his own sake. He does not want the added glory so that his passover will be less painful or easier. He wants his Father to be glorified by his work as the Son. He wants everyone to know that everything comes from the Father and returns to him. With the power Jesus has been given over all creatures, he hopes to give eternal life to all those whom the Father has entrusted to him. He prays so that his Father and mankind will be honored and served better.

Jesus' prayer is most comforting for us who yearn truly to know God as he is. In the idiom of the Bible, knowledge of God is not simply intellectual or affective knowledge; it is deep communion with the Father, thanks to Jesus Christ. Our expectant waiting is often painful to us. It seems that the Lord is awfully slow to manifest himself, that the world and its outlook steals him away from us in all sorts of ways, that our own efforts will lose out to the power of the world. Jesus knows all that. His priestly prayer is an uninterrupted prayer of intercession for all those who are aware of their selection and favor by God but who sometimes lose patience because their conflicts are too painful. He knows that they sometimes need to know that he will not abandon them even though he is away from them.

Jesus' prayer is not only consoling. It also sheds light on what our prayer should be. He prays that what happens to him will serve to give glory to God and to benefit those whom the Father entrusted to him. In our own life, too, there are moments that are particularly trying. We are tempted to pray for the alleviation or elimination of our fear, our suffering, our anxiety. That sort of prayer is not to be forbidden, of course. But the more Christ becomes our model, the more we will realize that true prayer seeks to ensure that the glory of God and the welfare of others will be salvaged if our trial proves too heavy for us and leads to failure. That is the prayer model, at once humble and loving, which Jesus proposes to us in this prayer to his Father.

The rest of Jesus' prayer is a rich source of encouragement for us. He dipicts the situation of the believer who is still living in the world and who is waiting for God's plan to reach its fulfillment. The Father has given certain men and women to Jesus, and the latter has given them his message. They know that everything spoken by Jesus comes from the Father. They firmly believe that they will obtain eternal life and live in communion with the Father, thanks to his Son. Is it not good to hear and appreciate those words in this period of waiting, when we may be tempted to lose patience? Jesus' very way of talking about his Father tells us that we are not forgotten, that we count in their eyes and share in their mutual love. We might also do well to recall all that Jesus does for us and that resides in us habitually: our recognition and acceptance of Jesus as God's Son and envoy.

Isn't that what the people gathered in the upper room did when "they devoted themselves to constant prayer"? When the Lord Jesus himself reiterates what he did for mankind to his Father and tells him that he is sure these people did listen to his message, then we can indeed rejoice. Perhaps we might even say that our faith and confidence in him are more vigorous than we ourselves imagined.

It is in this context that we can appreciate the point made in today's Epistle. We are blessed in our suffering to the extent that it is grounded in our faith in Christ: "Happy are you when you are insulted for the sake of Christ, for then God's Spirit in its glory has come to rest on you." It is almost too wondrous to believe! For when all is said and done, who or what is it that insults us? Is it not ourselves? The world in which we are according to Jesus' remarks in today's Gospel, is ourselves first and foremost. We give encouragement to conceptions, appetites, and desires that run contrary to God's Spirit. Insofar as we entertain them, we inevitably provoke inner conflicts that are extremely painful. But these very conflicts are signs that the Lord's Spirit will not let us be mired in the world. The insults and the uprooting provoked by them are signs of an inner disorder. At the same time they are signs of the work of re-ordering that is being carried on by God's Spirit.

The very same thing holds true for the insults that seem to be heaped on us by other people. They take hold over us and become painfully intolerable only to the extent that we are accomplices in them. When we seem to be the victims of other people, that is a sign of our own infidelity.

If we were willing to realize all that, how consoling it would be for us! It may seem cruel, but in fact it is liberative. We have no enemy but ourselves; and the Lord, through the presence of his Spirit, gives us the freedom to overcome that enemy. We need only be willing to "share Christ's sufferings." If we do, then we can rejoice when they appear in our lives; for that is a sign that he is quite near, even though he may seem to be far away.

And so we come back to what we were saying earlier. We are waiting for the Lord, and the wait is painful. But if we persevere in prayer and keep trying to discern the presence of his Spirit in the sufferings that attend us, we will be able to await his imminent return in peace and joy.

PENTECOST SUNDAY

Acts 2:1-11
1 Cor 12:3b-7,12-13
Jn 20:19-23

Jesus rose from the dead fifty days ago. Ten days ago he disappeared from the sight of his apostles. Before leaving, he told them: "You will receive power when the Holy Spirit comes down on you; then you are to be my witnesses . . ." (Acts 1:8).

Today we celebrate the coming of the Holy Spirit. Today the Lord fulfills his promise and gives us the Spirit. That is the basic fact affirmed on this feast: He is sent, he comes, he is present, he is at work.

The affirmation of his presence quite naturally arouses our curiosity. Who is he? Where does he come from? Where is he going? The questions get no response. We know not where he comes from or where he is going. He is vital but imperceptible, necessary but hidden. He cannot be seen or felt. He is everywhere and nowhere and he renews the face of the earth.

But we are anxious to discern him, and at the very least we would like to know the signs that will help us to recognize his passage.

Today's account of the Spirit's coming in Acts reports: "Suddenly from up in the sky there came a noise like a strong, driving wind which was heard all through the house where they were seated." And when Jesus communicated his Spirit to his apostles, he breathes on them and says: "Receive the Holy Spirit."

To express the presence of the Spirit of the risen Christ, today's texts pick up a favorite Biblical theme: the Spirit is the breath of God. He is so impetuous and intrusive that his actions are comparable to those of a mighty wind bursting through a house. What more expressive image could be used to talk about the Spirit than the image of a mighty wind.

The wind is not seen. We do not know its exact

source nor its ultimate place of rest. To be sure, meteorologists can offer us theories about the start and finish of violent storms. But someone who is overtaken by a storm wind still feels he is being enveloped by something powerful and mysterious. The wind blows and creates a violent stir. It bends things, breaks things, uproots things. It propels clouds, seeds, and dust particles. It devastates or fertilizes the soil. It is a master over life, sometimes bringing refreshment and sometimes consuming what it touches. And yet we cannot see it; we can only observe its many different effects.

The same is true of the breath that is God's Spirit. It too is impetuous and all pervasive. It too devastates, uproots, and destroys. It too refreshes, fertilizes, and transforms. And that is how it is described by God's word.

The noise of the great wind was enough to attract the attention of the Jews present in Jerusalem for the holy holiday. They came to see what was happening, and they were thoroughly astounded. An unbelievable surprise was in store for them: "Each one heard these men speaking in his own language." And they all wondered: "How is it that each of us hears them in his native tongue?" They had come from all the countries bordering the Mediterranean.

This was the first and most obvious and most spectacular sign of the Spirit's presence. They were separated from each other by different languages and closed up in their own individuality. Suddenly they could communicate unreservedly and they were able to understand each other. Those present were so astonished that they looked for plausible explanations, even going so far as to suggest that the apostles had gotten high on wine (Acts 2:13). Peter had to explain what was going on and reassure them. They were not the victims of drunkeness or of hallucination. It was something far worse. It was the beginning of a vast and formidable renewal, of a fundamental apocalypse. The Spirit of God had just burst into humanity in order to renew it, re-create it, perfect it. This violent wind would blow until the end of time. An inexorable force had been unleashed, which would tear down habits, mental outlooks, and even persons in order to refashion them in the image of Christ, the Son of God.

Some years later Paul wrote a letter to the Christians of Corinth. He had concretely experienced the presence of the Spirit. He glimpsed the Spirit at work—building the Church, bringing men together in the one faith, unifying them and baptizing them. Paul knows all that and he writes about it, and we can see the same thing today. There are men and women who can say, in all sincerity, that "Jesus is Lord." It is true for them. They are convinced. Their whole life depends on it, and sometimes they are willing to risk the loss of all human security for the sake of this conviction.

The people brought together by the Spirit can only be those who recognize that "Jesus is Lord." When they do, then each of them is entrusted with a function and given the resources required to fulfill it. They do fulfill it, docile to the Spirit who distributes his gifts as he chooses. No longer is their rivalry, jealousy, or domination in human relations. They are members of one body, the body of Christ. They all are different, but they all are necessary. In that body, union and communication between the members is not the result of individual initiative nor is it meant to serve the individual; it springs from docility to the Spirit and it is meant to promote the glory of Christ.

Today the world is in disarray. Everything seems to lead to an impasse. Never before has there been such an urgent desire to establish lines of communication, participation, and joint effort. But all these efforts seem to lead to ever more dismal and incomprehensible failures. All this bears eloquent witness to what the real presence of the Spirit entails. The Spirit gives the gift of tongues to human beings so that they can understand one another, but he only gives it to men who are willing to be transformed. He creates a new humanity where fraternity reigns, but where obedience also reigns.

If we ignore or reject this logic of the Spirit, then we will find it completely impossible to encounter one another truly. We will only be able to draw up alliances based on self-interest. They will inevitably lead to frustration and cause ever-recurring conflicts.

This is perhaps the most clearly paradoxical aspect of the Spirit's activity, as it is revealed to us today. He brings men together by pointing up their differences, giving them different functions, and offering them different gifts to fulfill these functions. At the same time he condems them to a painful solitude, which is part and parcel of their sharing in the unity of Christ's body. On the one hand he abolishes the old sociological categories: "Jew or Greek, slave or free." On the other hand he separates us from others. We can no longer find our comfort in them because we "have been given to drink of the one Spirit." He reunites us only insofar as we have gotten beyond any and every form of human dependence. That is how the race of human beings re-created by the Spirit shows up today.

The work which begins so rudely and spectacularly on this day of Pentecost will continue to the end of history. It is the Spirit's will that some of the baptized people who acknowledge Jesus as Lord should be active in reconciling their brothers and sharing the work of fashioning a new humanity. That is why the day of the Spirit's manifestation is also the day of the Church's birth. This Church will last to the end of time. To it are entrusted the signs that reveal the activity of the Spirit. In its ministers and members we may find the most scandalous inconsistencies and failings, and the powers of the Spirit can be used in a painfully unconscious way. That has gone on for two thousand years now. But that cannot prevent it from meriting the homage which Peter paid to Jesus: "Lord, to whom shall we go? You have the words of eternal life."

There seems to be only one thing for us to do, we

who are witnesses to the events of Pentecost and what has happened since. We must recognize the Spirit and give thanks for him. We must recognize the manifestations of the Spirit in ourselves and others, knowing well that such manifestations are given to us. Then we must thank the Father for giving us the Spirit and letting us know about him. In this way we will gradually turn away from ourselves and becoming capable of surrendering wholly to the breath of the Spirit.

TRINITY SUNDAY

Ex 34:4b-6,8-9
2 Cor 13:11-13
Jn 3:16-18

Last Sunday we celebrated the feast of Pentecost, the manifestation of the Spirit of truth who was promised by Jesus and who directs us towards real knowledge of the Lord. Today the Church wishes to glorify the Father who revealed himself to us by sending us his Son, and to savor our communion with Father and Son in the Holy Spirit. That is why she deemed it advisable to institute a special feast for the Holy Trinity.

The feast may seem astonishing to us in more than one respect. Do we not celebrate God at every Sunday Mass and at every instant of our lives? The very formulas of the liturgy direct our thoughts to God the Father, Son, and Holy Spirit. So why a special feast, especially in view of the fact that God ever remains a reality to whom we listen rather than one of whom we may speak? We do not serve him really. It is he who incessantly imbues us with his presence and transforms us with his Spirit, thus associating us with his love and rendering us capable of loving. Our love is but a reflection or embodiment of the love he gives us.

Our concern for improving the world and our collective introversion leads some to say that we must believe in man. The message and activity of the Lord in building up his kingdom are reduced to a frightening utilitarianism. We pretend that the Lord humbled himself to put himself at our service, that he took the form of a servant and died on the cross for this reason: and so we turn him into our household valet. Our faith and homage to him are gauged by the improving condition of man and his progress towards fulfillment.

Perhaps that is why the Church feels that this feast is advisable. She may feel the threat of a grave danger, of a blasphemous misunderstanding. Having shown us all the signs of God's absolute and tender love in the person of Jesus and the gift of the Spirit, she now wants to help us to go out of ourselves, to savor God's gift without grabbing it in a possessive way, and to reform our basic attitude towards it.

At God's command Moses climbs the mountain to receive God's revelation of a law that he is to inscribe on the stone tablets he has brought along. Perhaps Moses expected to receive a series of prescriptions. He receives something much more surprising and demanding—a revelation of God's love, tenderness, pity, and patience. In a word, he receives a revelation of God's fidelity. Fidelity says it all: God does not vacillate in his dispositions towards man. He sent out a summons to Abraham in Ur of the Chaldees, thrusting him into a nomadic quest for his God. From that time until the end of the world, when an apocalyptic cataclysm will definitively establish the kingdom, God will never cease to speak the same message to man, to propose a series of successive covenants that embody the same message: i.e., God is love. His message is: "Thou shalt love. . . ." He gives man his Son to save the human race, and his Spirit to bring mankind into communion with him through the recapitulation of all things in Christ.

Fidelity, a perduring good will and concern for the welfare of his stiff-necked creatures, marks his approach to man. He never ceases to offer man his free and indispensable love. That is the splendid import and power of the message given to Moses on Sinai.

But this fidelity is not a fearless rigidity. It is a continuing movement towards the creature he loves, a perduring force for creative fruitfulness. Each time we meet to celebrate the liturgy, the Church can only give us a small segment of God's word to ponder. We cannot cover the whole story of God's interventions on behalf of man. That would cover the whole history of the world! It is just as clear in the most clearcut manifestation of all, improbable but very precious: "God so loved the world that he gave his only Son." The fidelity of God is embodied in action, in the dynamism of his love which constantly works for the welfare of the beloved.

That is a human way of putting it all, to be sure. We tend to picture God involved in the unfolding web of history as we are, when we know full well that everything is the present for him. But so what? We are in time because God himself put us there and willed that our participation in his love unfold in the gradual progression of suceeding events. It is there that the fidelity and fecundity of his love is revealed to us.

God gave us his only Son, acceding to Moses' plea: "Do come along in our company." He does. He is present and alive with us in his Son and in what Paul calls "the grace of the Lord Jesus Christ." Jesus himself is the supreme grace that God gives to man, the most evident sign and testimony of his presence. We are aware of it from the day that God's Spirit overshadows a virgin named Mary. We listen to it at work in the words and actions of Jesus. We marvel at it in his death on the cross, we are astounded by it in his resurrection.

And John the Evangelist spells it all out: "God did not send the Son into the world to condemn the world, but that the world might be saved through him." Having completed the cycle of paschal feasts with Pentecost last Sunday, we know for sure that this salvation is the definitive fulfillment of creation.

It is here that a love of such fidelity becomes tragic. Its ceaseless fecundity makes it an indispensable necessity for man. Without it man can only end in violent destruction. The Lord respects man's liberty, but he also underlines the two poles of his option: "Whoever believes in him avoids condemnation, but whoever does not believe is already condemned. . . ." It is the great paradox of a liberty that can only choose between life and death. There are no varied or multiform ways of living, no choices between many different hypotheses. It is all or nothing. Father's love, manifested in Christ and stimulated by the presence of the Spirit, is tragic because it is decisive. It is not one gratuitous possibility among others; it is the very life of man. God's gift of liberty to man is the most wondrous summons to love, but it also represents the dangerous possibility of self-destruction. Many people fear it. They would have preferred not to be confronted with such a choice, which seems cruel rather than kind. But it is in his freedom to love or not that man is truly man. If this choice did not exist, with all its tragic aspects, man would be no more than a robot programmed in advance by an unconditional, absolute authority.

But what a dazzling destiny awaits those who choose to accept the Lord Jesus, who believe "in the name of God's only Son" with the help of the Holy Spirit. Everything becomes peace and joy in the communion effected by the Spirit.

We have heard Paul's words to the Christians of Corinth. They bespeak a light and flexible joy. The writer and his audience feel themselves enveloped in a thrust towards renewal that channels and intensifies their efforts, bringing them together in fraternal emulation and uniting them in the enthusiastic certainty that they have discovered an absolute love.

It is there that adoration and tenderness, gratuitousness and hard work, submission and liberty are joined in one united movement. Perhaps that is the aim of the Church in inviting us to contemplate the one God in three persons whom Jesus Christ revealed to us.

In the opening prayers the celebrant reminds us that God has permitted his faithful to see and know his glory. May he keep us firm in the faith of what we already know, and may he help us to make progress in docility to his "fidelity."

CORPUS CHRISTI

Dt 8:2-3,14b-16a
1 Cor 10:16-17
Jn 6:51-58

We are used to going to Mass and Communion. We try to be fully conscious and attentive, but we must admit that we often are prey to different thoughts and emotions that have little to do with what is going on. Besides, the danger of habit is very real; oft-heard words tend to lose their original power. Perhaps that is why the Church instituted the feast of Corpus Christi: to offset these problems and to give honor to such an important institution.

The Church gives us an opportunity to recall the inestimable treasure embodied in the sacrament of Christ's body and blood, and to commune with ever deeper concentration and intensity. Let us ponder the message that the Church has chosen for us.

Our Lord's words are astonishing, too much for his audience to bear: "I myself am the living bread come down from heaven. If anyone eats this bread he shall live forever; the bread I will give is my flesh, for the life of the world." Audience reaction is quick in coming: "How can he give us his flesh to eat?" There is no sense in trying to make up easy answers. Jesus' proposal is discomforting in its formulation. Who can take it cooly? Who can accept it as a reasonable statement? It is no more acceptable today than it was when Jesus first uttered it.

Before one accepts or rejects it, he does well to ponder it in the light of todays other two readings.

The selection from the book of Deuteronomy recalls Israel's sojourn in the desert right after its liberation from the Egyptians. The author draws spiritual lessons, helping the faithful to comprehend what God wanted to reveal to them through this long and seemingly interminable wait for the promised land. It is a lesson embodied in images, and it has great relevance for us today.

Yahweh led his people into the desert and kept them there for forty years. They are humiliated, they suffer hunger and thirst, they are threatened by serpents and scorpions. In the terrible wasteland of the desert their fidelity is tested to its very core. They learn that "not on bread alone shall man live" (Lk 4:4). It is God who will provide their food and drink; and they will win the promised land through his protection, not through their own efforts. Each succeeding generation of believers will thus learn that it is God alone who saved them from Egypt, protected them from danger, fed them daily with manna, and quenched their thirst with water from a rock. It is thanks to God's nurturing care that the Hebrew people survived the desert and attained the promised land.

The discourse in today's Gospel took place after Jesus had multiplied loaves and fishes miraculously to feed the hungry crowd that had been following him (Jn 6:1-14). Like the Hebrews in the Sinai desert, these people had followed the Lord and now were hungry. Following the lead of the Almighty in that earlier incident, Jesus feeds his people on this occasion. Thus the multiplication of the loaves and fishes is a replay of the Old Testament gesture. It serves as a starting point for Jesus to explain the underlying import of both the manna in the desert and the bread that was miraculously multiplied.

Just as the Hebrews in the desert and the Jews around Jesus would not have had life if it were not for the nourishment provided by God, so we will not know eternal life if it were not for a nourishment that will be the Lord himself.

Jesus tells his listeners that the "bread that comes down from heaven" is not like the manna: "Your ancestors ate manna in the desert, but they died." They may have ascaped the dangers of the desert, thanks to the manna, but their future was limited to the promised land. Our desert is the world, where the "serpents and scorpions" of temptation, hunger, and thirst torment us in all sorts of ways. The most trying temptations are often those least adverted to. If we refuse to absorb the nourishment offered us by the Lord, then we will be condemned to death as surely as the Hebrews would have been if they had refused the manna.

These two events—the manna in the desert and the multiplication of the loaves and fishes—will help us to grasp the rest of Jesus' discourse better. We have already grasped that the nourishment he offers is indispensable. He goes on to point out its effects.

"The man who feeds on my flesh and drinks my blood remains in me, and I in him." When the believer absorbs the bread that has been transformed into the body of Christ, he is no longer alone. He remains himself, but at the same time he receives the presence of the Lord and abides in him. The two existences are bound up with one another from that point on. Death becomes impossible because "Christ, once raised from the dead, will never die again" (Rom 6:9). This "living bread" is not a symbol, a sign informing us of Christ and his activity, a kind of privileged talisman. Jesus stresses his point: "I myself am the living bread. . . . If you do not eat the flesh of the Son of Man. . . ." He truly chooses to give himself as food to the believer, in order to nourish the vital power over which biological death has no effect. If it is not nourished adequately by this food, then the person will not be able to rise to eternal life with Christ.

Jesus offers a further explanation of this reciprocal indwelling by comparing it with the living union between himself and his Father: "Just as the Father who has life sent me and I have life because of the Father, so the man who feeds on me will have life because of me." It appears, then, that the union between Father and Son is the model for the union between the believer and Christ. Between the latter two there should be the same oneness of thinking, willing, and desiring that exists between the Father and the Son. What is more, if the Son lives through the Father, and if the believer who receives Christ lives through him, then the life they live is the very life of God himself. United with Christ, we are immersed in the life of the Holy Trinity whose feast we celebrated last Sunday.

Seen from this vantage point, today's remarks of Paul are obvious enough. "Because the loaf of bread is one, we, many though we are, are one body, for we all partake of the one loaf." Since the Lord dwells in those who eat his body, and since this unity of life with Christ introduces them into the inner life of God, all those who share in this sacrament are united with each other in the body of Christ. They form one entity with him, living in real, immortal communion with him. Together they form a new society: the sons of God gathered into one in his kingdom.

We could explore the implications of this reality *ad infinitum,* but there is no need to do that today. The important thing right now is to let ourselves be shaped by the message we have heard; to ask the Lord for strength to believe in it and to get a clear grasp of it.

Soon we will receive the Body of Christ. Let us make an effort to receive him with all the awareness at our command. Today the Lord has chosen to reveal to us that he has become our indispensable nourishment, that Holy Communion, the eating of his Body is the means chosen by his Father to transmit life to us through his Son. We now know that this Food gives all those who receive it effective communion with and in him.

COMMON SUNDAYS OF THE YEAR

2nd SUNDAY OF THE YEAR

Is 49:3,5-6
1 Cor 1:1-3
Jn 1:29-34

Isaiah, Paul, and John the Baptist speak to us about Jesus Christ. Today's words from Scripture do not attempt to free us from some defect or to teach us some truth. They wish to make us better acquainted with Jesus Christ.

As we listen to our three "prophets," one thing shows up quite clearly: their personal inability to recognize Christ or to speak suitably about him. Twice John the Baptist feels compelled to say: "I confess I did not recognize him." Paul explains that his call to be an apostle of Christ was God's will. Isaiah is able to describe the "Servant" only because God gives him that revelation.

These three men remain important figures in our spiritual tradition. Living in different ages and different circumstances, they spoke to us about Jesus in very precise and necessary terms. So it is highly significant that they should be unanimous in describing where their knowledge of the Lord comes from. There is no possibility of conspiracy or mere imitation here. John the Baptist did not ape Isaiah. Paul did not follow John's lead. Their times, their backgrounds, and their process of formation were too different. Imitation is out of the question because the personal history of each was quite singular. Yet, despite their differences, they all are convinced that their ability to speak is due to the direct, explicit intervention of the living God.

All three attest to their personal ignorance and all three trace their knowledge back to the same source. This makes their testimony highly persuasive. We can be sure that the message we hear today is not the invention of some mad visionary or some fanatical group. They can only tell us what they themselves have learned from God about Jesus Christ. Thus their teaching is of great importance for us. What do they tell us?

John the Baptist talks about a man named Jesus. There is nothing extraordinary about that, although we must admit that our faith in Jesus Christ often takes on a disembodied cast. When we think about him, we tend to conjure up a mythical portrait. We see him as neither man nor God, as someone set apart from others and preserved from the contagion of evil, hence as some privileged entity who has little in common with us. But that is precisely the starting point for the testimony we hear today. This man Jesus was born of a woman just as every other human being is. Isaiah's words tell us: "God formed me as his servant from the womb." He enjoys special protection, but that does not diminish his humanity one bit.

This man does have a singular destiny. Isaiah calls him the "Servant." John the Baptist gives him an even more curious title, "Lamb of God." And he gives him this title, not in any abstract way, but in a very concrete situation. Jesus is passing by and John the Baptist points to him: "Look! There is the Lamb of God."

Different as the two appellations are, they both indicate that Jesus is innocent on the one hand but on the other hand he will be punished by human beings as a guilty culprit. Thus Isaiah and John the Baptist proclaim his uprightness, his docility to God's orders. and his fate as a victim for the sake of others. The first letter of Peter alludes to "blood beyond all price, the blood of a spotless, unblemished lamb" (I Pt 1:19).

Jesus is the just man who will pay the price for others. He will be assaulted, tortured, and murdered by the very people he came to save. By depicting him as the "Servant" and the "Lamb of God," the two prophets also depict him as the one who inherits and fulfills the age-old promises.

John the Baptist tells us how he came to "recognize" Jesus in this light. Although Jesus was his cousin, John did not know him for who he was. God gave him a sign: "When you see the Spirit descend and rest on someone, it is he." And John can say: "I saw the Spirit descend like a dove from the sky, and it came to rest on him." He has no trouble in giving his own testimony: "Now I have seen for myself and have testified. 'This is God's chosen One.' "

The divinely inspired description of Jesus is quite explicit: Jesus is "God's chosen One." Years later Paul will refer to "Our Lord Jesus Christ, their Lord and ours." Words cannot go further here. All we can do is to look for synonyms, for expressions that will serve as more or less precise commentaries on what has just been said. It is fortunate that the divinely inspired descriptions are not weighted down or diluted with useless verbiage.

A man named Jesus is the just one who will be misunderstood, rejected, and finally killed. And this just one is the Lord of all human beings. That is the central statement made today, a statement so extraordinary that it could hardly have been invented by human beings unless they were enlightened about the matter by God himself.

John the Baptist explains himself further in rather curious terms. He talks about someone who is coming after him. That is Jesus, who is just a bit younger than he is. Jesus is completely unknown, while John is a celebrity in Israel who has enjoyed great success. But Jesus will gradually supersede him. He will become increasingly important while John will become less and less important. John tells us why: "Because he was before me." Jesus' importance does not lie in the luster of his virtue, in his ability as a wonder-worker, much less in his gifts as a popular orator. It lies in who he is. Although he was born after John the Baptist, Jesus existed before him. John knows that, thanks to a special enlightenment, and he says so.

Today's divine message does not just tell us who Jesus is. It also tells us what he is about. Since our three witnesses are very different people, it is not surprising that each explains Jesus' role in his own distinctive way. Isaiah describes his activity in two phases. First, he depicts the Servant offering salvation to his own nation and bringing together all the tribes of Israel. Then he goes on to depict the Servant as a "light to the nations" who extends his activity to the entire world. He fulfills the promises made to Israel, but he does not restrict God's salvation to one nation. The kingdom he announces is one in which separate nations and races will no longer exist as such.

But what is this "salvation" of which Isaiah speaks. The word is quite vague for people today. They do not feel that they are lost, hence they do not seek any salvation. They may experience certain difficulties and trials, but they hardly expect the solution to come from a God in whom they do not believe.

John the Baptist, too, has two expressions to describe Jesus' mission. Jesus "takes away the sin of the world" and he is to "baptize with the Holy Spirit."

Jesus takes away the sin of the world. It is some weighty obstacle, as it were. This prophet seems to be alluding to some sort of liberatoin that Jesus has come to effect. He seems to suggest that man's thinking and doing is confined by certain shackles which prevent him from attaining his full destiny. Christ comes to enlarge his perspectives and his possibilities.

Jesus also has come to "baptize with the Holy Spirit." As we know, to baptize means to immerse. Christ will regenerate man by immersing him in God's Spirit, by flooding him with the Holy Spirit. Man will then be profoundly transformed. One might go so far as to say that man is saved because he is annihilated and replaced by another who will always be himself, no matter what happens.

All that is implied in Paul's reference to those "who have been consecrated in Christ Jesus." He is referring to those who have been freed from the things that shackle their development and who have been imbued with the life-giving power of the Spirit. But Paul also reminds his audience that they have been "called to be a holy people." The work has already been accomplished by Christ, but it cannot be spread around unless man accepts it.

Today we have been given a basic message, so basic in fact that it might seem too general or too out of touch with our concrete lives. That is due to the fact that we, in our concrete lives, are generally unaware of the realities which go to make it up. We stay on the level of surface appearances. We do not advert to the fact that our most insignificant decisions and actions embody our most basic option: i.e., our acceptance or rejection of what we are told today about Jesus.

Today let us ask God to enlighten us all, as he enlightened Isaiah, John the Baptist, and Paul. And let us also ask him to give us the strength to bear witness to his light as they did.

3rd SUNDAY OF THE YEAR

Is 8:23b-9:3
1 Cor 1:10-13,17
Mt 4:12-23

Today we see Jesus officially inaugurating his public life. Not long ago, around the age of thirty, he had himself baptized by John the Baptist. Then the Spirit drove him into the desert, where he fasted forty days and was tempted by the devil. At the end of that period, according to Matthew's account, Jesus learns that John the Baptist has been put into prison—for what reason we shall learn later on. Then Jesus decides to leave the Jordan area and head northward to Galilee. He ends up near Capernaum, in the land of Zebulun and Naphtali. Matthew takes pains to be explicit on this point.

We have just heard a prophecy in which Isaiah mentions these two places. God once humiliated Zebulun and Naphtali, but some day in the future he will save and glorify them. The fact is that they had been overrun by Assyria in 734 B.C. In this prophetic text Isaiah proclaims their deliverance by the Messiah. Matthew the Evangelist has Jesus begin his preaching precisely in that region, in the land of Zebulun and Naphtali. We are suddenly offered a sign that is deliberately chosen by the Lord himself. He is going to fulfill the promises which were formulated by the prophets at God's behest.

The marvelous text of Isaiah still echoes in our ears. A great light dawns on those who had dwelt in a gloomy land. God is going to liberate them from the oppressor's yoke and the trappings of servitude. Traces of Isaiah's excitement and enthusiasm can be detected in Matthew's account of Jesus' initial preaching.

At first reading everything seems quite simple. There hardly seems to be room for additional comment. In fact, however, the Evangelist is evoking an explosive and dazzling happening. He situates Jesus' initial preaching in that sorely tested region of Israel. No reference is made to any organized public gatherings or to any preliminary efforts to round up an audience. Jesus simply starts to preach. We can picture him proclaiming his message as he moves through the lanes and village squares and stops by the village wells: "Reform your lives! The kingdom of heaven is at hand." For seemingly interminable centuries the whole nation has waited for a messenger who would proclaim this to it; now, finally, it hears the message.

The news, which was true for Jesus' audience, remains just as revelant today—and always. We, too, need only repent and be watchful. In other words, we must turn away from our selves and our interior shackles, we must lay hold of the light and liberty of the kingdom that is now offered to us. These are Jesus' first words. He announces some imminent liberation which can be expereinced by all who are willing to heed his hopeful proclamation.

We can picture him repeating this message to all he meets. They must have been thoroughly astonished. Continuing his journey, he leaves the village and skirts the shore of a lake. There he sees two fishermen casting their nets, weighted conical affairs that were dropped into the water to catch fish. It is a brief scene. Jesus bids Peter and Andrew to follow him, promising them that they will be fishers of men. They do not argue or ask any questions; they leave their nets on the shore and follow him. Further on, a similar scene takes place with John and James, the sons of Zebedee, who are helping their father to arrange his nets. Jesus simply calls them. The two young men leave their father and their fishing gear and take off with Jesus.

Two encounters with two sets of brothers take place, and four men head off with Jesus immediately. It would seem that some strong and convincing aura of calm authority emanates from Jesus because the four men follow him at once. They do not ask for reasons nor do they show any concern about what will happen next. There is also the fact that in Scripture the number "four" is the terrestrial number. Hence Matthew is pointing up the fact that Jesus is taking possession of all humanity by alluding to the call of "four" men. Jesus commands with all the authority of the one who has come to establish the kingdom.

This call also serves to illustrate the thrust of Jesus' first message. The invitation to reform one's life for the sake of the kingdom is accepted when one hears God's word and heeds the Lord's command. And that is how we will share the same experience.

Subsequent events move apace. Once these four men join him, Jesus seems to become more and more sure of himself. His work of preaching becomes more organized and success soon attends it. He speaks in the synagogues, proclaims the good news of the kingdom, and offers clear-cut signs of the veracity of his message. Matthew tells us that he "cured the people of every disease and illness."

Isaiah had intimated that when people perceived this great light, they would be as happy as they are at harvest time or when they are dividing spoils. Such happiness is indeed reflected in Matthew's report of Jesus' preaching. It is as if some happy news had just been announced, and we feel that we are at the start of some great achievement. This happening is so important that it will completely transform man's life. Henceforth human life will be dominated by a new master who will mold it to liberty and orient it to full and complete life by freeing it from the age-old shackles.

What a program is proposed to us today! What are we to make of it? Can we handle it? One might well argue that we are as blind and petty as Paul seems to indicate in his letter to the Corinthians. They have been offered the kingdom of heaven and they scarcely pay heed. They are divided up into factions, each claiming to be the most influential one. Some are champions of Apollos, some of Paul, some of Cephas, some of Christ. From Paul's words we can picture the scene well—people divided by petty rivalry and differing doctrines.

What local church community or diocese would not

merit the same rebuke from Paul today? What believer with an ounce of integrity does not recognize himself in Paul's description? Who of us does not have his pet ideas and preferences in the realms of politics and church life, arguing for them in such a peremptory way that other people and their ideas are excluded automatically? We know for sure that the Creed and God's word are to be interpreted in one particular way. We know for sure that the sacraments are to be administered in one particular fashion. So we use up a great deal of energy and ingenuity in proving that we are right and in condemning others.

Man's pettiness is quite unbelievable, yet it is as evident in the Church today as it was in Paul's day. God offers us his kingdom and reveals his power in the work of his Son, but we shrivel up in the dank atmosphere of petty quarrels over words or ideas. It is astonishing, but it happens every day.

Paul is obviously incensed and his tone becomes severe. There is only one Christ who was crucified for all. There is only one Lord who saves us, and who enlightens us from the day of our baptism on. To appreciate this fact we must get away from "worldly wisdom." We can only proclaim Christ and his cross. Paul, the highly educated and cultivated apostle, speaks out against "worldly wisdom." Intelligence is not the thing that enables us to be faithful to the kingdom. As soon as human capabilities are used to persuade or dominate others, they set up barriers and keep people out. They necessarily give rise to divisions in the ecclesial community.

Hence it is not possible for the preachers of the gospel to be "stars," each with his or her own fan club. If they recruit followers loyal to them, people who look down on others outside their club, then their message is a scandalous put-on.

If believers want to enter the kingdom, they cannot tolerate any wisdom except that of the cross. Any other wisdom would be their own wisdom. They would be proposing their own program, not that of the Lord. And we know from the pages of history what human programs are worth!

Today the Lord announces his kingdom to us. We can say that we have heard and heeded his message to the extent that we agree to wipe out our pettiness and open our hearts to the dimensions of the universe. If we do agree to do that, then Jesus' proclamation will fill us with real joy. We will come out of our selves and discover God's light.

4th SUNDAY OF THE YEAR

Zep 2:3;3:12-13
1 Cor 1:26-31
Mt 5:1-12a

Jesus has just started his public life. He has already proclaimed his message in the synagogues and elsewhere: "Reform your lives! The kingdom of heaven is at hand" (Mt 4:17). He has already called four men to leave everything and follow him. His fame has spread quickly throughout the area; now he is attended by large crowds. His message seems so important that they want to hear more about it.

"When he saw the crowds he went up on the mountainside. After he had sat down his disciples gathered around him, and he began to teach them." It is one of the most beautiful teachings ever: the Beatitudes. We will read this passage again on the feast of All Saints. At that time we will be celebrating the complete success of the Lord's work. Today we celebrate its inauguration, the appearance of the kingdom in germinal form. It is the prelude to the greatest happening of all time, the revelation of absolute, definitive happiness.

When we listen to Jesus' words, they sink deeply into us. They evoke strong and pleasant reverberations in our innermost depths, jibing with our noblest and purest aspirations. Everything seems feasible and directly within our grasp. All the painful and unbearable aspects of our lives are laid bare, recognized, and healed; suffering itself seems to become a source of joy. Everything seems possible for us once again. We feel a sense of wonder. Surely that is what the kingdom of God is! So why not lay hold of it immediately?

But soon that first impression grows blurred in our minds. We come back to ourselves once again. We realize that this is not the first time that we have heard these words and felt this way. The seemingly clearcut truth of the Beatitudes fades away and we are left with a feeling of weariness.

We have often tried to follow our innermost feelings of purity and nobility, but somehow we never were free to do it. It is as if some force got in our way and prevented us. And the saddest thing of all is that we have often felt we were finally free of some fault or obstacle, only to be hit with it once again. Lightning keeps striking the same spot over and over again.

We seem to be condemned to mediocrity. And when we think we have made some sort of progress, we suddenly run up against a stone wall and can go no further. The weighty impact of others, their aggressive actions and behavior, seem to turn us off our course and even ruin us. Fidelity ends up being as intolerable to ourselves as it is to them.

What is worse, when we begin to detect some semblance of fidelity, it seems that the spiritual progress intimated by the Beatitudes is always fleeting and beyond our grasp. We cannot even get a taste of it, much less savor its possession; it would be destroyed in the very act of enjoying it. So there is no real purchase point. We are wholly in the realm of unending desire. If we stop along the way to measure our progress, we nullify everything we have done.

While the Beatitudes may offer happiness to us, they never let us stop at the point we have reached. What they propose to us is a kind of death, a death so real that it does not even offer us the comforting thought that we are sacrificing ourselves for a good cause. This death is not an escape by any means. It is not some superficial evasion akin to masochism or suicide. Instead it is a dive into the deepest recesses of the soul in order to explore and uncover our most hidden capabilities. It comes down to choosing between actions and achievements that seem to offer us self-fulfillment and self-importance on the one hand, and a process of transformation that clearly seems to entail self-annihilation and unforeseeable results on the other hand.

We must remember Jesus' call to his first apostles. When they followed him, they were forced to abandon their work, their family, and their basic human situation. No equivalent return was promised or given to them.

Such is the proclamation of the kingdom which Jesus has just uttered to the crowd attending him. To us it seems way off-base. We might be inclined to assume that the first Beatitude on poverty of spirit, which inaugurates and personifies all the rest, is a hope offered to those who are suffering and a promise to restore their rights. We might also be inclined to think that we can begin to fulfill Christ's prophecy by promoting a just distribution of goods according to the needs of each person. In fact, however, this Beatitude has to do with something quite different, something much more basic and perhaps even tragic. Reading Paul's words in the light of Zephaniah, we can get a clearer picture of what is meant.

Paul says something frightening: God chose "those who count for nothing to reduce to nothing those who were something." That is why the weak and the foolish will confound the strong and the wise. Ordinary people and those who are despised will be first in the kingdom.

As Paul tells us, God made Jesus "our wisdom and also our justice, our sanctification, and our redemption." Hence we do not have a choice between several different hypotheses. It is Christ and his revelation or nothing at all. And if we are to heed Christ and his revelation, we must destroy in ourselves everything that counts for something. We must get beyond wisdom and force, sacrificing any and every satisfying result: "Let him who would boast, boast in the Lord."

Speaking of the start of the kingdom, Zephaniah referred to it as "the day of the Lord's anger." We must find shelter against it. As God tells us: "I will leave as a remnant in your midst a people humble and lowly . . . who shall take refuge in the name of the Lord."

What better commentary could there be on the Beatitudes which Jesus proclaimed to the crowd on the mountainside.

Suddenly Jesus' preaching, which began shortly before in an aura of gaiety and enthusiasm, takes on a dramatic aspect. The kingdom is ardently desired by human beings, to be sure. But it is also a gift from God which is brought to realization by the Beatitudes. With the help of today's three readings we have learned the conditions which God stipulates in order to perfect his creation for us and usher us into the kingdom.

Today the Lord demands that we realize and accept the fact that everything comes from him. If we try to merit or fashion on our own what only he can do, we will end up in a blind alley. Creation will reach its fulfillment only in a creature whose only ambition is to receive, who absolutely refuses to play the role of creator in any way.

The news we hear today is indeed very good news. True enough, it proclaims the "day of the Lord's anger." True enough, this anger has now been unleashed and will consume everything that counts for something; only what counts for nothing will be allowed to remain. But it is certain that the Lord never promised that access to the kingdom and the fulfillment of his promises would be limited to this earthly life. On the contrary, he has made us sharers in his own life. If we try to create or attain this life by our own wisdom and strength, then we are doing the exact opposite: we are trying to persuade him to share our life as human beings. The absurdity of that endeavor is self-evident.

Perhaps now we see more clearly what Jesus had in mind when he uttered his first message: "Reform your lives! The kingdom of heaven is at hand" (Mt 4:17). He seems to be inviting us to eradicate our own wisdom, to find our true source of strength in him. Then we will no longer be able to glory in ourselves as human beings; we will be forced to seek only the glory of God. That is the price we must pay if we want to win the happiness which Jesus proclaims today.

If we appreciate all this, then we will deserve to hear what Christ says today: "Be glad and rejoice, for your reward is great in heaven."

5th SUNDAY OF THE YEAR

Is 58:7-10
1 Cor 2:1-5
Mt 5:13-16

Faced with a surging crowd, Jesus clambers up a mountainside. His disciples gather around him and he begins to preach. First he proclaims the Beatitudes, pointing out the pathway that leads to the kingdom. But offering some heavenly recompense does not seem to be enough for him. Those who are willing to follow the pathway of the Beatitudes must also be aware of their importance here and now. That is what he brings out in the selection we have just read.

His words are important because they point up the radiating luster of those who accept Christ's notion of happiness, and also because they highlight the indispensable role of those who persevere in following him. We shall consider the import of the two expressions, "salt of the earth" and "light of the world." Then we shall consider the words of Paul and Isaiah to see how we can embody them in our own lives.

The Beatitudes—the last in particular—seem to be quite cruel. We get the impression that our life on earth is supposed to be that of a sorrowing, useless victim. Here Jesus wants to encourage his listeners by pointing up the authentic importance of his recommendations. It is as if he were telling them: "When you feel discouraged and your patience is exhausted, you must remember that you are the salt of the earth and the light of the world."

His subsequent words indicate that salt simply must be strong. If it deteriorates, it can no longer serve any useful purpose: "Then it is good for nothing but to be thrown out and trampled underfoot."

"You are the salt of the earth." You don't have to become it; that is what you are by your very nature. But you must be fully what you are, and your capabilities can be undermined by your evasions and remissness. The same holds true for "the light of the world." All that a light is expected to do is to shine. A city set on a mountain cannot be hidden, nor can a lamp be buried away. You, too, must let your light shine by practicing the Beatitudes; you must not tire of doing this.

But you do not let your light shine by showing off or emphasizing your own value and worth. You do it by obeying the light you have received from God: "Your light must shine before men so that they may see goodness in your acts and give praise to your heavenly Father." People will recognize the Father's glory and submit to him insofar as they see the good works of others. This is an important point, which can serve to correct a mistaken notion of what "witness" is supposed to be. The term "witness" runs through our ecclesiastical texts and is bandied about by many priests and people. We hear it so often that we may well be irritated by it, especially when it is used as a club to remind others of their obligations.

It is as if "witness" were a moral obligation to be fulfilled insofar as one is a believer. Earlier generations had a different term: "good example." One must give it in order to edify others and bring them to goodness. And this presumes that one believes in goodness oneself, even though he or she may not always be capable of fidelity to this goodness.

In the light of Jesus' words it would appear that witness is not an end in itself. Our conduct should not be motivated by a desire to "bear witness": i.e., by a desire to make others understand and appreciate something. That would be to slip into a subtle attitude of superiority, to imagine that one knows something which he virtuously tries to communicate to those who are ignorant of it. But the true believer does not act out of a regard for the opinions of others. He is faithful to what the Lord expects of him. It is the Lord who sets him up as the salt of the earth and the light of the world. He need only be consistent with the role he has been given and with the task the Lord sets for him. The rest does not concern him. In his goodness, Jesus tells us today that such fidelity is necessary and efficacious. But giving oneself an air of importance is certainly contrary to the Beatitude on poverty of spirit.

Isaiah and Paul bring this point home to us in today's other two readings. Isaiah describes the attitudes that will make us a flash of light in the surrounding darkness. Paul indicates the signs by which we can recognize whether we in fact are the salt of the earth and the light of the world.

Isaiah offers two sets of recommendations. Since we are familiar with Christ's words, Isaiah's words do not surprise us. Since he wants us to avoid penitential practices that cater to our vanity and our yearning for self-satisfaction, he points out that true fasting is to be found in serving others: "Sharing your bread with the hungry, sheltering the oppressed . . . clothing the naked . . . not turning your back on your own. . . ." Only then will your light shine, only then will your uprightness be evident, only then will your prayer be heard by God.

In a second series of recommendations, Isaiah indicates the things we are to avoid: "Oppression, false accusation, and malicious speech." The believer will be flooded with light insofar as he has attained this kind of liberation: "The gloom shall become for you like midday." By overcoming his aggressive impulses, he will be illuminated within. There will be no gloom in him, for he will know what suffices for himself.

We are often tempted to blame someone else for our own dark spots, our inability to see clearly, and our failure to make wise decisions. That is not right. Nor do we find real inner light by practicing a specious form of heroism or trying to do too such. Instead we must empty ourselves, digging out these features of our initiative and energy which seem to be important and effective to us. Only then will the light be able to penetrate the very depths of our soul and gradually dispel the nooks and crannies of gloom.

Here we encounter the message of the Beatitudes once again, expressed in a somewhat different form. It urges us to strip ourselves more and more, down to our very core. We must don a docility which will become wisdom for us. Then we will be the "salt of the earth" and our light will be manifested in our good works.

In today's reading, Paul indicates just how far-ranging this stripping of self must be. Left to ourselves, we might be inclined to regard the whole process as a trade of some sort: if we are willing to sacrifice and surrender ourselves, we will receive some satisfying spiritual compensation in return. Paul, who certainly was "salt of the earth" and "light of the world," indicates that he came to bear witness almost in spite of himself. He was salt and light only because of his faith and his trust in God's word. In himself he felt only "weakness and fear and . . . much trepidation." He refuses to bolster the strength of his message by appealing to intelligence or convincing argumentation. He preaches a message that is incomprehensible and intolerable on the human level: "Jesus Christ and him crucified." His speech is not convincing or persuasive on the human level, but it does possess "the convincing power of the Spirit." He fully commits himself to his task and surrenders himself to the point where he gives up the usual tactics for success. He puts himself in the hands of Another and looks on as the Spirit works through him to convince his listeners.

To arrive at such a peak of faith and self-surrender is a dizzying experience. If we truly grasp what Paul is telling us, if we appreciate the power at work and the demands it makes on us, then we will realize that there is no easy exchange at work here. It is a progressive crucifixion akin to that of Jesus. We can thank Paul for showing us that this is the way for us to take. If we take this road, then we are in the kingdom and we also make an effective contribution to the work of sharing it with others. We thereby prove the truth of what Jesus said in today's Gospel: "Seek first his kingship over you, his way of holiness, and all these things will be given you besides."

So let us turn to Christ, who has just promised us that we can be the salt of the earth and the light of the world if we are faithful to his Spirit. Let us ask him to carry on his work in us and to increase our faith and hope, for they are the roots of true wisdom.

6th SUNDAY OF THE YEAR

Sir 15:15-20
1 Cor 2:6-10
Mt 5:17-37

Jesus' message is one that bewilders us. Today he continues the sermon on the mount which we have been listening to the last few Sundays. From the Beatitudes themselves we glimpsed that his message is not an easy one to accept. But as his discourse proceeds and he spells out his message more clearly, we are even more astounded by what he seems to be demanding of those who believe in him.

Today's passage from Paul's letter to the Corinthians puts us on our guard against any quick or facile interpretation, which is always a temptation for us. To understand and appreciate the message of today's Gospel, we must first grasp Paul's point.

Paul, the apostle to the gentiles, is talking here about God's wisdom. He does not tell us what it is, he simply reminds us that it is quite alien to this world. He sets up an opposition between he wisdom of God and the wisdom "of the rulers of the age, who are men headed for destruction." The latter wisdom cannot satisfy us at all. God's wisdom, on the other hand, is "a mysterious, a hidden wisdom . . . what God has prepared for those who love him." He tells us: "Eye has not seen, ear has not heard, nor has it so much as dawned on man. . . . Yet God has revealed this wisdom to us through the Spirit."

It is a point of major importance. Before we direct our attention to Jesus' message, we must realize that his teaching is peculiarly his own. No other human being has taught it to him because man could not discover it on his own. The certainty of this fact has immediate consequences. It means that his message cannot be found in the world, in the mentality pervading the milieu in which we live; nor do we find any confirmation or support for it there.

If a person accepts and lives by Jesus' message, he will inevitably appear to be an odd creature in any societal group, even in the Church, paradoxical as that may seem. What Jesus tells us today is something that could not be figured out by human beings, no matter how intelligent or imaginative they might be. What is more, we must be willing to stand in contradiction to ourselves and to the human group in which we live, because the human element in us will not be able to tolerate Jesus' message and other people will not be able to comprehend it.

First of all, however, Jesus puts us on our guard against misinterpreting him. He is not presenting himself as an innovator who is going to contradict everything that the Father has revealed previously through the law and the prophets. Nothing is to be spurned. Nothing of what God has revealed will be bypassed without being brought to fulfillment. If someone neglects any of it or induces others to such neglect, he will be held accountable. If someone carries it all out and helps others to do the same, then he will be "great in the kingdom of God."

Jesus then recalls four commandments that are well known to his listeners. But instead of expatiating on them in terms of all sorts of juridical considerations. he stresses their implications for our interior life. Without omitting anything, he transforms them radically and offers us a singular brand of wisdom.

Instead of exploring them in detail, we shall try to pinpoint the overall lesson they convey to us. By reading them over once again, we shall be in a better position to grasp the thrust of certain details that might shock us at first glance.

The first two commandments mentioned by Jesus are absolute prohibitions on specific actions: murder and adultery. He goes on to explore the roots of these actions in the heart of man, man's inner complicity with them. According to Jesus, there is more than one way to kill a human being. Scoffing, spurning, and insulting are so many ways of killing. If we fail to show proper respect for our fellow man, we have already infringed on his life in some way. And if it is serious enough, it may even be a way of killing him. Thus any and every kind of interior malevolence must be ruled out. What is more, the energy invested in nurturing such malevolence must henceforth be invested in seeking ways to effect reconciliation. And this holds true even when "a brother has something against you."

The same applies to adultery. Consent to the desire, to the interior temptation, is already a fault. It is not enough to stay in line with the dictates of the commandment by refusing to engage in the conduct it condemns. One must also combat any and every form of complicity with the sin it condemns: "If your right eye is your trouble, gouge it out and throw it away. . . ."

The other two commandments mentioned by Jesus are not prohibitions. They have to do with commitments already made and the whole notion of terminating such agreements. Marriage and oaths made to God were conceived as contracts that one could terminate for good reason, e.g., because one of the parties had not honored the contract or because the implied commitments had been carried out. Jesus wants to move us beyond this notion of contract or temporary commitment towards the notion of an unconditional and definitive option. In this way he establishes the indissolubility of marriage and the definitive character of our fidelity to God.

Thus Jesus remains totally faithful to the law but transforms it completely. We greatly need to appreciate this, because we operate out of a legalistic mentality to a greater or lesser degree. Jesus invites us to get beyond this mentality in order to enter the spirit of the Beatitudes.

It is quite a process of development, and it enables us to discern what goes into the "wisdom" revealed to us by God. First of all, we see that man is stripped of everything that he automatically sees as important, of everything that the world regards as basic. We also learn that man can no longer belong to himself: "You cannot make a single hair white or black." He is no longer master of his spontaneous desires and appetites; he cannot exercise them as he chooses, justifying himself because he is not doing harm to anyone. Even the basic features of legitimate pride are taken away from him, because he must take the first step to reconcile himself with someone who is holding something against him.

Stripped of self, man no longer has any chance of backtracking. He cannot reconsider his commitments or break his contracts, even if he is the victim of another's weakness or malevolence. This stripping of the self is the price man must pay in order to develop another dimension of himself. Thus he can acquire some new intensity and value, but only if he is willing to divest himself of things which the world regards as indispensable.

The new dimension revealed to him is, first of all, the domain of his liberty. He is capable of persevering fidelity, no matter what the reaction of others may be. The perduring nature of his commitments points up the earnestness of his decisions and leads naturally to a radical self-transformation. This transformation comes about insofar as the roots of evil within him are destroyed; he is no longer under the sway of those impulses which are ready to lash out at the slightest pretext.

We now see clearly that this kind of wisdom cannot possibly be some sort of Platonic knowledge, some idyllic construct of the intellect however brilliant. Instead it is a progression in fidelity, entailing choices that may be painful and the obligation to persevere; only then can the choices bear their full fruit.

In this teaching Jesus draws the portrait of a new type of man. Liberty follows upon docility; it is not the possibility of carrying out all our whims and caprices. Fidelity to what is real means that we must persevere in the task of transforming ourselves, that we cannot succumb to the surface appearance of events. The human quality of our commitments is determined by their perduring nature, not by their subjugation to the vicissitudes of emotion.

That is the Father's wisdom which Jesus reveals to us today. We can choose between it and a seemingly easier type of worldly wisdom, but it is a choice between life and death. May the Lord's Spirit come to help us in making the choice of life!

7th Sunday OF THE YEAR

Lv 19:1-2,17-18
1 Cor 3:16-23
Mt 5:38-48

We are continuing our reading of the sermon on the mount. Jesus alludes to certain commandments of the Old Testament and spells out their full consequences. Last Sunday we were astounded by his demands, and in them we glimpsed the features of the new man he is proposing to fashion. Today he goes even further. He proposes that we be "perfect as your heavenly Father is perfect." Alluring as this suggestion may be, the pathway he proposes seems to be inaccessible and intolerable to us.

Jesus comments on two commandments that deal with our attitude towards our neighbor, and he extends their application greatly. The first is the old dictum, "an eye for an eye, a tooth for a tooth." In itself it does seem to limit one's "right" to vengeance when he has been wronged or exploited by someone else. But Jesus goes so far as to abolish the "right" completely. He rules out the possibility of forcing others to respect us. He even seems to favor cruel and unjust treatment of the believer by urging us to give up anything and everything readily when someone else makes a particular demand on us or mistreats us in a particular way: "Offer no resistance to injury . . . turn and offer him the other (cheek) . . . hand him your coat as well . . . go with him two miles . . . Give . . . do not turn your back on the borrower."

Some commentators feel that Jesus is deliberately being paradoxical in what he says here, and we might well agree with them. But the fact remains that his message is pointed and clear. It breaks down all semblances of personal reserve, ruling out any notion that we have some real or definitive right over anything. It tells the believer that nothing is his property, that he is always inclined to regard too much as his own. There is no doubt that many human beings find it truly impossible to give of themselves in the way that Jesus urges them to do here. His teaching is one that we cannot really endure. But at the very least we might be able to grasp the fact that we really do not possess anything, that we are inclined to hold on to too much. At the very least we might entertain the possibility of divesting ourselves completely of everything and consenting to this radical impoverishment.

Then Jesus goes on to comment on another commandment dealing with love of neighbor. Here he invites us to imitate the perfection of our heavenly Father, to love all human beings equally. We have no difficulty in loving those whom we particularly like, those who return our devotion, and those who thank us for our services to them. But as Jesus puts it, tax collectors and pagans "do as much." The ideal is to resemble our heavenly Father, who bestows sunshine and rainfall on all men equally, whether they are faithful to his commandments or not. Not only does God not punish us or destroy us for our failings, he also continues to lavish his attentive care on all of us, no matter how we respond to it.

We are summoned to give up all our preferences, to evince a sort of grand indifference. We are called to get beyond our personal preferences, to be indifferent to the favorable or unfavorable reactions we obtain, to keep on loving in a spirit of interior liberty that remains on an even keel. If we have not achieved this spirit of indifference, if we refuse to give up our personal preferences and choices, then we cannot be perfect as our heavenly Father is.

The whole message seems quite unreal. It seems to favor injustice, to confine the believer to a burdensome passivity, to scorn the impulses of spontaneity and generosity that well up in the human heart. Even worse, it seems to be a serious threat to the always precarious equilibrium of any society, be it the family or the nation, because it abolishes the "rights" of the human person. Such "rights" seem to be indispensable in protecting us from the weakness or malevolence of others, and thus Jesus' message seems to border on absolute folly.

Paul talks about this folly in today's Epistle: "If any one of you thinks he is wise in a worldly way, he had better become a fool. In that way he will really be wise." Worldly wisdom cannot bring us into the kingdom. It may be able to assure us relative tranquility during our life on earth, but it cannot get us any further than that. The fact is that we are not earthly in the last analysis: "Are you not aware that you are the temple of God, and that the Spirit of God dwells in you?" Thus Paul points up the value and inner consistency of the folly which Jesus propounds in today's Gospel. He reminds the believer that his innermost being is marked by the presence of the Spirit. The believer is a temple of God, a being in which God is present. Therefore "if anyone destroys God's temple, God will destroy him." That is what will happen if someone does not live in accordance with the dynamic thrust of the indwelling Spirit, if he is "wise in a worldly way," if he asserts his rights against other people, or if he chooses to confine his attention and his greetings to those who love him. It is not that God has vengeful thoughts towards him. The point is that "the temple of God is holy." Hence if someone lives in a way that is totally contrary to what he truly is, he is contradicting the presence of the Spirit within him. To work against the Spirit, who is fashioning God's perfection within us, is to effect a dislocation of our true self, to create a tension within the self that can only lead to disastrous ruptures.

If we want to live and to avoid destruction, then we are compelled to accept folly; "For the wisdom of this world is absurdity with God."

To help us with this whole matter, and to show us the supreme wisdom of this folly, Paul goes on to enlarge the vision and the perspectives of the believer. He shows us concretely what Jesus is talking about when he proposes self-abandonment and indifference to us.

"All things are yours, whether it be Paul, or Apollos, or Cephas, or the world, or life, or death, or the present, or the future." This is what happens when we follow the suggestion he gives us: "Let there be no boasting about men." When we do not look to the world or to others for security and satisfaction, when we accept self-abnegation and indifference, we are not hemmed in or mutilated. Instead we attain a liberty and a range that is universal in scope; and the more intensely we cultivate self-abnegation and indifference, the more real this liberty becomes.

In saying "all things are yours," Paul wants to keep us from attaching or limiting ourselves to one master. The Spirit is in each of us; no one contains him fully and completely. But it is not that simple to detect the particular reflection of the Spirit in every person or in every creature. We can only do it to the extent that we have liberated ourselves from our preferences and our tendencies to exclusiveness, to the extent that we display a universal benevolence which will help us to open our eyes more and more.

That is why Paul goes on to remind us that "you are Christ's." Possession by Christ guarantees us total self-abnegation and the vital energy we need. If the believer is Christ's, then he cannot hold back anything for himself. Everything he has, everything he can get, is the Lord's; it is not his own. He must use it as the Lord wills. In return, however, the Lord takes him in hand and his Spirit dwells in him. He belongs to the Lord. He is the temple, the dwelling place of the Lord's Spirit. How could the Lord possibly abandon him? Christ will not abandon him, no more than he was abandoned by his heavenly Father who raised him from the dead.

So the message makes sense after all. It is absurd only in terms of our own ideas and the mentality of the surrounding world. It is absurd because it is wholly different, because its methods and goals are totally different from those of the world.

The only important question is: Do we accept the kingdom proposed by Jesus? If we do, then everything will make sense. We will be gradually led to accept everything he teaches us today. If we do not, then we should not be surprised to find that he takes our refusal seriously and leaves us in our dark despair and our interminable torments.

When we first look at Jesus' teaching, we are inclined to ask whether it does or does not foster evil and injustice. Now we see that this approach is merely casuistry, a way to reject his teaching. It does not represent a disinterested inquiry into the truth of his words. Jesus wants us to learn what it means to live the holiness of God. It means giving up our inclinations to self-defense. It means cultivating an indifference that will allow our love to become universal. Only by undergoing this transformation will we be able to discover solutions to the concrete problems that will crop us. To attempt to solve them first is to engage in intellectual gymnastics and to go contrary to the life of the Spirit and his work of re-creation.

8th SUNDAY OF THE YEAR

Is 49:14-15
1 Cor 4:1-5
Mt 6:24-34

Today Jesus confronts us with a radical choice and compels us to make a basic, definitive option. Which master shall we choose: God or money? We cannot serve them both at the same time; they are incompatible and mutually exclusive. That says it all for us. Now how are we going to react? What choice shall we make? The rest of Jesus' discourse is meant to help us with these questions.

Jesus knows that our inermost desire is to serve God and be faithful to his word. He knows we are sincere. But he also knows that we are not properly enlightened and hence cannot choose correctly. So he chooses to attack our idolatry of money at its very roots. Once we set aside avarice and sinful delight in it, we can say that the most high-sounding justification for our worship of money is our concern for the necessities of life and the anxiety we feel about these matters. That is what Jesus discusses.

Using three comparisons that are highly poetic in their imagery, Jesus tries to show us the absurdity of our anxiety. The birds of the air do not sow or reap, yet they are nourished. No amount of worrying can change a man's height. The lilies of the field do not spin, yet they are clothed beautifully. Now if God takes care to feed the birds of the air and clothe the flowers of the field, will he not be even more industrious in caring for man? So Jesus concludes: "Let tomorrow take care of itself. Today has trouble enough of its own."

We must admit that these words are alluring. Enraptured by them, we feel that they are true, that it is absurd to be so concerned about our day-to-day life, that there are better things to do. But as we reflect further, things become a bit more complex.

Modern man is ill at ease. He is greatly concerned about his existence, and with good reason it seems. Do we have the right to leave him in his ignorance? Just because we are believers in Jesus, are we to live by caprice as the birds of the air and the lilies of the field? Man's uneasiness is justified. We need only look around us to see that. Hunger grows keener in most of the underdeveloped countries, while economic and social stability grows more precarious in other nations. Life in the great urban centers becomes more and more hazardous. Air pollution, traffic jams, and banditry are on the upswing. How are we to survive it all?

Are we to abandon others in their quest for solutions to these problems, on the pretext that we are obeying God's word? Is it Christian to refuse to share these concerns and thereby hasten the day of worldwide castastrophe? Even if we wanted to follow Christ's words literally, we could not. Our immediate responsibilities prevent us. Our family life and professional work impose constraints and compromises on us.

Pleasant as Jesus' words are, they do not seem to stand up in the light of real life. Do they not represent flight into negligence and irresponsibility, a cop-out that is scarcely compatible with elementary human fellowship and the obvious demands of evangelical charity?

Right away we are tempted to tone down Jesus' message in order to make it dovetail with real life. It is a detestable thing to do. God's word is not to be adapted. It is something we must hear and heed, something that should shape our lives. What, then, does it really say?

To begin with, it is obvious that Jesus is not urging us to laziness or negligence. Birds work incessantly at the task of finding their food, each species earnestly seeking its own proper diet. The lilies of the field keep plunging their roots more deeply into the earth in order to find the juices they need for growth and flowering. When Jesus tells us that each day has "trouble enough," that does not mean that trouble is going to be eliminated. It really exists, as we well know.

Looking at the text more closely, we note first of all that Jesus is teaching us a certain order of priorities: "Seek first his kingship over you, his way of holiness." Other things are not to be neglected, but they should be regarded as components of a more important and necessary ensemble—the kingdom of God.

It is an important revelation. We are not to mix up various domains indiscriminately, but we are supposed to look for some way to bring them all into harmony. If we strive for such harmony, we will find that the many problems vexing man cannot be solved if he, torn by anxiety, looks for the answer in money, economic power, or temporal realities. Money cannot calm man's anxiety, even though it may seem to be the most concrete and direct solution. It will only provoke new anxieties and tempt us to accumulate more and more of it.

This fact is verified by human history. Clearly man has no solution to offer for the problems posed by life. He is even more helpless when he lumps them together in order to get some overall perspective on them. He has no suitable proposal to make on his own. What real difference is there between Peking and New York? Materialism reigns in both.

In proposing a different set of priorities, Jesus invites us to adopt a radical switch in perspective. Compared with this revolution, that of the Maoists and their ilk seems quite tame; and the famous "class struggle" seems quite out of date. We do not get very far by limiting our efforts to a different way of sharing the pie, if the pie is poisoned to begin with. A more equitable distribution of property and income may prove our solidarity, eliminate certain abuses, and correct certain faults; but it does not really change anything. We are still looking to money to solve our anxiety; we are still engaging in a destructive form of idolatry.

If man first seeks God's rule and holiness, then all these other things will fall into place. It does not take much reflection to see that.

In recent years we have discovered that the earth's resources are not inexhaustible. Yet people continue to waste them in extravagant fashion. Groups and nations are unwilling to serve others. They want to insure their own success or domination, and so they use their resources in absurd ways. Man uses his intelligence to devise new engines of destruction that will kill even more quickly and surely. New appetites are aroused in people so that they will join the swelling ranks of a consumer society. And since there is never a proper balance between production and human appetites, man's anxiety continues to grow. People are tempted to hoard things, to pile up riches, as insurance against future needs. It is an absurd system that cannot survive because it keeps hacking away at the very ground beneath our feet.

Seeking God's kingdom and rule does not rule out development. Instead it promotes development—but in a particular way. It promotes development by putting everything in its proper place. Food is meant to sustain life, not to satisfy gluttonous cravings. Clothing is meant to shield us from intemperate weather, not to allow us to show off. If we drop our anxiety about money, if we first seek interior holiness and the proper order of things, there is no doubt that our order of priorities will shift markedly. We will find that we have an overabundance of what we need.

Is that a utopian dream? No, it is the height of realism. Yet man cannot see that. He prefers to dream of some chimerical paradise where every earthly craving will be satisfied to his heart's content. What we have in abundance is not a supply of consumer goods but a host of human beings who need help in their quest for God's kingdom.

This means that each of us must be willing to become a servant, as Paul indicates. As Paul sees it, his own personal worth is negligible. He will not waste his time examining his conscience *ad infinitum* in order to make sure that there is nothing for which he deserves reproach. He is even less concerned about what others think of him.

He simply wants to be faithful to the task entrusted to him. He turns his anxiety over to the Lord, knowing full well that "everyone will receive his praise from God."

"He who trusts in his riches will fail" (Prv 11:28). We all do to some extent. Will we have enough sense to serve the master who will give us an abundance of everything? We must remind ourselves that money is the root of inquity whereas the Lord is the prince of peace.

9th SUNDAY OF THE YEAR

Dt 11:18,26-28
Rom 3:21-25a,28
Mt 7:21-27

Today Jesus teaches us how to become real disciples who will enter the kingdom of heaven. His teaching may seem somewhat obscure, but it is very important.

He starts with a statement that is clear enough, one that seems chockfull of good sense. It is not enough to say, "Lord, Lord!" Our proclamation must be backed up by results, by coherence between what we say and what we do.

Then Jesus alludes to the day of judgment. He pictures those believers who have been content to proclaim their faith in him without really obeying him. They present their case for the defense. They have prophesied, expelled demons, and worked miracles in Jesus' name. In other words, they have really exercised powers given to them by Jesus. Prophecy, exorcism, and miracles are signs by which people can recognize the presence of Jesus. We are not dealing here with proponents of some false religion who are merely using Jesus' words to their own advantage. Nor are we dealing with sleight-of-hand artists who can trick onlookers. These people really are believers, who have been entrusted with spiritual powers by Jesus in order to proclaim his message and offer signs of its authenticity. And the tone of their defense indicates that they are dumbfounded by Jesus' accusing words.

His response is indeed surprising: "I never knew you. Out of my sight you evildoers!" It seems unbelievable that Jesus would claim he does not know people who have acted in his name. It is even more unbelievable that he should accuse them of being evildoers, when they have performed acts that enable human beings to recognize him as Lord.

None of this is logical, and we are greatly tempted to gloss over what Jesus says. Once again we try to tailor Jesus' words to our own standards of acceptability. But instead let us try to accept this astonishing yet important revelation.

It really is possible to proclaim the lordship of Jesus with prophetic words and miraculous deeds and yet not really know him. And since we then do not know him and he does not know us, our words and actions become iniquitous.

Those who act in the name of the Lord may really suffer from a split in their personality. They act in his name, but they carry out a purely external, social function which they do not apply to themselves.

The schism is not obvious, however, as Jesus points out in his subsequent remarks. He compares a house built on a rock with a house built on sand. They look no different on the outside. They both seem sturdy enough and fulfill their purpose adequately. No one could immediately detect any difference between them. But the contrast between them shows up when fierce winds blow and stormy weather breaks. The house built on rock does not crumble, the house built on sand collapses in ruin. Similar as they appear, their foundations were quite different. But it is only in a crisis that this underlying difference becomes evident to the observer.

The application of this simile to what was said above is clear enough. Two believers can use the same words, perform the same functions, and employ similar powers. No observer will detect any difference between them, and each may even have a serene conscience. Both may be quite generous and even heroic. Yet one is as solid as a house built on a rock, whereas the other is a house built on sand. That is Jesus' message for us today.

In all likelihood we are inclined to ask ourselves: To which category do I belong? Do I obey God's will and build my house on rock? Or am I content to utter words and perform deeds without giving any real inner adherence to them?

The fact is that our life is a many-sided affair and that we probably belong to both categories in one respect or another. There are some trials and severe tests which we manage to withstand without losing our inner peace or our confidence in the Lord. We manage to get through some sickness, or failure, or reversal of fortune quite well. But there are other trials that floor us completely. They seem too painful for us to endure. We pray fervently and persistenty, but to no avail. Someone close to us, whom we dearly love, betrays us. The behavior of some minister of the Church scandalizes us. We close up within ourselves, we cannot take it. The language of faith no longer makes sense to us, we are deeply troubled, and we give way to negligence.

Yes, our house is built on both rock and sand. Each storm is a flash of light, a sign from the Lord, enabling us to see where we really are. We can then get beyond our words, and the vague impressions of our own conscience to find out if we truly are docile to "the will of my Father in heaven."

Jesus' words about true and false disciples encourages us to be cautious in passing judgment on others or ourselves. They also leave us unsure about our own ability to enter the kingdom and offer us a sign whereby we can judge the degree of our personal fidelity to him. That sign is our ability to stand firm when trials and tribulations overtake us.

How are we to grow in this ability, which is the mark of a true disciple? Paul deals with this question in today's Epistle when he talks of God's holiness.

Right away he makes one thing clear: it is not our practice of the law nor our obedience to some rule, however stringent, that justifies us in the sight of God. We might have been inclined to interpret the warning of the Gospel in such terms, feeling that Jesus would surely recognize us as his disciples if we resolved to carry out generously some such resolution. Such a resolution might indeed raise our self-esteem, but that does not mean that God would share this esteem for us.

In God's sight we all are on the same level. No one

enjoys superiority. "All men have sinned and are deprived of the glory of God." We must first be convinced of this fact if we want to be recognized by Christ. We may have all sorts of spectacular talents and abilities, but we should not let this delude us. We are incapable of justice and holiness in the sight of God.

It is God who communicates this justice "through the redemption wrought in Christ Jesus." Hence we are "undeservedly justified by the gift of God." This is the second point in the revelation of God's justice. To be recognized as children of the kingdom we must acknowledge our personal inability and believe in the work of Christ, who gratuitously renders us worthy of the Father's love.

That brings us to the third feature of this justice. Believing in the work of Jesus means bringing our whole life and person in line with this faith. Obedience to our heavenly Father's will no longer means simply the faithful execution of some law or self-contained commandment; it means personal adherence to a wisdom that goes by the name of love. We know pretty much how we show commitment and fidelity to it, but we do not know where it will lead us or how we will get there. All we can do is to be docile to the breath of the Spirit, the Spirit of the risen Christ. We must remain open to it always, constantly renewing our resolve.

The book of Deuteronomy uses a marvelous image to express this suffusion by the Spirit: "Take these words of mine into your heart and soul. Bind them at your wrist as a sign, and let them be a pendant on your forehead." Those who cry "Lord, Lord" are content to wear them on their wrist and forehead. But if we take them into our heart and soul, then we show that we are willing to let the Lord work out his mysterious love within us.

10th SUNDAY OF THE YEAR

Hos 6:3-6
Rom 4:18-25
Mt 9:9-13

Jesus selects a new apostle today. As always, the call is direct and its acceptance is prompt. The man abandons everything and follows Jesus. But today's selection of an apostle has particular importance, for it is "a man . . . at his post where taxes were collected." That may not have any bad connotations for us, but it certainly did for Jesus' contemporaries. Tax collectors and other people of that ilk were regarded as untouchables and were labelled "publicans"; you were not to keep company with them.

The term "publican" derives from the Latin word *publicum,* and it applied to those who performed services connected with the public treasury. These men paid specified sums into the public treasury in advance, then reimbursed themselves by collecting tax payments from the public. Obviously it was easy for them to profit from all sorts of substantial windfalls of an illegal nature. That accounts for their terrible reputation. To induct one of these men into the band of apostles was to do something "scandalous." In fact, Mark and Luke go so far as to change Matthew's name to Levi in reporting the incident, so as not to cast suspicion on their fellow apostle and evangelist.

Jesus takes a notorious sinner and makes him an apostle, a pillar of his Church. a peer of Peter, Andrew, James, John, and the rest. We find it hard to imagine how intolerable that would be for the religious outlook of the people around Jesus. In their eyes a publican could not do good things any more than Abraham and Sarah could beget a child at their advanced age. Paul recalls that story for us in today's Epistle. It was hard for the aged couple to believe that they would beget an Isaac and have countless descendants, even though the Lord promised them as much. But Abraham did beget a son because "he was strengthened in faith." In like manner, a publican was chosen to be an apostle; and he eventually became one of the four evangelists.

After his call, Matthew apparenly held a banquet at his home. He invited Jesus and some of the people with him. He also must have invited his colleagues and friends, who are described in today's Gospel in a general way as "many tax collectors and those known as sinners." Jesus and all these people sit down at the same table to share the same meal. The narrator of the story does not give us any details about the meal or the way it was organized. He simply indicates that there were many guests. In any case, we gather that everyone there was relaxed and quite at ease.

The panorama moves away from the banquet itself and shifts to the vicinity of Matthew's house. Some Pharisees appear on the scene. Unlike the publicans and sinners around Jesus, they were men who observed the law strictly or had that reputation anyway. These practicing believers are astonished, but they cannot make their way to Jesus. So they question his disciples: "What reason can the Teacher have for eating with tax collectors and those who disregard the law?"

Their question is a legitimate one. Our natural tendency is to condemn the Pharisees out of hand, pointing to their systematic opposition to Jesus and his own vigorous condemnations of them. But here we wrong them in doing this. First of all, these men were believers in their own way and we are in no position to judge them. Secondly, our habit of condemning them makes us very much like them. Thirdly, their question is also our question in any case. They express sentiments that are very much our own. If we force ourselves a little, we can of course picture Jesus sharing a meal with people of ill repute. But it is an artificial stance on our part rather than a profound conviction. "Ordinarily," the Lord's companions are "the good guys." That is what we really think, and so we yearn to be worthy of him, to merit his favor or company. We have the impression that we must obey him in all things so that he will bless our efforts and find us worthy. We say to ourselves: "What will the Lord think of me?"

This outlook is encouraged by the teaching of Scripture on obedience and fear of the Lord. And we also find it in our treatment of other people. All too often we see traces of spiritual racism in our Christian communities. Certain people, who hold particular opinions or belong to a particular faction, are looked on with disfavor and ostracized for all practical purposes. In many ways we are the people of whom Hosea speaks. We try to make ourselves worthy of God's favor by holocausts and sacrifices.

Jesus' response comes ringing through the din of voices. First of all, he affirms the purpose of his mission: "People who are in good health do not need a doctor; sick people do. . . . I have come to call, not the self-righteous, but sinners." Now it is quite possible that the Pharisees would agree with that sentiment. It is his method or approach that they would criticize. In their own way, they too were concerned about sinners. To the latter they would recall God's law and then lambast them for failing to live up to it. That was the approach they took to bring sinners back to the path of righteousness. Jesus operates quite differently and goes much further than they would.

He makes it clear that sinners are called to share in the Lord's banquet. They will be rehabilitated, not because they have improved their fidelity to some set of laws, but because they have perceived the presence of their Lord and put their trust in him. Jesus does not proffer some external remedy, such as the medicine prescribed by a doctor or the harsh reproof of the Pharisees. Instead he proposes that they have faith in his presence, indicating that this faith can do the impossible.

Today's passage from Romans puts it this way: "Hoping against hope, Abraham believed." That is the situation of the sinner. He knows he is incapable of the slightest degree of fidelity, that he is unworthy of the Lord, that his urges make him an easy prey to his failings. But he also knows that he can be "strengthened in faith," because Jesus Christ was "raised up for our justification."

At first glance Jesus' acceptance of the invitation to dine with publicans and sinners may seem to be nothing more than the fulfillment of a mundane obligation; and the question of the Pharisees may seem to be nothing more than a jealous reaction to Jesus' growing influence. In fact, however, it offers Jesus an opportunity to show us a reality of the highest importance. When we realize that we are sinners who relapse over and over again, we must strengthen our faith in the activity of our Lord and put all our hope in him. Not only is this a precondition for his work of rehabilitating us; it is also a precondition for his presence, and without that he will refuse to admit us into his kingdom.

Jesus' response also helps us to grasp the unexpected import of this repast with the publicans: "Go and learn the meaning of the words, 'It is mercy I desire and not sacrifice.'" This response puts his message in line with that of the earlier prophets, such as Hosea. It also tells us which sinners have most need of his presence today. It is those who prefer to justify themselves by sacrifices and personal efforts rather than by offering their love. It is much easier for man to improve himself on the basis of some clearcut model than to love as Jesus did. But note what Hosea says: "Your piety is like a morning cloud, like the dew that early passes away. For this reason I smote them." The real sin, as Jesus points it out, is that of relying on one's personal efforts, of finding self-satisfaction in offerings and sacrifices, of looking for spiritual security there and refusing the important and wholly necessary gift of his love. If this gift is accepted, then faith and hope in the risen Christ have their full meaning. It is he who brings this love to reality in us. We open up to his presence. We hope against hope, "fully persuaded that God could do whatever he had promised."

If we are honest enough to recognize ourselves in the questioning Pharisees, then we have received a very worthwhile message. Insofar as their question is ours, we really are sick people in need of a physician. Our illness is lack of love, and the remedy does not depend on us. Our healing depends on our hope in the Lord. We cannot love properly any more than Abraham and Sarah could beget children at their advanced age; but everything is possible for God. If we hope in him, then he "will come to us like the rain, like spring rain that waters the earth."

11th SUNDAY OF THE YEAR

Ex 19:2-6a
Rom 5:6-11
Mt 9:36-10:8

Jesus has been passing through towns and villages, preaching in the synagogues, healing the sick, and encouraging the disheartened. But his work never seems to end. The people keep flocking to him, and he can read the distress in their eyes. They look "like sheep without a shepherd," he says. And he has pity on them.

That was his observation and his reaction some two thousand years ago. Are things very different today? We need only read a newspaper or listen to the radio to realize that they are not. People everywhere are upset and driven to dispair by the difficulties and the seeming absurdity of life. When we look at people around us, we get the same impression that Jesus got when he looked at the crowds around him. Even Christians no longer seem to know what master to follow, what person to trust. Once upon a time the Church offered them the consistency of a unified teaching, but now the barriers are down. They turn in every direction, "like sheep without a shepherd."

Noting the disarray and the lassitude of the crowd, Jesus has pity on all the people there. He turns to his disciples, but not for personal solace or support. His remark is one that we could not expect at this point: "The harvest is good but laborers are scarce." We know that the term "harvest," in the idiom of the Bible, alludes to God's kingdom. It is the time for reaping the grain and storing it in barns, and these images are applied to the end of time when the Lord will welcome the now purified elect. Although Jesus feels real pity for the dejected multitude, he sees in it a sign of the kingdom's proximity. His first words to his apostles are words of hope.

We detect the same note in today's passage from Romans. "When we were still powerless," and "while we were still sinners," Paul says, "Christ died for us." Christ took us in hand as we were and performed his work of transforming us, thereby justifying us in the sight of his Father. And Paul insists: "We shall be saved by him from God's wrath."

In a few brief words, today's message transforms our whole reaction. We are struck by the lethargy and prostration of those around us and of ourselves, even as Christ was. Our first reaction is to see it as a sign of absurd suffering and failure, which must be ended at all costs. The overall feeling is one of catastrophe. But Jesus reverses our perspective completely and injects an atmosphere of happiness. The situation proves that the time of the kingdom has arrived. We have already heard a similar message when Jesus proclaimed the Beautitudes. Today we see an application of the first Beautitude: "How blest are the poor in spirit; the reign of God is theirs" (Mt 5:3). These people must know that is true, so Jesus makes a point of telling them in the rest of today's Gospel.

Noting that the harvest is at hand, Jesus is worried about the scarcity of laborers. So he says to his disciples: "Beg the harvest master to send out laborers to gather his harvest."

So that is what he expects from us, especially at critical moments when human beings seem to be lost sheep, deprived of guidance and unable to find nourishment. He wants us to "beg the harvest master to send out laborers." People today instinctively tend to talk about commitment, direct service, and response to the anguished demands that rise on all sides. It is true that the Lord felt pity and spoke words of hope. But the first thing he says is that praying to the Father is the best way to flesh out this hope in the concrete. Upon reflection we realize that it is the one urgent demand imposed on all.

Today Paul tells us that it is Christ who saves us. If we realize this, then our first reaction would normally be to have recourse to this efficacious work, for none other exists. Prayer thus becomes the means of expressing our faith in the activity of the Lord, our desire to see his work carried out, and our certainty that we contribute to it by becoming attentive to what he is effecting in us rather than to the feelings we experience. In the face of human suffering, we must believe in Christ's hopeful word and we must beg the Father to send laborers to gather the harvest. That is what we are commanded to do today.

Then Jesus acts. He summons his twelve apostles, and Matthew is careful to give us their names. He probably wants to indicate that these twelve men have been specifically chosen by Jesus for a particular mission. In any case, that seems to be made clear from what follows.

First he gives them authority over unclean spirits, empowering them to expel them. Chosen from among men, the apostles cannot base their importance on their personal merit or on the quality of their personal prayer. Their importance derives from the fact that Jesus chose them and gave them certain powers.

Having chosen them and given them the necessary powers, Jesus then sends them out. They are harvesters who are to seek out "the lost sheep of the house of Israel," those people whose distress marks them as ready to enter the kingdom.

Jesus then goes on to describe proper conduct for those whom he has chosen, empowered, and sent out. He indicates what they are to say and do. They are to proclaim the kingdom, heal people, raise the dead, and expel demons. They are to do and say the same things that Jesus of Nazareth has said and done as God's envoy. In this way they will be recognized as his envoys. Finally, Jesus indicates the basic attitude that should dominate their words and actions: "The gift you have received, give as a gift."

Today Jesus tells those around him to pray that the Father will send sufficient laborers to gather in his harvest. We might well ask ourselves if that is our reaction when we look at the distress of other people and hear their call for help. Here Jesus underlines a universal obligation incumbent on the whole Church. By means of prayer it is to be the meeting point between the heartfelt cry of man, who no longer knows where to direct it, and the unfathomable love of the Lord, who comes to offer assurance of his kingdom.

To a handful of people, twelve to be exact, Jesus entrusts a specific mission and the power they will need to carry it out. It is not a universal charge. It is a particular role assumed by a small band of men, a modest group even in terms of the limited size of Judea. We could make many observations on all this, but the most important thing is to note what the Lord tells us. He chooses, calls, invests, and sends out. That is what he did for the generation of people he saw before his eyes.

He has always done the same thing at each critical juncture in the history of the Church. To a multitude of lowly faithful he gives the simple faith that inspires them to fervent prayer. To a handful of men and women he gives a special mission; they rise up as the undisputed guides for their age, bearing witness to his kingdom, manifesting his power, and exemplifying his strength in all sorts of ways.

To list them all would be a long and tedious task here. Indeed there may be some now whom we do not even know about. In any case we can be sure that the Lord will raise up people as he has always done in the past. But it is just possible that we will get the saints and the guides that we deserve. Perhaps our hearts must be purified by the persevering prayer of which Jesus speaks today in order for us to discern these saints and guides. We can be sure that the Lord will give us the guides we really need—if our hearts truly yearn for them, if our spirits are purified enough to discern them, and if our humanity is deep enough to allow us to trust in them.

In today's Gospel Jesus offers us a message of hope. Then he goes on to make it more concrete for us. During Mass today let us beg the Lord to strengthen our hope and faith so that we may be able to hasten the coming of the shepherds who are so sorely needed by the downcast multitude.

12th SUNDAY OF THE YEAR

Jer 20:10-13
Rom 5:12-15
Mt 10:26-33

Jesus is speaking to his apostles. He has given them a mission and entrusted them with the powers they need to carry it out. They are to seek out "the lost sheep of the house of Israel" (Mt 10:6). Now, before they depart, he feels obliged to warn them about the real dangers they will have to face. He tells them: "Be on your guard with respect to others" (Mt 10:17). He warns them about all the misadventures they will have because people will not tolerate their words and will take out all their aggressive feelings on them. Having described all the persecutions they will face, he tells them: "You will be hated by all on account of me." Then he concludes: "Do not let them intimidate you."

Three times Jesus warns his apostles not to be afraid to proclaim his message, and then he tells them why they can afford to be daring.

Today, as is the case every Sunday, we are struck by the relevance of the Gospel for our times as we read it. God's message always seems to answer some disquieting question inside us or to warn us about some danger. Today the Lord helps us to overcome our fear of talking about him.

It is not an illusory fear at all. In fact it is quite widespread. There are many priests and lay people who think that the time for announcing God's word directly and explicitly is either past or still in the future. Right now it seems more important to them to share the uneasiness of the world at large, to express unreserved solidarity with it, and to collaborate in the task of building it further. These believers are deeply marked by the outlook of the world, which sees the gospel message as abstract, useless, or outdated.

We must recognize the fact that this mentality has

been greatly encouraged by recent history or by the current behavior of those in charge of the Church. Were not statements made in recent decades about the incompatibility between certain scientific discoveries and theology? Condemnations were issued in the name of doctrine, then later rescinded in the name of that same doctrine. Such an approach would hardly lead large sectors of the public to believe that the gospel message can be taken seriously or have any permanent value. And then one thinks of the difficulties raised by recent statements of the popes, in which they recalled important points of Christian morality—such as the whole matter of contraception. There is such a wide gap between their teaching and current mores that some people are dubious about the timing of such statements while others doubt the truth of them. When someone notes the confusion and uncertainty of believing lay people and ministers of God's word and sacraments, one may well wonder whether they are animated by the same faith. All these things help to raise suspicion in the minds of some about the truth of the gospel message. They encourage many believers to keep silent, or to water down their convictions, thus widening the gap between human beings and the word of God. Believers are afraid to speak out because they no longer are deeply certain or because they do not want to seem to lack solidarity with the rest of mankind.

The fear is not illusory. Jeremiah experienced it and described it for us in vivid terms. We can almost hear the cries of his detractors: "Denounce! let us denounce him!" And we can feel the thirst for vengeance on him: "Then we can prevail, and take our vengeance on him."

Jesus addresses each one of us today, trying to protect the integrity of our faith and to safeguard the boldness of our witness.

First of all, he makes a point that is just plain common sense; then he draws a logical conclusion from that point. Everything will end up out in the open and known, says Jesus. People cannot hide the truth forever, as we see over and over again. For all man's attempts to conceal the truth, the real story eventually comes to light. Hence there is no reason for us to hide or keep silent about the things that we are holding in our hearts, the words and truths that Jesus has entrusted to us. They will be revealed in any case.

At this point Jesus gets down to brass tacks. He knows very well that one may deny or casts doubts on plain common sense. He wants to answer one possible objection that is very real. After all, the apostles are risking their lives in this whole matter, as Jesus himself admitted. He must take this eventuality into account and point out what the real risk and danger is here. He makes a distinction between those who can kill the body and he who can cast the soul into "gehenna." The danger of bodily death is not the most serious risk, for that is the fated lot of all physical existence on this earth. Eternal life does not reside in the body alone. The real danger would be to let the tempter rob us of that eternal life. And that is precisely what would happen if a person refused to speak the whole truth taught to him by the Lord. Jesus would be forced to deny him in turn before his heavenly Father and to condemn him to a death of the soul, for that is precisely what the person himself chooses by fearing to speak of Jesus.

Jesus seems to sense that he has just uttered a truth which is hard to understand, so he explains himself. He uses the beautiful image of the sparrows that are sold in the marketplace. They are so little regarded that they are sold for "next to nothing." Yet each one of them is under the watchful eye of our heavenly Father. As for us, every hair of our head is counted; we are worth more than an entire flock of sparrows. The only risk that his faithful witness faces is the risk of bodily death, and that is not the essential thing. No one can rob him of his soul if he does not consent to it, and he can put infinite trust in the protection of his heavenly Father.

It is not a statement designed to give consolation to

excessively timid emissaries. Far from being haphazard, it ties in with the ensemble of Christ's work in the universe. Paul explains the point to us in today's selection from Romans, which complements the message of today's Gospel.

Paul begins with Adam, with the start of the human race. He tells us that death entered the world through the fault or sin of one man. Death is rooted in sin. Whether human beings are guilty of sin or not is not at issue here; they all must bear the consequences of Adam's sin. Hence we are not necessarily dealing with a punishment inflicted on all men. Instead we are dealing with a general condition imposed on all. Some fatal destiny, resulting from an incapacity known as sin, hangs over each and every human being.

Thus Paul starts from the reality of death, a universal and irreversible power which is evident to all. But then he goes on to say that another reality is superior to the reality of death. The first Adam, who was the origin of death, is merely a type of another man, of "the man to come." Paul is very clear on this latter point: "But the gift is not like the offense." Death might possibly be powerful and inescapable in every case. But in fact the power of death has now been destroyed by "the gracious gift of the one man, Jesus Christ." And this gracious gift, this grace, reaches all human beings.

Hearing Paul's words, we understand Jesus' teaching more clearly. Bodily death, which might be inflicted on us by the enemies of God's word, is negligible because it has already been destroyed by the life which Christ gives us. His life is more powerful than death. That is why he can say: "Do not fear."

There is no flaw in Jesus' line of argument. His logic is unassailable, yet its harsh rigor is hard to take. Jesus does not seem to take due account of human frailty, for man will always be frightened by the risks that he treats so off-handedly here. Perhaps that is why he goes on to make a kind of deal with those who are willing to proclaim him before human beings: "Whoever acknowledges me before men, I will acknowledge before my father in heaven." The risk accepted by those who bear witness to him will entitle them to share in his kingdom. Refusal to bear witness to him, on the other hand, will lead to their exclusion from the kingdom.

There may well be times in our lives when our fear of failing to show solidarity with other human beings will have to give way to our fear of failing to show sufficient courage and boldness in proclaiming God's word. In concrete life it will always be difficult to strike a proper balance between the proper boldness and the danger of rash, useless temerity. We know full well that any line of conduct and every attitude is open to criticism. None is completely good or always right. Sometimes silence will be preferable to untimely proclamation. But such silenct must never be prompted by personal fear of endangering one's own reputation or upsetting one's own inner comfort.

Making some concrete resolution is not the important thing right now. The important thing is to pinpoint our conscious or hidden fears, to ask the Lord for delivery from them, and then to pray that our inner hope and trust will be intensified.

13th SUNDAY OF THE YEAR

2 Kgs 4:8-11.14-16a
Rom 6:3-4.8-11
Mt 10:37-42

We have just heard the final section of Jesus' discourse in which he sends out his apostles to proclaim the imminent coming of his kingdom. He has already selected his apostles, conferred a mission on them, invested them with spiritual powers, and offered them advice and admonitions. Now he goes on to trace the spiritual physiognomy of a true apostle: that is, what his underlying outlook should be and what conditions must be met if he is to radiate the message of Christ.

Much of what Jesus says today is very familiar to us. His words are quoted frequently to describe the absolute nature of attachment to the Lord. It would be quite easy to comment on them in terms of their universal application, thereby passing over their narrower application to the mission of the twelve apostles in today's selection. That approach would broaden their scope, but it would also dilute their intensity. If we limit the message and our commentary to the twelve, we will find that Jesus' words have great force indeed.

What we have here is a series of three statements about the demands made on the true apostle of Christ, and then a series of three statements on the impact of his work on others. The two sets of statements are connected by a comment which explains the "why" of the first three statements and the "how" of the second three statements.

In the first set of statements Jesus lays claim to first place in the life of his apostle. If a person loves father or mother, son or daughter, more than Jesus, then he is not worthy of Jesus. Indeed the apostle must give preference to Jesus over himself: "He who will not take up his cross and come after me is not worthy of me." To follow Jesus is to give him priority over one's personal desires and one's most noble and generous plans. The apostle must sacrifice his own independence and let Jesus take him where he will. He must let Jesus fashion his holiness in his own way and at his own pace. even though that may upset the lethargy or impatience of the apostle himself.

There is an obvious progression and buildup in these first three statements. Jesus gradually lays hold of the person down to his very depths, demanding docility on every level. Every person and everything else must take a back seat to Jesus. In certain circumstances the choice he asks of us may seem to be cruel and intolerable, a veritable crucifixion. No evasion is possible, and Jesus tries to explain why this harsh demand is justified: "He who serves only himself brings himself to ruin, whereas he who brings himself to nought for me discovers who he is."

In all probability Jesus realizes that he is demanding complete self-detachment in the order of priorities he proposes here. He knows that his apostles will feel they are sacrificing something basic and essential when they obey him. The person who follows Jesus will experience a feeling of vertigo. The love demanded by Jesus will lead to a sort of destruction, as if the human element in the apostle were being deliberately denigrated and set at nought. Jesus does not deny this impression. Indeed he points to this feeling as a sign that the apostle is successfully following in his footsteps.

Much the same thing is said by Paul in today's Epistle. Once again we detect the same juxtaposition of death and life. We must pass through death in order to find life. "We have died with Christ" because we were "baptized into his death." Indeed "through baptism into his death we were buried with him." How can we help but take these words at face value? We are tempted to interpret such language symbolically because that would appeal to us more and safeguard our thirst for power and success. Unfortunately such an interpretation would go against the whole thrust of the gospel message, of the Beatitudes especially. Ordinarily God makes his presence manifest in ways that give us the impression we are suffering some sort of destruction. Only rarely does he do it in ways that give us a feeling of inner euphoria, and then it is usually to encourage us or bolster our perseverance. We must lose our life, allowing the Lord to extinguish our thirst for selfish existence; if we do not, then all is lost indeed.

If a person is willing to lose his life for Christ's sake, then he will "discover who he is." He will truly be alive, as Paul tells us: "We believe that we are also to live with him. . . . You must consider yourselves dead to sin but alive for God in Christ Jesus." Life will be found once again because the risen Christ will never die again.

It all becomes terribly logical when we agree to this course. The emotional sacrifices and the priorities demanded by Christ are no longer mutilations but transformations in our way of loving. They teach us how to love properly and truly, that is, with a concern for others rather than for ourselves.

Having urged the apostle to accept an inner death, Jesus then indicates what the impact of the apostle can be. Once he agrees to follow Christ wholeheartedly, he will truly be the emissary of the Lord. It is not enough for the Lord to choose him, endow him with power, and send him out. If he is to proclaim the kingdom, then he himself must fully accept the message he is going to proclaim to others. The powers of spiritual healing must first be applied to himself before he can apply them to others. Only then will those who accept him be truly accepting Christ and the Father who sent him.

It is an important point. If an apostle has not brought himself to nought for Christ's sake, then he is incapable of truly proclaiming the kingdom. If an apostle has been willing to bring himself to nought so that he can become a child of the kingdom, then he will stimulate others to discover the life of the kingdom as well. Indeed the person who accepts a true apostle will find Christ and his

Father. The apostle will perceive this, however. He must be willing to lose everything for Jesus' sake, to believe what Jesus has told him. That is all there is to it. He cannot plot his success on a chart or measure his effectiveness on a graph. Sometimes other people will proclaim their willingness to follow the Lord, but the apostle will never be able to know who was the instrument of the Lord in their case.

These words should suffice for the apostles. Out of consideration for them, however, Jesus warns them about possible distortions. They may be tempted to reduce their mission to role-playing, to passing themselves off as prophets or holy men. If people accept them as such, that will certainly help those people to make some spiritual progress. Those people may even become prophets or holy people in turn. The apostles will have accomplished something, but that is all they will have accomplished. They will not have introduced people into the kingdom. By passing themselves off as prophets or holy men, the apostles will be focusing people's eyes on themselves and limiting the potential spiritual progress of their listeners. But if they have truly set themselves at nought, then they will be leading people to Christ and to his Father rather than to themselves.

Thus Jesus against stresses the goal which the apostle should have in mind. He is not supposed to play a certain role for the edification of others that will bring self-satisfaction. He is supposed to die with Christ in order to "live with him."

Finally Jesus urges his apostles to neglect nothing in their concern for others. The slightest service to others, even a glass of fresh water, is a service to their Lord and a promise of greater discoveries in their future. That is what happened to the woman of Shunem who welcomed Elisha into her home. She saw him as "a holy man of God" and extended hospitality to him, going so far as to construct an abode for him on the roof of her house. In return Elisha won a favor for her from God, enabling her to become a mother even though her husband was advanced in years.

So there we have the words Jesus spoke to his apostles when he sent them out to proclaim the kingdom. With the help of today's other two readings we have been able to explore their meaning more deeply. What do thy signify for us in the concrete? Each one of us will have to ask the Lord about that; there is no general, all-inclusive answer. Let us open our minds and hearts to his presence so that he may give us an answer and thus enable us to "discover who we are."

14th SUNDAY OF THE YEAR

Zec 9:9-10
Rom 8:9,11-13
Mt 11:25-30

When we read or listen to the gospel message, we often have a feeling of deep inner contentment. It has a ring of truth that convinces us and seems to offer us fulfillment. But as we contemplate the weight of the seemingly simple words and their implications for us, then our contentment gives way to anxious questioning and a feeling of dizziness.

Such is our reaction as we listen to Jesus' admiring comments about his Father and the conclusions he draws from them. He reveals man's limitations and inadequacies on the one hand, and then he goes on to spell out the demanding attitude we must display so that the Father can reveal his kingdom to us.

He makes the point simply and clearly. His Father has hidden the kingdom from the learned and the clever. At first glance this might seem to be an ambiguous statement, for in Scripture wisdom is the supreme virtue and the children of the kingdom are enjoined to act with more cleverness than the children of the world. But today's Epistle helps us to understand the point at issue here. Paul reminds his listeners that they are in the Spirit, not in the flesh. So the learned and the clever of whom Jesus speaks might well be those who wish to limit the source or content of our knowledge to what the human mind can observe or keep track of, who feel that there is nothing above or beyond that limited area.

Notice that Jesus' words do not represent a condemnation or rejection of the human mind or its capacities. He is not against man's efforts or discoveries, but he does seem to suggest that they are relatively limited when it comes to knowing God and entering his kingdom.

We are well aware of the results that flow from setting such limits on man's knowledge and refusing to open up to anything beyond the sensible world. People who do that will inevitably find themselves crushed under an intolerable burden and yoked to an intolerable chain, even though their approach might have seemed perfectly reasonable at the start. As the burden grows heavier on their shoulders, they will feel more obligated to this present temporal world. Their solidarity with it, which is legitimate in itself, will become an exclusive thing which shuts them up in the present world and absorbs all their creative capabilities. They are doomed to a suffocating kind of death that is the result of their own self-imposed limits.

It is not an imaginary hypothesis. That is what today's gospel message tells us. It permits us to glimpse two potential dangers. On the one hand there is the danger that people will place too much confidence in the systematic formulation of their faith. On the other hand there is the danger that people will allow scientific discoveries to topple their faith.

Among the first group are those who entertain too much certitude about the particular way in which their faith is systematized. They know how to express a particular content in a precise way, and they attach absolute value to their particular form of expression. They walk around as wise and clever people who have constructed an intelligent synthesis. By closing in their faith in this way, they actually kill it. It no longer generates life for the kingdom. Instead it becomes a system on which one builds or with which one demolishes others. The history of the Church is filled with that sort of thing, bearing witness to the thrust away from the real kingdom.

The second group of people, who allow their faith to be undermined by scientific discoveries, are quite similar to the first group. If scientific progress does win us some new and real knowledge, if it does not simply propose an unjustified hypothesis, then it cannot help but give us greater insight into God's creation. It may point up the errors in our earlier synthesis, and that is always a good thing even though it may propel us into the unknown. Or else it may enrich the store of knowledge we already possess.

The kingdom itself does not lie at the end of a reasoning process or generous human effort, but every advance in human knowledge and human character can help man to perceive it better.

The Father's pleasure is to reveal his kingdom to "the merest children." In other words, he reveals it to those people who choose not to limit themselves to what man can discover on his own, who are modest and humble and open enough to recognize and admit that they depend on Another. This Other, the Holy Spirit, can bring them to life; so says Saint Paul. The Father and the Son cannot be known by man on his own. They know each other, however, and the Father can be known by "anyone to whom the Son wishes to reveal him." The Son can help us to detect the presence of the Spirit by showing us, through the example of his own life, how a person speaks and acts when the Spirit dwells in him.

The "merest children" put their trust in Jesus, who describes himself as "gentle and humble of heart." Zechariah pictures him as "meek and riding on an ass; on a colt, the foal of an ass." Jesus does not seek to dominate or enslave us; rather, he promises to give solace to our souls. He does not seek resignation or capitulation from us, he offers us liberation. The person in whom God's Spirit is at work is not dispensed from man's lot of suffering and death, but his soul is comforted in that he finds his fulfillment in this suffering and death. What is an overwhelming burden for some becomes a life-building thing for others, thanks to the work of the Holy Spirit. Instead of being locked up in a world that cannot please them or satisfy them, the later are able to develop the full potential of their souls.

Trusting in their master, who is "gentle and humble of heart," they share in the glorious future that will be his: "His dominion shall be . . . to the ends of the world." They will never be abandoned by him. They will always be free to submit themselves to him. What is more, "the warrior's bow shall be banished, and he shall proclaim peace to the nations." Thus the peace which Christ promises to his disciples is not a myth; it is a direct consequence that will accrue to all those who have come to learn that his "yoke is easy and (his) burden light."

Having grasped the point being made today, we are anxious to know whether we are ranged with the clever and the wise or with the merest children. In all likelihood we belong to both groups in one way or another. If we were only members of the first group, we would not have grasped Jesus' teaching at all. If we were no longer members of that group in any way, we would no longer ask ourselves the question. Jesus knows we need help in choosing the right path, so he goes on to tell us some of the things we should do in order to be more solidly ranked among those whom the Father favors with his revelation.

First he says: "Come to me." That should be our first step. We should refuse to get wrapped up in the loneliness of self-absorption, which is so painful and heavy to bear. We must accept the fact that we cannot liberate ourselves on our own, that we need the Lord. To go to him is to break the vise-like grip of a self-enclosed world and its smug self-satisfaction.

Then he says: "Take my yoke upon your shoulders and learn from me." He seems to be suggesting that we often bear heavy burdens which are of no advantage to us at all, that we afflict ourselves with heavy labor and suffering as if we were still debtors "to the flesh." Such burdens can only crush us; they do not purify or save us. So we must trade in those burdens for the authentic ones that the Lord himself offers us. For only he knows the yoke and the burden that will help us to become the "merest children" whom the Father favors with his revelation.

To move towards Christ is to decide firmly to wear his yoke and bear his burden. It is to live by the Spirit, to "put to death the evil deeds of the body." In short, it is to distinguish what is real from what is illusory. The things that the clever and the wise can put together are indispensable, but they are never sufficient and we must be able to get beyond them. To accept a kind of dying is to accept a transformation of self. In so doing we do not despise or reject the achievements of the clever; rather, we seek ot put them in our service where they belong. If that is the tack we take, then the Spirit within us will be able to give us life and the Son will be able to reveal his Father to us. As Zechariah puts it: "Your king shall come to you."

Today's message is important for all of us, whoever we may be. No matter how strong our faith may seem to be, no matter how vast our knowledge or generosity may be, we may be among the wise and clever people to whom the Father refuses to confide his secrets. That is the case if our outlook is that of a person who focuses on himself and keeps everything else out. The "merest children," by contrast, are never satisfied because they know that God will ever remain unknown and that his outpouring of love will depend on their acknowledgment of need.

15th SUNDAY OF THE YEAR

Is 55:10-11
Rom 8:18-23
Mt 13:1-23

From the opening words of today's Gospel we know that Matthew wants to tell us something very important. He sets his scene with masterful simplicity. Every word suggests that we are going to hear a major address. Jesus heads out of doors for the seashore. The crowds gather around him, so he pulls out from shore a bit in a boat in order to be better heard. Then he begins to speak.

But why does he speak in parables? His apostles will soon ask him that very question. Certainly his stories are great, delivered with all the finesse of a great storyteller; but they are also quite puzzling and mysterious. Why doesn't he just come out and say what he means? Then there would be less need for discussion afterwards, and his words would have a great range of influence. Jesus, however, does not seem to share this opinion and he explains why.

As he sees it, a person must already have some sort of preparation in order to understand the word of God. This is not true of everyone. Those who have some sort of preparation, who have already begun to plumb the mysterious reality of God, will be further enlightened by Jesus' message. Those who are still on the outside, on the other hand, will not understand much. They will sink deeper into their ignorance and their inability to grasp the mystery. They will see and hear Jesus without being able to understand. But his words will permit them to sense the existence of a mysterious reality, thus serving as a standing invitation to probe more deeply into it.

That is the invitation addressed to us today, and our response to it will affect the whole course of our lives. It is a critical issue—no mistake about that. Many generous people and virtuous prophets waited their whole lives for the revelation granted us today but did not receive it. They wanted to see and hear what we do see and hear, but their wish was not granted. It is to us that Jesus recounts the simple story of the farmer who "went out sowing."

We can picture the farmer scattering the seed around him with an ample motion. It falls all over, some on the footpath, some on rocky ground, some on thorny bushes, some on good soil. It is a simple and seemingly innocuous story. What does it really have to tell us? Yet Matthew sets his scene with meticulous care and indicates that a large crowd was present. He clearly is trying to suggest that Jesus is revealing an important mystery to us.

Is not Jesus the farmer who "went out sowing"? As the farmer scattered his seed, so Jesus scattered his words among the crowd assembled on the shore. What did they pick up in his words? In all likelihood the degree of individual comprehension varied widely, as is the case with most audiences.

In his parable Jesus described exactly what happened when he himself spoke to people. He is the farmer who went out sowing in his field. The seed is his message—something more than human words. It is the word of God. The people gathered around him are the people of God, the descendants of the prophets, priests, and kings whom God raised up over the centuries to put new life into their hope and their patient wait for the one who would definitively establish the kingdom. There they stand around the seashore, the natural heirs to whom God's message was addressed. Jesus speaks to them. As the Gospel puts it: "He addressed them at length." And the people probably do not even realize that they are witnessing and participating in a major moment in the history of mankind.

Just as the farmer scatters his seed on the varied soil around him, so Christ offers the one word of God to the varied audience in front of him. Some listeners accept it, some reject it; some are overjoyed by it, others remain untouched. Yet for all it remains a fertile seed. The kingdom is inaugurated in this necessary encounter between the word of God and the human race, between the message of Christ and the audience around him.

That indeed is the important happening which takes place as Jesus speaks to the multitude. The kingdom is inaugurated, the new man begins his existence and formation under the guidance of God's word. The full fruitfulness of this divine word will become a reality to the extent that the new man accepts it as he should. Once a field has been seeded, its appearance will change considerably. In like manner world history is about to be wholly transformed, because Jesus has just sown the seed of God's word in it.

Starting from this basic message of the parable, we can easily grasp Jesus' later explanation of it to his disciples. He recounts the story again and applies it to different individuals. The first time he spoke to all; this time he enables each individual to situate himself vis-a-vis this "seed."

Once again we go back over the different kinds of ground on which the seed fell. But this time we are on somewhat different terrain. We cannot tell for sure now whether the "seed" is simply God's word or is also the ground to some extent. In any case we do feel that it has to do with an intimate encounter between God's word and man, so intimate in fact that they mingle with each other to form a single reality. They need each other. God's word is made for man; it can only take root in him. Man is made for God's word; he can only bear fruit through it.

First of all we have the person who does not grasp the word. The footpath is too rough or hard for anything to penetrate it. The seed rolls off and is snatched up by the birds of the air or by the "evil one." Sometimes we are like that. We are given plenty of signs, we hear the same divine message several times, but it says nothing to us.

Sometimes we do hear it and we accept it joyously.

It is like a flash of brilliant light, and we yearn to carry it out immediately. A sudden intuition strikes us and we decide to act on it immediately. But in reality we are akin to the rocky ground. Obstacles, sometimes very mild in themselves, stack up against our good intentions. The taunt of a neighbor or considerations of human respect are enough to dispel our firm resolve.

Sometimes we come to understand and even love God's word. But we cannot possibly carry it out. We have certain responsibilities and tasks, we are part of society and certain demands are made on us. Even if we are not seduced by the lure of riches, we find that certain yearnings and desires are transformed into basic needs; the word of God is shoved into the background. This, too, is something that we all have experienced.

Finally there is the good soil which produces "a hundred or sixty or thirtyfold." Are we sometimes like that? Probably, but we never know when we are because spiritual fruits cannot be counted or measured. In any case we like the notion of being good soil. We know that we have been one or more of the first three types of ground on occasion. Now we would like to be the good soil. But how? That is what Paul tells us in today's Epistle.

If we are to become what we are supposed to be, we must first know exactly the state we are in and what we are supposed to become. In one of his finest passages Paul describes them to us.

First, Paul describes the present state of affairs: "The whole created world eagerly awaits the revelation of the sons of God." Creation is not yet fulfilled. Nor is mankind, the conscious soul of creation. They are waiting and yearning for God's revelation.

Paul then goes on to describe the state of those who have received him: "All creation groans and is in agony even until now. Not only that, but we ourselves, although we have the Spirit as first fruits, groan inwardly. . . ." Insofar as we accept the Spirit, we simultaneously nurture two feelings. We are filled with hope because the fulfillment of creation is imminent, but we suffer from the pangs of childbirth through which we and the world are going. The kingdom was inaugurated when Christ began to speak. But it will be completed only when God's word "shall do my will, achieving the end for which I sent it."

We become good, fruitful soil by accepting God's word, which is the answer to our anxious waiting, and by letting it transform us no matter how painful that process may be.

16th SUNDAY OF THE YEAR

Wis 22:13,16-19
Rom 8:26-27
Mt 13:24-43

Last week Jesus told the parable of the farmer who went out sowing, thereby giving us an important piece of news: the kingdom has been inaugurated. Like the sower moving through his field, Jesus spreads the seed of God's word all around him. This seed is entrusted to the soil, which symbolizes the crowd gathered around him. Each individual listener will welcome the seed of God's word and make it fruitful in his own way, depending on the dispositions of his heart. The central event in the story is the encounter between God's creative word and humanity. The new age, so earnestly awaited by generations of holy people and prophets, has been inaugurated.

Today Jesus continues his teaching on the kingdom, still using parables. Having proclaimed the inauguration of the kingdom, he now talks about its further development and history. His message, proclaimed from a boat anchored offshore in front of a pressing crowd, will produce fruits that will develop over the course of time and be harvested at the end of human history.

And yet his proclamation of the word was hardly spectacular. At most he spoke for a few hours before a few hundred people. In his whole lifetime he may have been heard by thousands of people at most. His words and deeds will be reported in a relatively small book. What is all that when we compare it with the billions of human beings who have lived on this earth in the past or who will live on it in the future? A few million words, perhaps, spoken to some thousands of people: it appears to be ridiculous!

Jesus accepts this basic fact. His initial work is akin to a mustard seed, one of the smallest of plants. To those who might ridicule such an insignificant beginning Jesus replies that he is fully aware of the disproportion between surface appearances and the true importance of the event. But then he quickly warns us not to make a hasty judgment. The little mustard seed should not be despised because it will become "the largest of plants." It will become so large that it will shelter all "the birds of the sky" in its branches. He seems to be suggesting that all mankind will be able to come together in the branches of his tree, since it will be large enough to shelter everyone.

The start of the kingdom is indeed unspectacular. Jesus tells us not to let that fact bother us. Indeed he goes even further. With the parable of the leaven in the dough he seems to be telling us that this initial obscurity will be permanent. The amount of leaven in the dough is relatively insignificant, and it will disappear completely into the overall mix. We know, in fact, that the leaven can go to work only if it is wholly mixed up in the preparation. It disappears in the batch of flour, but the flour in turn is wholly transformed by its intangible presence. In the end we have a whole new reality before us.

The point and purpose of the story is clear enough when we ponder it. The kingdom may have modest beginnings, but it develops from there. It remains invisible until it has completed its work of transforming the world, but that should not lead us to doubt its existence.

Hence we are confronted with a dynamic perspective. The kingdom, inaugurated by Jesus' proclamation of God's word, will not impose itself imperiously on all creation right at the start. Working modestly and imperceptibly it will slowly and gradually gather up the whole universe into the peace of the Lord. But what does that mean in the concrete for us who hear this message today? What will the kingdom look like to us now, and how are we to behave? The parable of the good grain and the chaff, explained by Jesus himself, answers these questions.

During the period when the kingdom is growing and the work of transforming the world is going on, the kingdom will be present everywhere but it will not be clearly evident or completed anywhere. The son of man sows God's word and it bears fruit in the world. At the same time, however, a weed grows up too; and it sometimes threatens to choke the good seed.

In the parable the workers seek out the owner of the field. They do not understand how or why this weed is able to grow there. Where does it come from? That is our question, too. How can it be that the world is not good? How is it that the members of the Church have such evident defects? Why do believers lack docility when it comes to the teachings of God? We could ask countless questions of this sort that deal with the existence of evil and its scandalous, intolerable reality.

Our feeling is that the weeds must be torn out at once, as the workers in the parable suggest. It suggests to us that they are indeed industrious and "committed" to their task. Since things are not going in accordance with what is true and right, they propose to correct the situation immediately. They will do what must be done; they will tear out the weeds. That line of argument has often been used in the Church, giving rise to crusades, religious wars, and expulsions known as excommunications. We are not condemning those actions here, for that would amount to falling into the same off-base approach. We simply want to acknowledge the existence of "weeds" in our history and the tendency to rip them out at once as the field workers propose in the parable.

But let us not stop at past history, let us look at ourselves today. It is clear that racism is not a dead issue by any means, and that we are constantly tempted to condemn or exclude what does not seem to fit in with our personal conception of good.

But the reply of the owner in the parable comes back at us: "Let them grow together until harvest." The real sorting will be done then, for only then will true discernment and judgment be possible. Until then everything is inextricably mixed up; we cannot root out the weeds without destroying the wheat at the same time. Jesus explains that "the harvest is the end of the world." And it is his envoys who will be charged with the task of doing the sorting.

Today we are given a revelation that is a bit baffling, but the point is already suggested by the first two remarks about the mustard seed and the leaven. The start of the kingdom is imperceptible, and its integration into the universe is so discreet that it forms one whole with the rest of creation. Hence it is present everywhere but nowhere fully realized. Insofar as creation is still moving forward towards the kingdom, it is inevitably ambiguous. This ambiguity itself is universal, evident in both societal groups and individuals, in the Church and believing faithful. Hence goodness and purity and truth do not exist in any clearcut form; nor is evil to be found in its pristine form. No individual and no social group is in full conformity with the kingdom; but none is alien to, or excluded from, the kingdom either.

The same thing can be said about the declarations and actions of the individual or the group. No person or group can refrain from speaking or acting, of course. Such abstention would already represent a definite stance. External manifestations are always ambiguous in concrete circumstances. We are never faced with a choice between one action that is absolutely good and another that is absolutely evil. In varying degrees and circumstances each and every choice is both good and bad in one way or another. This ambiguity exists even when we make a moral decision that is in conformity with a duly established law and that is confirmed by the highest religious authorities. For even that decision can be prompted by various motives that water down the quality of the love we think we are displaying. The most elementary laws of psychology tell us that, and Jesus confirms the fact today in talking about our participation in his kingdom.

So what are we to do? First, we must accept the reality which the Lord has revealed to us today in the Gospel message. Accepting it, we are compelled to live with an uneasy conscience. We cannot possibly be fully satisfied with what we are and what we do because we are in a continuing process of transformation. Hence we must reserve judgment on everyone else. We cannot impose our opinions on others on the pretext that ours are better than theirs. Elements of good and bad are to be found in all opinions. It is an uncomfortable situation in which to live. We can tolerate that discomfort only to the extent that we place our security in the Lord's promises. Only then can we enjoy the promise of the Beatitudes. Beyond that, "we do not know how to pray as we ought; but the Spirit himself makes intercession for us." That is truly encouraging because "the Spirit intercedes . . . as God himself wills."

17th SUNDAY OF THE YEAR

1 Kgs 3:5,7-12
Rom 8:28-30
Mt 13:44-52

In the last few weeks we have listened to parables which were meant to help us grasp the nature of Christ's kingdom. Jesus has tried to convince us of the importance of the happening that is now in process of realization. He has also tried to stress the seeming modesty of the whole affair, thereby helping us to draw some sensible conclusions about it. Today he urges us to seek out the kingdom and accept it wholeheartedly. So far, acceptance of the kingdom may have seemed to be an optional thing, however desirable it might be. Today we glimpse the fact that the kingdom is indispensable. Each of today's parables stresses this point in its own particular way.

First, we have two parables that deal with preferring the kingdom. Very similar to each other, their message seems to be identical at first glance. The man who finds the treasure in the field and the merchant who discovers a rare pearl "went and sold all . . . and bought." Both parables breathe the same atmosphere of joy, precipitate action, and preference for one thing above all others. Both the finder of the treasure and the merchant are taken aback by their discoveries. Everything else seems unimportant by comparison. So they liquidate their past, sacrifice their other possessions, and use every means they can to carry off this exclusive investment. They do it in such a way that there is no turning back later. If this venture should fail, they will have nothing. The risk undertaken is total.

In both we detect the joy of an exciting discovery. It fulfills all their aspirations, so that everything else loses its value and can be liquidated with a feeling of contentment. We also note that the treasure and the pearl will require them to sacrifice all their other possessions. One cannot possess anything else when one possesses the kingdom. The kingdom is all-embracing and totally absorbing. Possession of it and service to it allows for no turning back, no possession of other things.

Yet, for all this, the choice seems to be made with a happy, light-hearted spirit. There is no element of constraint or pressure in this option that eliminates all other options. There is no element of anxiety in this risk, which binds the chooser to a reality that is both mysterious and strange.

But if the two people in the parables arrive at the same outlook, the parables do indicate that they got there by different ways. The point seems to be that we can get to the kingdom by different pathways.

The man who found the treasure in a field was not looking for anything. It seems that he stumbled on this wondrous thing by chance. We feel the same way sometimes when we are blessed with a happy turn of events, and we exclaim: "It is providential." But the finder here does not want to sneak off with the treasure surreptitiously. "He hid it again," so that he could be assured of its future possession after he had bought the field. Yet one might debate his honesty here. One might say that he should have told the owner of the field about the treasure before bidding for the field. Such detachment would have been nobler than his sneaky honesty. That may well be, but it appears that the finder of the treasure can think of only one thing now: possessing the new-found treasure. "Rejoicing at his find," he is carried away to such an extent that prudence and common sense are blown to the wind. The only important thing for him now is to get possession of the treasure. His sharp dealing stresses the importance of the treasure that has suddenly come across his path.

The merchant, on the other hand, has been on the lookout for pearls. His line of work compels him to keep an eye out for pearls that are even more valuable than those he has aleady found. Then he spots one that supasses all the rest. Folly takes over and he throws professional caution to the wind. He liquidates all his assets to get one pearl. The value and importance of his discovery takes precedence over everything else.

Whether it be a sudden, unexpected find or the object of a lifelong search, the kingdom is the supreme treasure. It eclipses everything else. Once it is discovered, everything else loses its savor and importance.

Then comes the final parable, that of the net. Comforting at first, it soon sounds a tragic note. To those who have anxiously searched for the treasure of the kingdom but have not yet had the joy of finding it, the first section of the parable offers the insistent message that they must keep looking for this priceless pearl. The kingdom is like a net cast into the sea; it will not be drawn up until it is filled. Until the proper time comes and the harvest is ripe, until the catch is complete, everyone will have their chance to find the priceless treasure. But at the end of this long period of patient waiting, when it is clear that everyone has had a chance to choose freely, the net will be hauled on board and the sorting will begin. "That is how it will be at the end of the world," says Jesus.

And it is here that the tone of tragedy enters the score. Jesus does not say much about the fate of the just. He concentrates on the fate of the wicked. It is as if he were trying to convince us that the risk of opting for the kingdom is not as grave as the risk of opting against the kingdom. Those who refuse the kingdom, the wicked, will be hurled "into the fiery furnace, where they will wail and grind their teeth." We have heard similar words in previous weeks, when Jesus spoke of the wheat and the chaff. Let us be honest for many people his words are intolerable!

After all, they say, is he not offering us a choice akin to blackmail: you are free to accept or reject my offer, but it will go hard for you if you reject it; you will suffer cruelly in hell. Some preachers of previous generations frightened people with grotesque pictures of hell, and common sense has revolted against those images.

But now many have gone from one extreme to the other, as happens so often. Now they reject the idea altogether. They justify their rejection, of course. They say that hell is incompatible with God's goodness. They challenge someone to explain what "everlasting fire" and the "gnashing of teeth" might mean. Since the notion of hell can hardly be envisioned on the basis of man's experience here, they find it simpler to reject the whole idea.

The fact is that we cannot picture hell any more than we can picture heaven from the vantage point of our life here on earth. And we must readily admit that it is a little presumptuous to limit God's love and his goodness by the measure of our own imagination, shaped as the latter is by our own disappointing experience of man's disordered affective life here. We must make an effort to get beyond our instinctive repugnance for the notion of hell, for this repugnance is a sign of our own spiritual indigence. To do that, we must pay heed to what the Lord tells us today.

First of all, he tells us that the kingdom is life. Outside of it lies death, which is pure torture for man because it stands in radical contradiction to his most basic makeup and orientation. But man cannot be forced to opt for the kingdom. If it were not possible for him to refuse the Lord, to live by the inner lights which the Creator has granted him, then he would be a robot without any liberty at all. We might well prefer to be without any liberty, for that would eliminate many risks; but it would be odd indeed if God were to mutilate his creature in that way.

So his threat of punishment for those who reject the kingdom is not blackmail. It is a revelation of our liberty, of the thing that gives us our dignity as human beings. It makes us realize that man's authentic life is to be found in love, not in compulsion.

For those who accept God's offer, the situation is a happy one: "God makes all things work together for the good of those who have been called according to his desires."

Concluding this series of parables, Matthew refers to "the head of a household who can bring from his storeroom both the new and the old." We have learned much from the things we have been told; old truths have come to life and taken on renewed importance. We must keep going back to God's word, which we already know, so that it may continue to nourish us further and give us new life.

18th SUNDAY OF THE YEAR

Is 55:1-3
Rom 8:35,37-39
Mt 14:13-21

We have just heard the account of the first multiplication of loaves. Matthew and Mark also tell us of a second such incident. In the four Gospels we find six accounts of a multiplication quite as spectacular as this one.

Our first impression is one of great perplexity. It is hard for us to accept the reality of the story told to us. We readily tend to seek some symbolic interpretation of the story, one that would satisfy our concern for verisimilitude. We would prefer to regard it as a legendary story, a miracle story, imagined by the apostles to convey an important teaching to us in a vivid way.

Among all the miracles of Jesus it is the most difficult one to accept. To cure the sick, expel demons, and raise the dead is to engage in spectacular feats, to be sure. But we can easily see the verisimilitude of such accounts. We can point to occult forces, more or less magical in nature, whose existence is indicated by certain clues in our own human experiences. Jesus could have been familiar with such forces and mastered them to benefit others. But nothing similar is possible in today's case. Loaves of bread and fishes are material realities familiar to us all. They can be split up of course, but we find it hard to believe that they can be multiplied *ad infinitum*.

A collective illusion is out of the question. There may have been some twenty thousand people around Jesus that day. Yet, after the food had been distributed to them, there were twelve baskets of food left over. The noticeable surplus is a sign of the event's reality. If some sort of mystification had been involved, people might have thought they had eaten their fill; but there would not have been any leftovers! So the event really took place as it is related, and it was Jesus who took the initiative and willed its occurrence.

The crowd did not ask anything of him. The people simply were there. This is clear from the gospel account.

Jesus had just heard the news of John the Baptist's death. "He withdrew by boat from there to a deserted place by himself." The people around him caught wind of his departure. In all likelihood they saw his boat moving away towards a distant shore and it was easy to figure out where he was heading. We can readily imagine the surge of emotion that went through them as they saw their prophet head away. We can see them surging on towards the place where he would land. They do not want him to go away from them. They want to see him. So there they are. They then see his pity for them as he heals the sick among them. Time passes, they are still there. They have no thought of leaving him. Why should they worry? Jesus surely will provide for them.

The apostles quite reasonably suggest the only solution that seems sensible. Jesus should dismiss the crowd so that the people can find food for themselves somewhere. They do not ask him for anything, nor do they seem to have any inkling that Jesus can do something in this particular situation.

Then Jesus speaks, refusing to send the crowd away. It is as if that action would refute the confidence that people have placed in him. It is not possible for him to send anyone away. So he gives the apostles an impossible order: "Give them something to eat yourselves." They reply pointedly. They have only five loaves of bread and two fishes. They cannot feed such a crowd.

Jesus has the bread brought to him. He blesses it, breaks it, and passes it out. In his hands it becomes inexhaustible. He keeps giving it out; it keeps multiplying. The apostles take it from his hands and distribute it. The surplus is so great that they fill baskets with the leftovers.

The point of evident importance is the place of Jesus in the whole event. The people had come to him, probably without anything specific in mind. They simply had enormous confidence in him. The presence of the apostles merely highlights the paucity of resources available. They will distribute what Jesus provides; the crowd will accept it. It is Jesus Christ, the Lord, who holds center stage.

In this incident we have a concrete illustration of the point made by Paul in today's Epistle: "Who will separate us from the love of Christ?" He goes on to enumerate all sorts of trials and sufferings, both physical and emotional. Such things usually trouble the people who suffer them, causing them to lose their inner peace of mind and to doubt the presence of the Lord or his goodness. They leave a deep mark on people and foster a sense of despair. For Paul, these things are negligible: "We are more than conquerors because of him who has loved us." After listing some of the terrible threats that a human being may face in this life, he concludes that nothing "will be able to separate us from the love of God that comes to us in Christ Jesus, Our Lord."

If we are willing to accept the full reality of Paul's words, we must admit that they are as astounding as the incident in today's Gospel. We are being asked to accept the existence of a love whose ties with us are stronger and more lasting than any terrestrial reality or any earthly creature. We are quite aware of the formidable power and constraining influence that human life can exert over us. Yet Paul tells us that nothing in this life can break the bond that links us to the love of God. In short, man possesses an invincible liberty. He is free to maintain a link with God's love for him, no matter what trials or forces may threaten him.

Paul adds that this love "comes to us in Christ Jesus." Could this fact be better illustrated than it is in the miracle of the loaves and fishes? The crowd simply had to present itself to him. The apostles, fulfilling their role as intermediaries between God and man, simply had to accept what Jesus gave them and make it available to the people around them. It is Jesus who willed the whole affair, who did not neglect anything that would render the Father's love present. He calls upon his Father and the bread multiplies above and beyond the needs of those present.

Needless to say, our critical sense might well come into play at this point. There are many questions we would like to ask. How can he let so many men, women, and children die of hunger today all over the world? How can he permit the murderous cataclysms we witness? These and many similar questions may lead us to doubt the veracity of Paul's statements and of Matthew's report on the loaves and fishes. But if we pose questions in this way, we run the risk of never finding any answers. The Lord is not speaking to us today in order to answer our problems, though our problems may indeed be excruciating ones. Nor should we try to judge the truth of God's word on the basis of the short-term experience we have had of it. The only approach possible for us is to accept it without reservations. If we choose to debate God, his word will never be believable.

Isn't that what Isaiah tells us today? "Why spend your money for what is not bread?" That comes down to asking: "Why use your energy for things that are not essential, necessary, and truly nourishing?" His message continues, becoming bold and insistent: "Heed me . . . that you may have life."

We do not get a satisfying response from God by calling him to account and questioning the veracity of his message. He responds to us when we listen to him unceasingly. Then his response is as bountiful as it was when he fed the thousands of people who were hungry. If his love is not evident to us, that is due to our lack of hearing him. We get caught up in various lines of reasoning which create such confusion in us that nothing else can get through. We must heed him always and accept his message unreservedly. Only then can we see things as God sees them. Only then do we see the uselessness of the questions we are inclined to raise when he reveals his love to us. Only then do we realize that the absence of a solution casts doubt on our ability to hear him, not on the truth of God's word.

The multiplication of the loaves and fishes caused us some perplexity. In a short while the Lord will be present in the bread and wine of the Eucharist. If we had doubts about the reality of the gospel miracle, we might also be skeptical about the content of our faith in the Eucharist. In deep humility let us ask the Lord to increase our faith and to help us heed him continually.

19th SUNDAY OF THE YEAR

1 Kgs 19:9a,11-13a
Rom 9:1-5
Mt 14:22-23

With five loaves of bread and two fishes Jesus had just fed "five thousand, not counting women and children." Apparently fearing that the enthusiasm of the crowd will turn the event into a popular demonstration or a personal triumph of some sort and thereby destroy the spiritual sense he intends, he prepares a hasty departure from the scene. He orders his apostles to ship out and wait for him on the distant shore.

There then takes place that fantastic incident in which Jesus and Peter go to meet each other on a storm-swept sea.

The scene is scarcely imaginable, but it does evoke sympathetic reverberations deep within us. It strikes home in that part of our selves where we experience things intensely without being able to express them or explain them. Distinctive as the experience is in the lives of the apostles by virtue of the peculiar set of circumstances surrounding it, its spiritual reality is not alien to us.

The apostles are in the boat, "already several hundred yards from shore." The wind is gusty, the waves turbulent; navigation is difficult. Suddenly, not long before dawn, they see a figure coming towards them; the figure is walking on the water. They think it is a ghostly apparition and cry out in fright. At once the figure speaks to them: "Get hold of yourselves! It is I. Do not be afraid!" It is Jesus, identifying himself. With his usual impetuosity Peter blurts out: "Lord, if it is really you, tell me to come to you across the water." If the Lord is doing that, he wants to do it too. Jesus is quick to encourage him: "Come!" Peter leaves the boat and heads over the water to Jesus.

That Jesus can walk on water is something which fits in with the other things we see him do in the gospel accounts. He has just fed more than five thousand people with a few loaves of bread. Why should he not be able to walk on a storm-swept sea? The thing that really astonishes us is that he would share this capability with a simple fisherman upon the latter's request.

Astounding as it may be, Peter's adventure here is matched by incidents in our own life of faith. Now and then we do see, in fleeting glimpses, what a believer should really be like and what the Lord expects of us. We suddenly discover some particular aspect of the person of Jesus, and we say to ourselves: "That is what I wish for with all my heart!" We do not take due account of the fact that we are moving into the realm of the improbable, that we are asking for things beyond our human capacities. Yet it is only then that faith really begins.

The divinity of Christ, the necessary mission of the Church and her supernatural powers, our own risen life with Jesus—these are just a few of the truths that go to make up the revelation which guides our whole existence. Is it not beyond the power of human beings to adhere fully to those truths and to organize one's life around them? Indeed it is, and few manage to do it. Paul himself is disconsolate in today's Epistle. His faith in the risen Christ is total, but at the same time he feels his fellowship with his people: the Jews. He enumerates what they have received, noting that it was enough to enable them to believe in Jesus. But they did not believe in him. They would have had to get beyond the point they had already reached, rediscovering the truth they already possessed on another level as it were. God always operates that way with us. Each time we try to fix the content of of our faith in some hard and fast mold, it escapes our grasp. Faith requires a continuing process of rupture with the past and movement towards the future, in an atmosphere as risky as that which surrounded Peter when he tried to walk on water.

The risk that Peter took was very real, and we are not surprised by what happened next: "When he perceived how strong the wind was, becoming frightened, he began to sink." Peter had put himself in an impossible situation. To be sure, he had received the Lord's command and the corresponding capability to carry it out. But he could not avoid the sudden discovery that he was in a superhuman situation. His fright was the most natural thing in the world.

Right away he feels the effects of his fear; he begins to sink. It is the very thing that God warns the prophet Jeremiah about: "Be not crushed on their account, as though I would leave you crushed before them" Jer (1:17). Fear shrinks a human being, rendering him incapable of seeing his action through to the end.

This fear experienced by Peter is something we know very well. It is that fear of ourselves, that feeling of deep insecurity, which grips us when we are uncertain where we are because our faith has committed us to a pathway whose stages and direction are not well marked out. It is our fear of others, of what they might say or think about us. It is our fear of some heavy past that weighs upon us, or of an uncertain future that lies in wait for us ahead. It is our fear of certain trials we may possibly have to face. In short, it is all those uneasy feelings and presentiments that assail us and grow into some real sort of terror.

We are only too familiar with the ill effects of such fear. We see countless examples of its ravages in our day-to-day life. People, paralyzed by timidity or by the conviction that they are bound to fail, end up as failures because they do not dare to try. The same holds true in the religious realm. Our fear of evil makes us vulnerable to it. That is only logical, because such fear indicates that we are already dominated by evil. Excessive audacity is no better. The only proper attitude is one of total confidence in the Lord.

That is what Jesus seems to be telling Peter after the latter has cried for help: "How little faith you have! . . . Why did you falter?" The force of the wind got the better of Peter's confidence. He let fear take over, and frittered away the power of the Lord. Paying too little attention to the Lord and too much attention to the threats of wind and wave, he could not help but sink.

We are given an important lesson here. God may ask the believer to go beyond himself. The believer will be able to manage this feat insofar as some sort of harmonious communion exists between his human capabilities and God's Spirit. But the process itself may well provoke fear in the believer's heart. He will find himself in a totally new situation where the old ties of security no longer help him. If he opens the door to such fear or yields to it in any way, then he will be doomed to failure.

There is only one course open to him, and Peter tells us what it is when he reacts to his distress: "Lord, save me!" His fear had been a kind of rejection of the Lord insofar as he let it water down his confidence. Only the Lord himself can restore the presence of his power within us when we have let it slip away by our neglect. After all, which of us can fashion what is really divine? It is the Lord's work, as today's Gospel indicates: "Jesus at once stretched out his hand and caught him."

Peter's cry for help is an admission of helplessness, and his humility will allow him to be saved. Peter had failed to show confidence in Jesus at one point. Jesus' subsequent reaction reveals how true and effective his mercy really is.

Peter's experience in today's Gospel helps us to appreciate how we make progress in our faith. It is not a straight-line process. It is not like pouring water into a container, where the water mounts slowly to the top from the constant pressure. Our progress in faith is due to summonses which urge us to surpass our human limitations. Secretly lured by this invitation and inwardly persuaded of its truth, we are completely disposed to commit ourselves to the task of fleshing it out in reality. But if the spirit is willing, the flesh is weak. It panics when it perceives the consequences that will flow from the spirit's choice. If our spirit lets this reaction take over, we are doomed to failure; only the Lord can get us up and on our way again. He lays hold of us once again, and we can experience this "hold" on us. It comes across to us as the only source of solid strength and the only thing that will enable us to fulfill the goal he proposes to us.

These experiences are repeated in our lives over and over again. We make a little progress, then we slide back again. Some divine impulse moves us forward, then we run into a blind alley, then the Lord starts us moving once again. As we experience these things over and over again, we gradually develop a heartfelt conviction about God's presence and draw into closer intimacy with his Spirit. Holiness no longer is envisioned as the pursuit of some carefully worked out project or the imitation of some model or the fleshing out of some personal ideal. It now is seen to be communion with Christ's Spirit, who keeps inviting us to imagine and create the improbable; to peacefully accept the unexpected.

Today's Gospel ends up by telling us that the apostles in the boat showed their reverence for Jesus: "Beyond doubt you are the Son of God!" As we participate in our Eucharistic sacrifice today, let us ask the Spirit to open our eyes so that we, too, may recognize and acknowledge his living presence.

20th SUNDAY OF THE YEAR

Is 56:1.6-7
Rom 11:13-15,29-32
Mt 15:21-28

Today Jesus makes someone importune him for a favor. On many occasions we have seen him work miracles without any prompting at all. He does not even wait for people to ask him for a miracle, he simply goes ahead and heals the sick or raises the dead. But today it is quite a different story. A Canaanite woman, not a Jewess, leaves her house and goes after Jesus. She pleads with him insistently, despite his rebuffs, and ultimately persuades him into granting her request.

Jesus' apparent cruelty is astonishing. At first he does not respond when the woman begs him to deliver her daughter from the clutches of a demon. The apostles grow insistent too, but Jesus maintains that he must reserve his powers for the people of Israel. The woman prostrates herself in front of him. Jesus' refusal seems to border on tactlessness. It is not right, he says, to take the bread of his Israelite children and throw it to alien dogs.

Not only is the Lord reluctant; his reasons for refusing her seems quite intolerable to us also. Is it not contrary to God's universal love to reserve his benefits to a single people, to leave this sorrowing woman unanswered and uncomforted? Once again we are tempted to look for some reasonable explanation, to figure out what the Lord was trying to get across. But the fact is that Jesus offers no explanation whatsoever. In the end he simply says: "Woman, you have great faith!"

Who is this woman? From her very first words on, the woman in question behaves like a mother who is profoundly distressed by the plight of her child. She does not ask Jesus to have pity on her child, but on herself. It is her own suffering that she puts first, even though it is her child who is under the domination of a demon.

The plight of her child is painful to her, and she asks the Lord to pity herself. She becomes doggedly insistent, so much so that the apostles are moved to intercede with Jesus and to try to change his mind. The woman throws discretion to the wind, and we must admit that her example of the crumbs from the table is adroitly used.

In all this she shows up as a typical human being, no better or worse than any other. Her ardor, her passion, her weakness makes her very close to us.

But though she is one of us, her behavior vis-a-vis Jesus reveals a deep awareness of who Christ is. She calls him, "Lord, Son of David." She recognizes and acknowledges his sovereignty, prostrating herself before him. It is a sign of homage due only to the Almighty. She knows Jesus has the power to free her daughter from the grip of the demon, so she will insist as much as she has to. Her faith is simultaneously knowledge and fidelity, strong enough for her to overcome all obstacles and to commit herself wholly to forceful pleading.

Her attitude tells us what her faith is, and the gospel account makes a point of her background. She is not a Jew, not a member of the chosen people. She is pagan in background and upbringing. She knows very well that the Jews call her people "dogs"; yet, by the same token, it is through the Jews that she comes to know and accept Christ.

Paul focuses on this very point in today's Epistle. Speaking of his fellow Jews, he says: "Their rejection has meant reconciliation for the world." He seems to be suggesting that the Israelite nation was separated and set apart from other human beings so that human beings could be reconciled with each other and with God. At first there seemed to be some basic opposition between the Canaanite woman and the Jews; now the Canaanite woman seems to be the heiress to the spiritual treasure of the Israelite nation.

While the faith of the woman finds its origin in the Jewish people, it also presupposes qualities that are brought out in the account itself. First, we see her humility; it preserves her from humiliation. She knows her faith is a free gift, that she could not discover it or fashion it on her own. It is something created by another, something to which she has no right, hence there is no reason for her to feel humiliated by a rebuff.

This fact gives rise to a second quality in her: docility. She is ready to accept God's way of doing things without any reservations. We are astonished by Jesus' cruelty, but the woman herself does not even seem to notice it. She is ready for any and every reaction of the Lord, however unexpected that reaction might be. Paradoxically enough, it is this very docility which gives her the energy and perseverance to keep at her insistent plea for help.

Such is the faith of this woman, a faith which Jesus notices and praises. And one of the most original aspects of her spiritual life is the relationship between the faith of this Canaanite and the Jewish nation. Regarded as an outsider, she still was able to know and recognize Christ—thanks to the Jewish people.

By the same token, her faith in Christ might well help the Jews themselves to recognize Jesus as the Messiah described by the prophets and awaited so long.

What happens to this Canaanite woman is very important. On the basis of the relationship between her faith and the existence of the Jewish people we can get a better appreciation of the relationship between the Church and non-believers. In his letter, which we read today, Paul helps us greatly to do this.

Clearly enough, the Epistle talks about "setting apart": and the Gospel talks about the priority of the Jews. But if we take a close look at what is said, we discover that this priority does not exclude anyone. It is a pedagogic device willed by God so that everyone can better appreciate his message and adhere to it.

Paul tells us: "God has imprisoned all in disobedience that he might have mercy on all." It is obvious, then, that no one is superior or more perfect. All men are separated from God by some sort of radical lack of docility. It makes them unsuited for the kingdom that he has promised them. To all human beings God offers his mercy, and only his mercy can bring them to reconciliation. Already initiated, this process of reconciliation will continue on to its fulfillment because: "God's gift and his call are irrevocable." Having inaugurated this revitalization of the universe, God will continue to offer it to all human beings whoever they may be.

But he has set the Jews apart. Living in the midst of other nations, they are a sign of his mercy; throughout the course of human history they remind people of God's presence and activity, of the bond of union between God and humanity. This reminder will help other peoples to discover him, know him, and adhere to his message. In this way the chosen people will fulfill its mission even though it may not rid itself of its own disobedience. And the faith of alien nations will help the Jewish nation to recognize and exorcise its own disobedience.

So there is a necessary and fruitful interchange between the "setting apart" of the Jews and other nations. No one is superior to others. Each can help the other. The Jews are the sign of God's activity; converted pagans are a stimulus to authentic conversion, helping the Jews not to rest content with being a sign, for that may prove to delude them.

We can readily see the applications of all this to the Church. Needless to say, we must avoid a too facile comparison between the Church and the Jewish people. But if we look for analogies, we can see one feature of the Church which may help to clarify our faith a bit.

The Church, too, is "set apart." In the midst of nations it is a sign of the Lord's activity. It is also the trustee of the Spirit's creative energy, by virtue of God's word and the sacraments. Hence it is the indispensable instrument of the universe's evolution towards its true destiny. But that by no means implies that it will be collectively holy, or that its members will be faithful and docile to the whole gospel message. The earthly Church is no better than other societies. Christians are no better than other people. The Church and its members need the help of God's mercy as much as other individuals and groups do. It will be stimulated to seek this help insofar as it discerns the activity of the Spirit and the impact of God's word among other peoples. The activity of the Spirit, of which the Church is the instrument, will stimulate it to fidelity and lucid self-criticism in the light of the gospel message. The Church proclaims the gospel message but all its members do not remain faithful to it. It rediscovers that message with the help of those who have come to believe in God's word.

In this way the prophecy voiced by Isaiah will find fulfillment: "My house shall be called a house of prayer for all peoples."

21st SUNDAY OF THE YEAR

Is 22:19-23
Rom 11:33-36
Mt 16:13-20

We have just heard a conversation between Jesus and his apostles. Jesus starts the conversation off: "Who do people say that the Son of Man is?" He wants to know what people think of him, and the apostles report what they hear: "John the Baptist . . . Elijah . . . Jeremiah . . . one of the prophets." Jesus presses his inquiry, as if he really wants to know something else: "And you . . . who do you say that I am?" Peter blurts out: "You are the Messiah . . . the Son of the Living God!"

In a single sentence Peter says it all. Jesus is not simply the Messiah that has been expected for centuries. He is also our Lord, our God. We are so used to hearing these words of the Gospel that they may seem quite banal to us. In reality they are astonishing.

A simple fisherman, brought up in the religious tradition of the Hebrew people where the name of God was not pronounced for fear of blasphemy, dares to utter these words. It is not simply the astonishing fact that he can picture a human being as God. He dares to apply this appellation to the carpenter of Nazareth, the son of Joseph and Mary. He says what a pious Jew would hardly dare to say: "You are God!"

Right away Jesus tells him where this knowledge came from: "Blest are you, Simon, son of Jonah! No mere man has revealed this to you, but my heavenly Father."

Thanks to a revelation from the Father, Peter has faith in Jesus. Jesus in turn displays his confidence in Peter. On Peter he will build his Church, "and the jaws of death shall not prevail against it." And that is not all: "I will entrust to you the keys of the kingdom of heaven. Whatever you declare bound on earth shall be bound in heaven; whatever you declare loosed on earth shall be loosed in heaven." Peter will be given the power to let people enter the kingdom or to keep them out.

The Church, the community of believers, is not Peter's, of course; it is Christ's. It is Christ who gets it together, builds it, and directs it. But Peter is the foundation on which the various parts of the Church are assembled and brought into harmony. What is more, he enjoys the power of binding and loosing. Nothing is pure or completed in the earthly Church as it journeys towards the kingdom. Peter will have the task of serving the Church by showing discernment. It is he who will be able to judge whether the members of the Church are living in conformity with Christ's plan. That is the mission entrusted to Peter.

In entrusting Peter with this role, Jesus shows us the role and importance he wishes to give to the Church. If man wants to know Christ and live in communion with him, he cannot eliminate the Church. Nor can he erase Peter's work of discernment. Man cannot pretend to go to Christ without going through his Church as it is: i.e., a human and spiritual society. He cannot pretend to meet Christ directly on his own without relying on the Church. Listening to Christ's words today, we know that is impossible. If we presume to do that, we are trying to cut Christ down to our own measure, to fashion Christ according to our own standards of convenience, to reject Christ as he reveals himself to us.

We can always ask ourselves why Jesus decided to do things in the particular way that he did. Couldn't he have revealed himself directly to men and communicated his Spirit without going through a community that will ever remain fallible? Of course he could have done that! Paul seems to anticipate our question in today's Epistle: "Who has known the mind of the Lord? Or who has been his counselor?" That is the way the Lord wanted it. It is up to us to accept that fact.

What a liberation awaits us if we grasp that fact and accept it! A host of problems fades away. We can see the life of the Church in a very positive light—despite its evident divisions and debates, its anxious searching and its evasions.

First of all, we realize that the Church is not the guardian of some venerable human culture or civilization. It is not a dispenser of moral security or comforting religious stability. It is not the protector of some particular political or social order.

The Church was set up to help us discern Christ's activity in ourselves and the world; to help us live in accordance with Christ's activity so that we might gain access to the kingdom.

Peter was given the keys of the kingdom. The Church was set up to let us into it. Jesus often speaks of the kingdom in his gospel, but never in direct terms. He speaks in parables, as if the kingdom would always remain somewhat alien even though it was a visible thing that we could experience. It is a mystery, both familar and distant. It will elude our grasp until all creatures have been gathered together in Christ. Here and now we are on the road, and the Church helps us to move forward. It is from that perspective that we must judge and serve and use the Church.

But we are always inclined to judge the Church in terms of what we are and how we need the Church. We keep forgetting or ignoring its true purpose. We may be inclined to be progressivist or conservative, to be passive or active. Such inclinations stem from temperament, education, and personal need. Following these inclinations, we may support some change or seek to preserve an age-old structure. When we do these things, we may be helping a society to evolve further or to remain faithful to a tradition, we may be displaying fidelity to some aspect of our personal vocation; but we are doing what suits us and we have not taken one step towards the kingdom.

The latter is something quite different. Moving towards the kingdom does not entail some prolongation of our selves through action, however generous that action might be. It entails a willingness to pass from this world into the kingdom.

This is the essential work of the Church that is known as baptism. It is not operative solely during the few minutes when the sacrament is conferred. It is prolonged through our whole life. It effects our transformation, our re-creation, through the formation of what Paul calls the "new man." That entails a twofold movement: detachment from self and attachment to the Lord, destruction of the pagan and construction of the believer, passage through death to life.

From this viewpoint it is clear that the Church, such as it is today, is perfectly suited to our passage into the kingdom. As we can tell from many signs, the Church is simultaneously intolerable and necessary, irritating and valuable, for every believer. Some find the Church irritating and intolerable because she is so unwieldy, slow, and caught up in compromise. Others feel the same way because of her bold steps forward and the things she so willingly leaves behind.

At the same time, however, both groups know that she is necessary and precious. Only she possesses the words of life. Only she has at her command the creative energy of the sacraments. Only she opens the doors to the kingdom.

Playing out the stakes of incarnation, with all the blemishes and scandals that entails, the Church summons us as we are. In all sorts of ways she rouses us and forces us to make a choice. We must either get beyond our selves and live for Christ, or cling to our own ideas—be they egotistical or generous-minded—and thereby refuse Christ.

Today we are going to offer our thanksgiving sacrifice to the Father. Let us thank him for giving us Saint Peter and the witness of his total faith. Let us thank him for having set up the Church and putting it at our disposal. The Church, such as it is, leads us to him.

22nd SUNDAY OF THE YEAR

Jer 20:7-9
Rom 12:1-2
Mt 16:21-27

Peter has just recognized Jesus as the emissary of the Most High, as the Son of God himself. Jesus has made him the rock on which he will build his Church, and entrusted the keys of the kingdom of him. It would seem that Jesus' teaching and activity has begun to bear fruit, enough at least to spark faith in his apostles and allow him to lay the first foundations for his Church. That Church will be the instrument of man's salvation.

Jesus will now be able to help his apostles make considerable progress. He will provide them with more precise knowledge about the way in which he himself is obedient to his Father. Then he will draw the necessary conclusions with regard to those who believe in him.

We soon see why Jesus has to spell out his teaching right after Peter has professed his faith and been entrusted with the mission of serving as the foundation of the Church. His words will scandalize the leader of the apostles, causing him to say things which Jesus must reprove harshly.

The apostles have begun to realize the great things that are expected of them. Their mission will be very important for human beings, so they cannot have a mistaken notion about the way in which they are to carry it out. They could destroy themselves if they interpreted it wrongly. Their mission really will jeopardize their spiritual destiny.

For this reason Jesus tells them what it will entail for himself. He will suffer at the hands of all the important people in Israel—the chief priests, the scribes, the elders, the Sanhedrin. Both the temporal and the spiritual authorities will help to put him to death. After his death, he will rise again.

Peter will not tolerate any such thing. Such a forecast

of failure, he thinks, could only cause a decline in popularity and block the success of his mission. So Peter takes Jesus aside and explains that he should not say such things. Moreover, Peter really loves Jesus and he finds such a finale quite painful. He cannot accept the idea that his friend and master will suffer an infamous death.

Peter's reaction is the reaction of many generous people who are anxious about the effectiveness of their work in the service of the Lord. Peter reacts that way precisely because he has recognized the Messiah and Savior in the person of Jesus. Jesus must be recognized and acknowledged by everyone, by the leaders of the nation in particular. That would mean success. Lack of such recognition would be failure and defeat.

Jesus' response to Peter has the sting of a whiplash. The leader of the apostles is still reacting as a campaign manager would. His thoughts are man's thoughts, not God's. He is putting obstacles in Christ's way, undermining his fidelity to the Father.

But aren't Jesus' words too cruel for human beings? Wasn't it natural for Peter to resent the idea that Jesus would be maltreated and even tortured? Could any red-blooded man react differently? Jesus' reaction is pointed in any case: "Get out of my sight, you satan." "Satan" here means "adversary." Peter's thoughts are still those of man. He is not yet fully transformed. But even though he may not be able to accept God's will in this matter, he must not be allowed to put obstacles in the way of God's unfolding design.

Jesus asks a lot of Peter. There is one kind of love which is loaded with an understandable modicum of pity. It has all the appearances of being high-minded and dedicated to a good cause, but in reality it is an obstacle to the realization of God's plan. This pity is really a way of protecting our human thoughts, and to that extent it is a devilish thing.

"Jesus then said to his disciples. . . ." He knows that Peter's reaction is not peculiar to him alone. So he goes on to present a very important teaching that is reiterated more than once in the Gospels. We can never exhaust its content. To follow Christ is to deny oneself and take up one's cross. We find and save our life if we lose it for his sake. If we gain the whole world and lose ourselves, we have lost everything.

It is harsh, demanding talk. Yet it is put in such general terms that one could interpret it in a way that would suit him perfectly. That evasion is frequently the tack taken by believers. The other two readings today, however, allow us no such equivocal interpretation.

Paul develops his line of thought in three successive stages. He thus links up his thought with that expressed by Jeremiah and helps to explain the import of Christ's words to his disciples.

"I beg you . . . to offer your bodies as a living sacrifice holy and acceptable to God." That is the indispensable starting point. The inner sacrifice of our person must be real and unreserved. It must be made to the Lord himself, as to someone whom we know and trust completely. Otherwise the self-abnegation involved would be wholly unjustified.

What occurs then is a real interior communion between the Lord and the believer, a communion that grows more and more intimate as inner obstacles are wiped out by God. As Jeremiah puts it: "You duped me, O Lord, and I let myself be duped; you were too strong for me." Recognizing that the Lord is stronger and more important and therefore offering oneself to him unreservedly is the first step. But that is not enough. Even though we may have given up everything, we are always quite ready to take it all back. The subtle maneuverings of the human heart encourage that sort of recovery on the flimsiest of pretexts. It is a fact which Peter experienced when Jesus told him about his upcoming passion.

Hence Paul puts us on our guard: "Do not conform yourselves to this age." Even though we have generously offered everything to the Lord and put ourselves entirely at his disposal, our outlook may still be modelled on that of the present world. But the kingdom progresses according to God's way of thinking, not according to man's way of thinking. That is the point of Jesus' words to Peter, is it not? The aims and methods of the world are so different from those of God that the man who wants to remain faithful to God must ever stand in opposition to the world. As Jeremiah puts it: "Whenever I speak, I must cry out, violence and outrage is my message." This message is intolerable to the world, so intolerable that "the word of the Lord has brought me derision and reproach." After we overcome the interior obstacles, we must overcome the obstacles and seductions of the outside world. The word of God leads him who proclaims it into solitude and loneliness. Fidelity to God makes the believer different from other men. To save his life he must choose between the approval of the world and the self-abnegation of solitude. He must take cognizance of the fact that we always tend to model ourselves after the world, as the history of the Church proves over and over again. Is it to be expected that our age will avoid the mistakes and disorders which have happened over and over again?

Admittedly our human sciences now provide us with rare insight into the motives underlying human actions and the constraints to which we are subject. We might well be inclined to think that we are above and beyond the mistakes of the ignorant generations of the past. But such an outlook is a delusion in two respects. First, the human sciences cannot know man as he truly is because their investigative tools only allow for the observation of external phenomena; there is much in man that escapes the most precise tools and the keenest minds. That is the first illusion: man thinks he knows everything, but there are things of which he is ignorant. Secondly, the human sciences proffer solutions which are necessarily offbase because they touch on only one aspect of the real. That is our second mistake: relying too heavily on the human sciences and their solutions.

What, then, are we to do? Paul tells us: "Be transformed by the renewal of your mind, so that you may judge . . . what is good." That takes us pretty far. First we lose our life by offering ourselves to the Lord and refusing to model ourselves on the present world. Then we find our life again by being transformed, so that we can then discern what is good and make sound judgments. Until that happens, we cannot see or know correctly. Knowledge of Christ, acceptance of God's ways, and faithful efforts to turn his plan into reality are the end result of a personal transformation that endows us with new capabilities and a new lucidity. The apostles were not able to comprehend Jesus. Jesus did not prove anything to them. Instead he tells them to undergo a self-transformation, for only that will give them "understanding."

Then the whole process becomes irreversible. The new understanding takes over. Jeremiah tried to rid himself of it, but he could not: "It becomes like fire burning in my heart, imprisoned in my bones." It is a vivid image, and it needs no commentary.

Let us pray for one another, asking the Spirit to transform us so that we grow in fidelity to God's ways and hence in our communion with him.

23rd SUNDAY OF THE YEAR

Ez 33:7-9
Rom 13:8-10
Mt 18:15-20

Today Jesus gives some instructions to his apostles as he discusses the life of the future community of believers. On first reading his words we are shocked. Our attitudes have progressed on such points as respect for other people and their freedom, so that these counsels on fraternal correction seem to be a bit strict and out of tune. Besides, it becomes harder and harder to determine precisely in what circumstances these instructions of Jesus are to be carried out. Sin seems to be less and less tangible a thing to lay our hands on. Each individual determines for himself what the standards of morality are—both those that are universally recognized and those that have now faded away. Jesus' rather "judicial" talk about "witnesses" and "recourse to the community" does not suit us at all.

But Jesus is giving us the word of God here, and we cannot reject it. For it offers us something that we cannot do without. To grasp his point, let us start with the words of Ezechiel and Paul in today's other two readings.

Ezechiel's message is a major one. God addresses him and gives him various instructions. The prophet is a man personally chosen by God to be a "watchman" over the house of Israel. He will listen to what the Lord says and convey God's message to the people of Israel. If it has to do with man's faults and aberrations, the prophet is obliged to pass the message along to men out of obedience to God. The justification and salvation of the prophet depends on his obedience to God.

Two points are worth nothing here. The message comes from God. The prophet is his intermediary. He is obliged to transmit the message to those for whom God intends it; if he does not, he will be punished.

The terse words from the letters to the Romans seem

to be quite different. But they, too, are valuable in helping us to grasp the message of the Gospel. Paul tells us that the whole law is summed up in the commandment to love: "Love is the fulfillment of the law." Here Paul is not adding anything of his own to the gospel message. He is simply reiterating what the Old Testament said, and what a scribe said in answer to a question put by Jesus one day. But this reminder puts us in the proper frame of mind for interpreting Jesus' words to his apostles today. There is no question here of using today's Gospel text to justify sneaky surveillance of our fellow believers or invidious comparisons between ourselves and others. It is not an excuse to set up a tally sheet for judging people's moral worth. Jesus' counsels must be regarded as expressions of his love.

This point is made clear in the Gospel itself. If we start with the final section of today's Gospel and go back from there, reading it in the light of the other two texts for today, we will understand Jesus' point readily enough.

Jesus says that when two or three believers are gathered together "in my name," he himself is present. "In my name" is an expression that crops up frequently in the gospel texts, and we know that it has real meaning. The person who is living in the name of Christ is one who has been chosen and recognized by him, and who agrees to live in conformity with his teaching. Such a person wants to identify himself with Christ as much as possible. When several people of like mind join together and try to flesh out this desire jointly, then Jesus is present. It is no longer simply a get-together of several believers, a mere conglomeration of individuals. The group itself takes on unity and inner consistency; it becomes something more than the sum of its individual members. The group thus formed becomes united with Christ.

Hence it is not surprising that the prayer of this group should be efficacious. Its prayer to the Father is not just the accumulated opinion of the individual members; it is the plea of Jesus himself to his Father. By virtue of their coming together, the believers are immersed in the loving relationship that exists between the Father and the Son. The group is the Son addressing his own prayer to the Father: "I know that you always hear me" (Jn 11:42).

The consequences become quite understandable and logical. Going back over the Gospel, we find this remark on the connection between the community of believers and the salvation of each individual: "Whatever you declare bound on earth shall be held bound in heaven, and whatever you declare loosed on earth shall be held loosed in heaven." If we grasp the fact that the community of those united in Jesus' name is actually the presence of the living Christ, then we can readily see that this community can speak in the name of the Lord himself and that its decisions embody his will.

That brings us to the instructions which Jesus gives at the start of today's Gospel. They follow this remark of Jesus: "It is no part of your heavenly Father's plan that a single one of these little ones shall ever come to grief" (Mt 18:15). What concerns Jesus is the spiritual attention we should pay to the welfare of our brother. Helping our fellow Christian in trouble, who is the victim of some sin or other, is an obligation imposed on us by love. We must do this if we are to be faithful to God's work.

As we noted above, God imposed on Ezechiel the obligation of proclaiming his message. That obligation is a standing one, but now it falls upon the community of believers who embody the Lord's presence. Because Christ is present in the community, the community is obliged to be docile to his presence and love; and his will is that everyone be saved.

The effort to bring back members of the community who have lapsed in their fidelity to God is an attempt to serve the Lord and flesh out his presence. The tie between heaven and earth takes on new and deeper meaning, because the things that are bound or loosed by the community on earth will be bound or loosed in heaven.

Insofar as the community comes together in the name of Christ on earth, it will be brought together in heaven. Insofar as it attaches individuals to Christ here on earth, they will be attached to Christ in heaven also.

Thus our Lord's instructions are not meant to foster a rating system among believers. They are an obligation based on love of neighbor. We must try to help other people even as we would like to be helped in a similar situation.

Hence Christ's teaching is not only legitimate but quite sensible. His instructions are not the cold dictates of juridicism. They are meant to help us remain within the boundaries of love, to avoid turning fraternal correction into a personal affair where one individual tries to teach a lesson to another individual.

We start with a man-to-man approach, then two or three people take over if the first approach does not work. If that fails, then the community takes over in order to show the brother in trouble that the Lord is involved here. But "if he ignores even the church, then treat him as you would a Gentile or a tax collector." From the standpoint of today's other readings, this means that the cure for the individual in question is beyond man's capacity, even though the people involved may be faithful servants of God. The important thing is not to turn it into a matter of personal honor, so that one vows to straighten the other person out at all costs. To do that would be to go contrary to love; to let the instinct for domination over others take control. Pretending to act "in the name of the Lord," and for the other's good, we would actually be succumbing to the worst sort of hypocrisy.

At the start of our meditation we were astonished when Jesus told us what to do "if your brother should commit some wrong against you." We gradually came to see that it was the application of a general truth—the living presence of the Lord in his Church—to a particular case. Since no one is exempt from failure or error, we might well start by accepting the fact that others could perform this duty of fraternal correction and spiritual support for us. That would be the best preparation for fulfilling this duty with sensitivity and kindness in the case of others. By accepting the counsel of others and giving counsel in turn, we will be manifesting our fidelity to the name of Christ.

Let us make our own the words that Francis of Assissi expresses in his commentary on the *Our Father*: "May we love our neighbors as ourselves, drawing them towards your love as best we can."

24th SUNDAY OF THE YEAR

Sir 27:33-28:9
Rom 14:7-9
Mt 18:21-35

Jesus has just been talking to his apostles about unity in the community of believers, and how this is a sign of his presence. Peter is a man of wide experience who knows that human relationships are no easy matter, that fierce arguments and conflicts can arise, that such things must be kept in line if the unity of the community is to be safeguarded. So he asks Jesus: "When my brother wrongs me, how often must I forgive him? Seven times?"

Peter's question makes good sense. Its relevance is brought home to us every day. Belonging to the community of believers does not rid a person of faults. It does not mean that henceforth one will never wrong other people, or even one's fellow believers. And we all experience the malevolence of others, the ill effects of their prejudices on our reputation, our possessions, and our freedom. How much of this should be taken? How many times should we pardon them?

The question is harder than it may seen at first glance. We all realize that if we keep forgiving rude and dishonest behavior, we run the risk of encouraging others to remain in their evil ways. We then become their accomplices. Moreover, pardoning can often show up as weakness, as an abdication of our own personality and a lack of respect for justice. The dictum, "an eye for an eye," comes readily to man. Indeed it may even seem too restricting when we yearn really to get revenge on people for the way they have treated us.

In answering Peter, Jesus simply gives him a different digit: "seventy times seven times." What he means is that there is to be no mathematical calculation at all, that we are to keep pardoning people indefinitely. We must keep pardoning again and again. The answer must have been as hard for Peter to take as it is for us. Sometimes we pretend to go along with the idea, but we have our subterfuges: "I'll forgive, but I won't forget." Is that real pardon? It would be better for us to admit that we are incapable of the pardon Jesus demands. So Jesus tells us a parable to show us the importance of his injunction and how we can measure up to it.

It is the story of the king who decides to settle accounts with his servants. One of them owes a huge amount. Threatened with punishment for non-payment, the servant begs the king for pardon. Pardon is granted on the spot; the whole debt is erased. On his way out, that servant meets someone who owes him a mere fraction of the amount he owed the king. But despite the pleading of this other person, the servant of the king maltreats him and has him put into prison. Distressed witnesses to this event report it to the king. The king is greatly incensed, summons the servant to him once again, reproaches him for his lack of pity, and has him put into prison until he pays back "all that he owed." The servant will stay in prison forever because he can never pay back the sum he owes.

Jesus draws his own conclusion from the parable: "My heavenly Father will treat you in exactly the same way unless each of you forgives his brother from his heart."

The story is quite interesting because it teaches us an important lesson. We certainly share the astonishment and distress of those who saw what the servant did to his debtor right after the king had forgiven him. The attitude of the servant is intolerable. It reveals his greed and his hardness of heart. In fact it is unjust in legal terms. The amount which the third party owed the servant no longer belongs to the servant because the latter owes much more to the king. It is really the king who has a claim on the debt of the third party.

We can draw some important conclusions already. We all are in the same situation as the servant who owed the big debt to the king. God gives us his grace and pardons our sins. The believer differs from the non-believer only in that he knows his real situation vis-a-vis God whereas the non-believer does not. We must not forget this basic situation when we attempt to straighten out matters with other human beings. Peter had phrased his question in such a way that it was an affair between him and other people. Jesus injects another note that corrects Peter's presentation. The argument is never restricted to a debate between human beings; God himself is always involved. And both adversaries are equally dependent on God and his mercy.

What is more, everyone on earth lives for God. He is their only judge, the true goal of their existence. Paul tells us as much: "None of us lives as his own master and none of us dies as his own master. . . . Both in life and in death we are the Lord's." We are the Lord's property; indeed all human beings are. So we have no right to anything, even when someone seems to wrong us.

It is only in this perspective that we can begin to understand the unremitting kind of pardon which Christ proposes today. It is only in this perspective that we can begin to carry out his proposal in our everyday life. The first step is to realize where we stand vis-a-vis God.

We may still be operating in terms of merit and spiritual progress. We may still believe that our generous-hearted and sometimes heroic virtue can win us the Lord's favor. If that is the frame of mind we are in, then today's lesson is meaningless to us. We cannot help but repeat the behavior of the king's servant, operating in terms of creditor-debtor relationships. We may be fine servants of the Church. We may be greatly respected in the Christian community. But we have not yet found our way into the kingdom which Jesus speaks about today.

On the other hand, we may be persuaded of the truth of this parable, which reminds us that we all are basically dependent on God's mercy. We may appreciate the fact that we belong to him and that only his grace enables us to enter the kingdom. If that is so, then we can begin to establish relationships with other human beings that are in accord with Jesus' teaching today.

In the latter case the problem posed by Peter is no longer a problem for us at all. If we are sensible enough to seek and obtain God's mercy, it becomes impossible for us to be harsh with those who are our debtors. Pardoning offenses, which had been a problem, now becomes a test. We are believers insofar as we pardon; insofar as we do not pardon, we have not yet begun to believe. We may talk theology, feel religious sentiments, and participate in liturgical actions; but our faith is not real because it has not yet transformed any bit of us.

So what are we to do? First we must recognize and acknowledge our true situation. Without this lucidity we cannot get anywhere. We must acknowledge the fact that we do not believe as we should. Then we must imitate the behavior of the servant who owed so much to the king. We must bow down before God and ask him to accomplish his work of transformation within us. Finally, we must obey him completely in the concrete instances where we are given the opportunity and the possibility of pardoning others. Then we will be able to pray as he himself taught us: "Forgive us the wrong we have done as we forgive those who wrong us" (Mt 6:12). Insofar as we share God's mercy with others, he will show greater mercy to us: "Blest are they who show mercy; mercy shall be theirs" (Mt 5:7).

At this point we can easily forsee the effects that pardon obtained and pardon proffered to others will have on us. We will gradually approach the radiant love of our Father more closely. We will be willing to receive the benefits of his unique goodness in overflowing measure; hence we will be able to put the whole notion of pardon behind us. Liberated from all possessiveness, we will no longer possess anything of our own. No one will be able to wrong us; offenses will no longer exist. They still exist right now because we are propietors who defend our rights; in reality we are the slaves of the things we so earnestly try to protect. If a person wants to be truly free to love as Jesus teaches him today, then he must arrive at the point of entrusting himself completely to the mercy of God and erasing all other forms of attachment. He will no longer extend pardon at all. He will be pardon incarnate, in the image of God himself. He will be invulnerable to the attacks of others, however violent or insidious or savage they may be.

None of us has arrived at that stage of liberty yet. But at least we may now realize that no one else is to blame. Our own inconsistency and opacity is at fault. So we can turn to the Lord, living in the Eucharist we shall soon receive. May he give us the joy of experiencing his love and the desire to be wholly imbued with it.

25th SUNDAY OF THE YEAR

Is 55:6-9
Phil 1:20c-24,27a
Mt 20:1-16a

We have just heard a well-known parable. the parable of the last-minute workers. The story is well constructed, designed to provoke our astonishment and make us share the scandalized feeling of the all-day workers. How unjust the owner seems to be when he pays the wages at the end of the day!

The owner of a vineyard goes out to hire laborers. In both the Old and the New Testament, the vineyard symbolizes God's work in the world. It is Israel in the Old Testament, the Church in the New Testament. The workers idling around the marketplace are those who have abandoned the Lord. The Father never ceases to be concerned about them. They are called hour after hour because God calls whom he wants, when he wants, and how he wants. Then, at the end of the working day, it is pay time.

The picture is carefully drawn. Starting with the latest arrivals, the owner pays each one a denarius. The early workers see this, of course, and they are outraged when they are not paid more. Angry, they express their discontent: "The last group did only an hour's work, but you have put them on the same level as us who have worked a full day in the scorching heat."

This brand of discontent crops up elsewhere in the gospel accounts. We see it in the elder brother of the prodigal son, for example. He has worked loyally at his father's business, yet his father has never given him anything to enable him to have a party with his friends. So he becomes indignant when his father puts on a lavish banquet for the returning prodigal who has wasted his portion of his inheritance in debauchery.

The early workers, like the elder brother of the prodigal son, are deeply disturbed. Their sense of justice has been offended. From a human standpoint their attitude is perfectly logical. When it comes to our line of work, we are clearly operating in terms of efficiency and profitability. Each person wants to get a salary that is proportionate to the work he has done, to the skills he has contributed, to the responsibilities he has discharged. From our personal point of view, which dovetails with the moral teachings of the Church in this case, the attitude and approach of the owner seems unjust.

We hear the same sort of complaint when people are talking about eternal salvation. Some Christians complain about their treatment. They have been faithful, perhaps heroically so, all their lives. Yet other people, who seem to have led loose lives for years and years, need only "shape up" at the last minute to gain the same eternal reward.

Then the owner replies: "You agreed on the usual wage, did you not? . . . I intend to give this man who was hired last the same pay as you." We are operating on the juridical plane of contract and in terms of the owner's absolute authority. The contract provides for the usual wage of a denarius and the owner, who obviously stands for God here, can dispose of his goods as he chooses. Moreover, his logic may well escape man's view of things. As Isaiah puts it: "My thoughts are not your thoughts, nor are your ways my ways, says the Lord."

His reply is clearly authoritarian. It does not seem to reflect any love on the owner's part for the early workers whose sense of justice has legitimately been offended. Is the "shock" intended? Does it not seem that the owner wants to "shake up" the protesters, to make them realize that there may be another logic besides their own?

Perhaps we may come to see the whole scene in a different light. If we look at the situation more closely, can we not say that it is the early workers who enjoy a privileged place in the story? To be sure, they have "worked a full day in the scorching heat." But the owner has allowed them to escape the anxiety of enforced unemployment and the restless quest for daily food. The workers hired at the end of the day were not so fortunate.

The same applies to those faithful who have heroically maintained loyalty to God throughout their lives. They are privileged beings by comparison with those who came to the Lord only at the end of their lives. Isn't that what is suggested by Paul's cry of faith and love in today's Epistle? "For, to me, 'life' means Christ." Or again: "Christ will be exhalted through me, whether I live or die." His labors and sufferings do not really matter. What matters is his enthusiasm at being in the hands of the Lord, at enjoying the privilege of being laid hold of by the Lord and living in intimacy with him.

The owner asks the early workers: "Are you envious because I am generous?" It makes us stop and think again. Perhaps it is the late arrivals who should be jealous. They were admitted to the vineyard only at the last hour; only then were they allowed into the intimacy of the Lord.

And so we gradually perceive the underlying meaning of this parable. In the kingdom we are in a realm of goodness, mercy, and gratuitous gift-giving. We are liberated from the world of right, profit, and fair exchange. The logic is wholly different from our own logic. In the kingdom we must be willing to accept dependence on the Lord and put ourselves in his hands. We are invited to accept the fact that God is God, not ourselves sublimated to the highest degree of perfection. We tend to make him a super-judge, who ranks people good or bad and deals with them accordingly. But in reality God is love. And Saint Paul tells us about love: "There is no limit to love's forbearance, to its trust, its hope, its power to endure" (1 Cor 13:7).

That is why "the last shall be first." Far more than others, they will come to discover and accept the gratuitous mercy of God. Their participation in the kingdom will be spontaneous and immediate because they will see it as a gift, not as something due to them. As Paul puts it: "It is not a question of man's willing or doing but of God's mercy. . . . God has mercy on whom he wishes. . . . Who are you to answer God back?" (Rom 9:16.18.20)

That is how the kingdom appears to us today from Christ's words. It is both alluring and somewhat abstract. Perhaps it is up to us to make it concrete, and it is here that the ramifications of the parable may well startle us if we take the parable seriously.

Unjust retribution and the proper sharing of goods and responsibilities are the underlying justification for the existence of labor unions and trade associations of all sorts. They are debated subjects, giving rise to strikes and what many call the "class struggle." But if we consider all these things in the light of the gospel message, then the so-called revolutionaries are not really revolutionaries at all. The real revolution is not to be found in seeking respect for human rights and equality in this area. Such improvements are always imperfect, always open to further correction, always the breeding ground for conflict and war. So long as one stays inside this system, war will be inevitable and peace a utopian ideal. Peace will only be possible if we grasp the point of today's parable about the last-minute workers.

In the parable, the salary is not based on competence, or profitability, or the extent of the worker's responsibility. It is based on the need of each worker. If we consider the matter seriously, we will realize that this approach is completely opposed to the outlook of the present day. Everyone today clings to his own hierarchy, whether he is a Marxist or Non-Marxist, a collectivist or an individualist. Each one defends the rungs of his own ladder, because his system reassures him and stimulates him to use his energy.

Things are quite different in the gospel's scheme of things. Each person has received talents from God, different in nature and amount. Each person is obliged to put them to good use for the benefit of others. In this way he will gradually move away from egocentrism and towards greater love. In this way the kingdom of God will gradually be built up on earth and bring all men the peace they so ardently desire.

In short, we shall remain in the realm of violence so long as salaries and rewards are based on profits, returns, responsibilities, and competence. We must come to realize that the universe and the fruit of man's work are made for all men. We must come to the point of letting each receive according to his needs. Only then can we hope to live in peace some day. But will man be willing to work without the stimulus of profit, without being able to satisfy his vanity or slake his thirst for domination over others? That is the real question confronting us, and it will be answered one way or another. If we refuse to give up old incentives and instincts, the answer will be a violent one. If we are willing to uproot the old bad habits in ourselves, then peace may prevail.

Is that a utopian dream? Yes, if we try to go it alone. But if we are willing to accept God's word, it becomes a realistic hope.

26th SUNDAY OF THE YEAR

Ez 18:25-28
Phil 2:1-11
Mt 21:28-32

Today Jesus addresses his remarks to the chief priests and elders of the Jewish nation. They are the nation's guides and leaders. Chosen from among the higher-class people of the country, they are considered to be particularly well versed in their religion and its Scripture. They have the reputation of being upright men who faithfully observe the law. By virtue of their conviction and their social role, they are the most determined champions of the nation's traditions and the ones least inclined to accept changes in the interpretation of its Scriptures or the practice of its moral code.

Inevitably, then, Jesus will meet great resistance among them in proclaiming his kingdom. For while his proclamation claims to be in full conformity with the age-old law, it is also new and revolutionary in the way it comprehends and applies that law.

We may regard ourselves as convinced and generous Christians, as upright people who know what the Lord expects of us and feel sure that we are faithful to his demands. Insofar as we see ourselves in this light, we are akin to the chief priests and elders whom Jesus addresses today.

It is the brief and simple parable about the two sons. A father possesses a vineyard, and he has two sons old enough to work in it. He asks the first to go and work; he says he will, but then he does not go. He asks the second to go and work; he says he will not, but then he regrets his refusal and goes out to work in it. Jesus asks his audience: "Which of the two did what the father wanted?" They reply, quite sensibly: "The second."

Since he is speaking to the notables of the Jewish nation, he applies the parable to them and their situation. He obviously wants to shock his listeners, to apply the parable to them in a pointed way and get a reaction from them. He compares them to publicans and prostitutes, to those who are held in the least esteem by the people: "Tax collectors and publicans are entering the kingdom of God before you. . . . Yet even when you saw that you did not repent."

That is the parable and the lesson which Jesus offers to those who think they are upright. Let us make a few remarks about the parable, for that will help us to profit more fully from the lesson that Jesus gives us today.

The second son in today's parable started out by saying no to his father's request. Then, it seems, he reflected on the matter further. He saw his disobedience for what it was, repented, and ended up obeying his father. It was his awareness of his refusal that prompted his remorse and led him to obedience. A refusal contrary to God's will, an act of disobedience consciously adverted to—that is what enabled the son to change his attitude towards the Lord and to correct it. Now the publicans and prostitutes, labelled as sinners by the Jewish people, cannot have any illusions about their situation vis-a-vis God. Hence they are in a position to glimpse the holiness God proposes to them, to desire it, and then to flesh it out in reality. The publicans and prostitutes mentioned in our gospel text illustrate what we all in fact are. Because God sends out a summons to us, we come to see our spontaneous refusal to do what he wants. We are then in a position to measure the great gap between what we really are and what we should be. And that is the first precondition for gaining entrance into the kingdom.

The first son in the parable acceded to his father's request at first, but in the end he refused to obey him. The second son refused at first but ended up going anyway. His inconsistency is tolerable because it marks a forward step. The inconsistency of the first son, on the other hand, represents a copout. How could he make a pledge and then refuse to act on it?

The fact is that his sort of inconsistency is inevitable

once a person believes he is upright. Such a person is convinced that he has already gone to work in the kingdom, which is symbolized by the vineyard. He thinks he is faithful, so he gradually becomes incapable of seeing the real progress he might be able to make. Deep within him there remains a firm refusal to change in any way. Why should he bother? He is a just and upright person. He is sure that he possesses the truth and is faithful to that truth. Those who think differently from him cannot possibly be speaking in the name of the Lord.

That is why the priests and elders of the Jewish people did not repent after they heard the preaching of John the Baptist and saw publicans and prostitutes being converted. They did not realize, they could not realize, that they were being given an example. With his strong words Jesus is trying to help these "upright" people to discover their lack of uprightness.

All of us believers are prey to the inconsistent behavior of the first son in the parable. We are convinced that we have not refused the Lord in any way. We always say the right thing because we are used to using words and ideas that find their inspiration in God's word. Thus we readily fall prey to delusion. We are so clever in our way of speaking and arguing, so sure that we know and accept God's demands. So we stay where we are and what we are. We are determined not to change, and we use all our energy and zeal to change others.

Today, then, we are warned about two types of inconsistency that we can readily find in ourselves. One is to refuse the Lord at first and then to obey him; that is less serious. The other is to say yes to the Lord at first and then sneak out of our commitment. That is the fate that awaits us if we are convinced of our own spiritual worth. We are subject to both types of inconsistency at times, now to one and now to the other. How are we to free ourselves from both of them and achieve inner unity and the harmony of the kingdom? Paul tells us in today's selection from his letter to the Philippians.

He pleads insistently with them "in the name of the encouragement you owe me in Christ, in the name of the solace that love can give, of fellowship in spirit, compassion, and pity." He wants them to "make my joy complete by your unanimity, possessing the one love, united in spirit and ideals." There is only one real sign of our participation in Christ's kingdom: our unity as believers whereby we participate fully and unreservedly in the one love of God.

Paul's point is important. The only way to extricate ourselves from the inconsistencies mentioned in the Gospel is to grow in love. It is useless to engage in a laborious effort at inner analysis, to be constantly suspicious of our inner impulses and decisions. We gradually rid ourselves of inconsistency and participate more fully in the kingdom to the extent that we develop our love in the community of believers.

Paul then goes on to show us how we can become indifferent to self and more attentive to the will of the Lord. We must adopt a certain attitude towards ourselves and towards other people. We must always consider others superior to ourselves, and have greater concern for their interests than for our own.

Hearing this advice, we immediately raise a host of objections to it. We feel that Paul is spurning any and all sense of objectivity; that we do meet people who in fact are of less worth than we ourselves are. It hardly seems that flying in the face of reality will produce any good fruits. But we must admit that the objection is quite theoretical. Any comparison that would lead us to conclude we were better would probably cause us to regard ourselves as upright people, and we know where that will lead us. Paul's approach is quite positive when we examine it closely. It will help us to react in ways that are replete with sound humility.

We can now understand and appreciate the advice he offers next: "Your attitude must be that of Christ." In incomparable prose Paul describes the whole destiny of

Christ. In his constant and progressive process of self-abnegation, Jesus went from the state of being divine to the humiliating death of the cross, leaving it up to his Father to raise him from the dead and to restore him to his dignity as Lord. If one wishes to acquire the love that will liberate him from his inconsistencies and integrate him into the kingdom, he must be willing to follow the same route. The one true ambition of man is to follow Jesus on the pathway of self-denial and to let God use him and resurrect him when and as He wishes. From a human standpoint, any and all fidelity to love will appear to be a process of self-denial in which one puts all his hope in the Father. If this process is not to be pathological, it must be carried out with increasingly precise obedience, with a deep desire to devote one's whole heart and soul and mind to God as the great commandment bids us do.

If we do that, then one day we may be able to say yes to the Lord's commands and proceed to do them promptly.

27th SUNDAY OF THE YEAR

Is 5:1-7
Phil 4:6-9
Mt 21:33-43

"My friend had a vineyard . . ." That is how Isaiah begins his magnificent paean to God's love for his people. We cannot fail to recognize the grandeur and evocative power of his words. In relatively few words he sums up the whole drama of Israel and humanity vis-a-vis God and his love.

God created man out of a deep concern and tenderness. Then he chose a certain group of human beings as the guardians of his promises. This group was to make him present to all humanity. He reared and trained the men and women of the Israelite nation to be ambassadors of his joy and tenderness. But instead of producing the good fruits of fidelity and peace, they produced jealousy, violence, and hatred. God looked for good grapes but received wild berries. Hence destruction is unavoidable for these people. It will be God's way of chastising them for their wrongdoing. He expended his love lavishly to create and cultivate them; now it will turn back on his unfaithful people and lead them to their destruction.

Isaiah concludes: "The vineyard of the Lord of hosts is the house of Israel." Israel was chosen by God to be his witness among the nations. Its curious and burdensome privilege was to suffer the torments of the nations in its flesh, while at the same time it was to act as their ever alert conscience.

Can we not say that this "vineyard" is every society chosen and loved by the Lord even though it does not know him, even though it proves to be a disappointment and hence is doomed to death and disappearance.

This prophecy of Isaiah is especially courageous. It is not easy for a prophet to reveal to his friends and companions their infidelities and the inevitable consequences. Perhaps that is why this passage retained such an important place in the religious history of Israel. When Jesus picked up the image of the vineyard in his conversations with the chief priests and elders, they knew what he was referring to at once. Indeed Jesus sets out the lines of his story in a way that is quite reminiscent of Isaiah. He talks about the man "who planted a vineyard, put a hedge around it, dug out a vat, and erected a tower."

But his story soon takes off from there and goes its own way. The owner of the vineyard sends out servants, one after the other, and ultimately his own son. The servants are turned backed or killed, and the same fate awaits his son. Jesus will go on to draw lessons from this story.

The way in which Jesus transforms the motif of Isaiah is most important. He stresses the repeated sending of emissaries, the persevering solicitude of the owner and the almost incredible lengths to which he carries this attitude. Despite the repeated rebuffs, despite the maltreatment of his emissaries, God keeps sending the messengers which the people need so badly. The reference is clear. Throughout history God has raised up numerous prophets, but the people never listened to their message. They rejected them, maltreated them, even went so far as to kill them. Finally he sends his own Son, who now speaks to the chief priests and elders.

While God perseveres in sending emissaries, the tenants become more and more aggressive and hostile to them. When they see his Son, they say: "Let us kill him and then we shall have his inheritance." That is what they do. Israel is no longer the vineyard of which Isaiah speaks. Now it is the tenants who wield the powers of the kingdom and are entrusted with the task of using them as God wills. We are given an important message here, and there are at least two points worth noting.

The most serious fault of the tenants is obviously their refusal to accept the prophets and the Son that the Father sends them. Jesus tells us the roots of this fault: the tenants wanted to expropriate the vineyard and make it their own. It is understandable enough. They have invested their labor in it, they have increased its value, they have enabled it to produce good grapes. Why should their hard labor benefit a distant owner who never appears on the scene, who is content to send deputies?

The same temptation is obviously the one that entices the chief priests and elders to whom Jesus is speaking. They succumb to it to the extent that they use the law and the prophets to bolster their own personal authority and to block progress towards a fuller discovery and appreciation of God's message.

But here Jesus' point applies to a wide range of people beyond the circle of his immediate listeners. It underlines a danger confronting any and every community of believers, any and every church. The ecclesial community is chosen by the Lord and designated to be the trustee of the kingdom's creative power in the midst of humanity. Hence this energy should be used as the Lord intends: i.e., to bring all men to liberation. Unfortunately the ecclesial community will always be tempted to use this power of the Spirit to its own advantage. It will be tempted to surpress every provoker who might undermine its prerogatives or challenge the God that it claims to have a hold over.

The Son was indeed killed by the Jews who were in Jesus' audience, but that sort of murder is still with us. Every time we attempt to make the kingdom our own personal domain, every time we focus all our attention on the success of some project which we feel will serve God and man, then we engage in the hypocrisy of serving our own feeling of self-importance. We expropriate the Lord's vineyard for ourselves, serving ourselves under the guise of serving the truth. And isn't that the spirit of pharisaism so justly condemned by Jesus? So there we have a warning.

Next there comes a whole process of substitution. The son who was killed, the stone that was rejected, becomes the cornerstone. The dead one is raised to life again. The murderers, who had no right to commit such a terrible transgression, will be dispossessed of their managerial position and their entire mission. As Jesus puts it: "The kingdom of God will be taken away from you and given to a nation that will yield a rich harvest." Insofar as Israel is concerned, the prophecy takes effect at the death of Jesus on the cross. Insofar as the Church is concerned, it takes effect when Christ's community is given control over the power of the kingdom on the day of Pentecost. This power will not be taken away from it. But it can be taken away from a person or a group of persons who might still be killing the Son today and expropriating the kingdom for themselves. That is what happens when someone tries to be something besides a useless servant. For then the Spirit can no longer use us because we lack docility. The kingdom can no longer be built up through us.

The warning is meant quite seriously, and it places a heavy obligation on us. It compels the believer to devote his whole mind, his whole will, his whole store of physical and phychic energy to the construction of the kingdom. At the same time he must not seek any results for himself. Indeed he is not even allowed to work up a project and devote his energy to it, for that would be riddled with ambiguity. Gratuitous love is obligatory in God's kingdom. Nothing else is allowed there.

How do we arrive at that? Paul tells us in another of today's readings. He realizes that there is a basic human repugnance for such purity. He knows that we are incapable of managing it on our own, however much we may want to. So he offers us sound advice: "Present your needs to God in every form of prayer and in petitions full of gratitude."

Such service to the kingdom calls for deep-rooted fidelity and renunciation. It cannot help but bring out our personal incapacities and inner conflicts that are sometimes insoluble. There is only one thing for us to do: to put ourselves in the Lord's hands so that he may plant his kingdom in us. It is in this way that our membership in the Church will gradually be divested of all that is dangerous in it.

At the start of our meditation we could hardly have imagined that the text of Isaiah, picked up again by Jesus, would lead us right to the core of our own selves, show us our terrible frailties, and invite us to such a basic conversion. In the course of today's Eucharistic sacrifice let us offer ourselves to the Lord and unite ourselves with his death. Let us ask him to destroy our old selves so that we may be associated with his resurrection and so that he may turn us into new creatures.

28th SUNDAY OF THE YEAR

Is 25:6-10a
Phil 4:12-14,19-20
Mt 22:1-14

We have just heard a well known parable. In fact, until the last revision of the liturgical readings and their organization into a three-year cycle, this parable was read twice a year: on the tenth and the nineteenth Sundays after Pentecost. We might well wonder if it is possible to say anything more about it. But the other two readings for today will suggest applications we might not have imagined previously.

It is the story of the king who is going to celebrate his son's wedding. He organizes a lavish banquet and sends out his servants to find the invited guests. Right away we realize that we are in for an important teaching. Isaiah says: "The Lord of hosts will provide for all peoples a feast. . . ." Quite often in the Bible the gathering of all men into the joy of the Lord after their life on earth is presented as a joyous and lavish banquet. For then "the Lord will wipe away the tears from all faces."

Indeed this is one of the most important parables Jesus has ever told. It highlights for us the real meaning of this world, the importance of his word which tells us the meaning, and the insistent nature of his repeated invitations to share the kingdom with him.

The story begins happily enough. Everything is going to be great. At last human beings will come to know the happiness they have sought so insistently. Yet, unbelievably enough, the guests refuse the invitation when they actually receive it.

Even in human terms, their behavior is incomprehensible and absurd. When a king or a president or any important personage holds a reception and sends out personal invitations to his friends and acquaintances, they would never entertain the idea of declining. It is good form to attend, and people go out of their way to arrange their date-book accordingly.

In today's story it is God who invites them, and they refuse. Here we have a capsule summary of the whole history of salvation. It is a history that does not run smoothly. The Lord sends out repeated summonses but his efforts often prove to be abortive failures.

The appeals become more and more insistent and compelling. There are three series of invited guests. The first set refuse without offering any explanation: "They refuse to come." The king tries to attract the second round of guests by speaking in terms that will please and delight them. They too refuse, preferring their own agenda to that proposed by the Lord. Or else they turn hostile, maltreat his messengers and slay them. In the case of the last series of guests, the king sends out strict orders; they are no longer free to choose on their own. First, he punishes the guests who killed his messengers. Then his servants "rounded up everyone they met." But even that tack does not meet with complete success. One person at the banquet does not observe the proper protocol. He is not dressed properly for a wedding banquet, and so he is thrown out.

We must not delude ourselves about all this. The people described in the parable are not mythical creatures; their reactions are our own. Unfortunately for us, we often tend to regard gospel stories as little fables when someone in the story comes to a bad end. For example, we are all too ready to equate the first set of guests, who were invited but preferred to go their own way, with the Jews. They were then replaced by the pagans, who had not been invited at first. If we interpret the story that way, then we are behaving exactly like those who reject the invitation; we are assuming that we are already seated at the banquet table. If we do not watch out, we may end up outside like the guest without a proper garment.

Yes, the story is about us. With great care and attention the Lord faithfully prepares a suitable destiny for us. Using our liberty in a wrongheaded way, we refuse it and choose another one for ourselves, entangling ourselves in a painful, desperate, absurd bondage.

What is even more paradoxical is the fact that we are absurd and that God—the king who organizes the feast and invites us to it—accepts this absurdity. He takes our foolishness into account. We are free to refuse him. He shows us that there is even greater liberty in persevering love. God keeps sending new servants, one wave after another. Who are these servants?

Our immediate tendency is to equate them with people who have received various sorts of special mandates authorized by some religious community. We think of the prophets and wise men, of the priests and levites in the Old Testament. We think of the bishops and priests in the case of the New Testament, or perhaps of the baptized in general who bear witness to the evangelical way of life. All this is true, of course, but the Bible sees things somewhat differently.

Quite often the Bible presents certain people, even pagans, as the servants of God—insofar as these people are instrumental in carrying out his will. Nebuchadnezzar and Cyrus are viewed in these terms. Then there are the angels, mysterious messengers whom God uses to reveal his will and to collaborate in the task of effectively insuring salvation. God can also use events in history to reveal his plan and to stimulate confidence in his ability to assure man of happiness.

All these various kinds of servants continue to appear after the foundation of the Church. In the first place we have the Church, its ministers, and all the baptized. They embody God's permanent and personal invitation to us. But they are not the only servants of God. We run into such servants constantly, even though we may not recognize them as such or may even reject them. It may be some person we hear, some event that overtakes us, some trial we endure, some joy we experience. These persons or events may send out a summons to us, force us to make a choice. In so doing, they too are servants of God appealing to our liberty.

Thus today's parable becomes quite concrete and its application to our lives direct. We can even grasp the meaning of the most disturbing and mysterious remarks. Jesus says: "The invited are many, the elect are few." On the basis of what we have said above, we now realize that the Lord is always present. His interventions are manifold and constant. Unfortunately we perceive few of them. Many of them come to nought because we overlook them or reject them. Our mind and heart tend to be oddly restrictive, confining themselves to their own petty desires and ambitions for the most part. The effort at maintaining our personal defenses keeps us locked in our insipid pettiness.

Today, once again, the Lord calls us: "Everything is ready. Come to the feast." All we have to do is accept his invitation. To be sure, we must wear the proper garment. We must change our lives in some respects. We are afraid to do that because the things we already know, however confining they may be, do offer us some comfort. The Lord asks us to listen to his summons, to abandon our narrow conceptions and our absurd logic. He asks us to give up our frightened imagination and our calculating mind for the sake of another wisdom. His wisdom calls for boldness and inventiveness, two qualities that are greatly wanting in our supposedly creative age. The "novelities" of our day are merely extensions of past things; they have nothing to do with creation at all.

All this presupposes a radical change in outlook and perspective. Paul explains it to us in stages. First of all, we must be at ease in a wide variety of circumstances—amid both plenty and want. Our serenity must not depend on such things, for that would be a subtle form of idolatry—all the more pernicious inasmuch as it would seem to be legitimate and reasonable.

Once free of such enslavement, we can then learn to echo Paul's own sentiments: "In him who is the source of my strength I have strength for everything." Accepting Christ's invitation, we do not just share in a festive gathering. We also share in his strength and power when we become part of his kingdom.

Let us pray for each other, asking that each of us will be attentive to the servants sent to him by God and will know enough to welcome them as messengers with good news. Only then will we begin to enjoy an era of joy and peace such as the world has never seen before.

29th SUNDAY OF THE YEAR

Is 45:1.4-6
1 Thes 1:1-5b
Mt 22:15-21

Today's Gospel describes a trap that is laid for Jesus by the Pharisees. Envious of his success with the people, they want to get him to compromise himself by taking a stand on dangerous issues. The plot is well hatched. They make a temporary deal with the Herodians, the partisans of Herod who are on the side of the Roman Empire. Then they carefully work up a question and head off to find Jesus.

Their approach is particularly cunning and spiteful. They start off by praising Jesus' fidelity to truth and his courage in voicing it. He is no respecter of persons or circumstances, they say. Then they pose a thorny question: "Is it lawful to pay tax to the emperor or not?"

The situation is quite delicate. Jesus must give a yes or no answer, and either answer will put him in an impossible situation. If he answers yes, the Pharisees will cry bloody murder because he has taken sides with the Roman invader and betrayed God Almighty. If he answers no, then the Herodians will denounce him to the Romans as a political threat. They will have him condemned as a rebel who opposes the law of the occupying power. Jesus will be forced to compromise himself no matter which answer he gives.

His difficulty is compounded by the general atmosphere in which the question is asked. Jesus' interlocutors are not looking for truth, they are trying to down him. An honest response is never possible in such an atmosphere of confrontation and hypocrisy. Truth only reveals itself gradually to people who are willing to submit to it; it does not come to those who seek to use it for their own selfish ends.

Yet Jesus must give an answer. Silence itself would be interpreted in the wrong way. He must find some dialectical approach that will silence his examiners, giving him a chance to make a sound point without favoring either side.

Jesus first reproaches his questioners for their hypocrisy, thus showing that he has a clear awarness of the situation. Then he has them produce a coin of tribute and describe the image on it. They tell him that Caesar's image is on it. He then replies: "Give to Caesar what is Caesar's, but give to God what is God's." His interlocutors are taken aback. They cannot rebut his answer or reproach him for it, so they back off.

Jesus' reply is rich in meaning for us, so much so that it has often been taken out of context and used to support the most contradictory theses. The fact is that Jesus does not give a direct reply to the question at all; he does something better. He transforms the whole question at issue and pursues it to its ultimate conclusions. He does not give a yes or a no answer, which would set up a definitive opposition between God and Caesar and make a sharp break between them. Instead he indicates that man has obligations which make him subject to both Caesar and God, but in a hierarchy which he does not choose to define further. The point is that man has complementary duties and obligations. How are we to determine what they are? How are we to spell them out more precisely? Today's other two readings can help us here.

Isaiah speaks to us about Cyrus. He develops Yahweh's thinking with respect to this pagan king of the Persians. Cyrus does not know anything about this God of the Jews; he worships his own gods. He carries out his policies as he decides, seeking to bolster his own best interests. He is not encumbered by spiritual considerations such as those that enter into the decisions of the Israelite nation. But this pagan king is known by Yahweh. His ignorance of Yahweh means nothing, for he is raised up by Yahweh to play an important role in the destiny of the Jewish people. Cyrus is unaware of all that, but he is part of God's picture anyway. Hence he must also be taken into account by anyone who claims to be faithful to Yahweh.

In the text of Isaiah, Cyrus is the Caesar of today's Gospel. He is a pagan who does not know the Jewish law, hence he is an enemy of God in the eyes of the Israelites.

In Paul's letter to the Thessalonians we read his greeting to that community. It is a church, a community to which the believer belongs in body and soul. His membership indeed is something more than that of someone in the old covenant, because the Church is the living body of Jesus Christ. Paul gives thanks to the Lord for this Church. Its faith, hope, and charity are the work of Jesus himself. This community is not man's work, for it is rooted in the power and the activity of the Holy Spirit. Each member has been chosen and each has received the light of the Holy Spirit. That is why and how he has been made an integral part of the community.

Both Isaiah and Paul provide us with an excellent commentary on Jesus' reply to the emissaries of the Pharisees. Jesus made it clear that we have duties to Caesar, who symbolizes contemporary society, and to God, who is the absolute master of all. Paul and Isaiah indicate how these duties are to be carried out in proper proportion.

Clearly every human being, whether he is a believer or not, is an integral part of some temporal society. The believer is also immersed in another society, in a spiritual community. So there are two different powers, alien to one another by virtue of the plane on which they are situated and the means they utilize.

Cyrus and Caesar represent the terrestrial organization of human life, with all the political and economic implications that it entails. Every human being—whether he is a believer or not, whether he is aware of a spiritual life or not—is inevitably a social being who receives benefits and services from society and pays back what he owes in the approriate way: e.g., in income tax. Every human being is responsible in his own way for the sound functioning of the human group to which he belongs, and ultimately for every human group. The latter concern brings him into the whole area of national and international problems: e.g., social justice, world hunger, etc. They are the logical extension of man's work and responsibility insofar as he is linked, wittingly or unwittingly, with the whole of creation.

Now within the human race some people have been enlightened by the Holy Spirit and gathered into a living communion. The Spirit's power and activity gathers them together, transforms them, and guides them so that they behave in conformity with Jesus Christ. They are members of Christ, subject to the Spirit who guides them towards the kingdom. At the same time they are members of human society, subject to its demands. Living in human society, they struggle to win respect for human solidarity in all its dimensions.

Now while these two powers or authorities are distinct, they are linked with each other by virtue of their origin and their goal. Cyrus did not know that everything came to him from Yahweh, yet he was part and parcel of the carrying out of God's plan. The final goal of every creature is to be reunited, recapitulated in Christ. This holds true for individuals, and for the societies composed of believers and unbelievers. But in between the origin and the goal lies our time of passage on earth. It is a time of journey, a journey that must be undertaken so that Caesar, unaware of man's real origin and goal, may gradually be transformed within by the Spirit and constantly revivified by the members of Christ.

Hence the latter cannot set up camp outside the earthly city, even though they cannot legitimately identify themselves with its goals either. They must be present in the city, performing every type of service that human solidarity demands and doing it even better than others. But they must also keep calling this earthly society into question, for they know its true origin and goal as well as the kind of wisdom that will get it from one to the other. The absolute imperative of service to God and man cannot exclude anything; but man's inner unity is not to be found in confusing the two domains.

We must develop the right attitude to suit each individual case. There will always be a trace of ambiguity involved in it. We must take due account of the immediate environment around us and also temper this with our adherence to the wisdom of God's Spirit. Our attitudes will be the fruit of this twofold effort.

30th SUNDAY OF THE YEAR

Ex 22:20-26
1 Thes 1:5c-10
Mt 22:34-40

We are in an atmosphere of confrontation and harsh debate. First the emissaries of the Pharisees and the Herodians questioned Jesus about paying taxes to Caesar. Then the Sadducees come to question him and are silenced. Today the .Pharisees renew their offensive. Successive waves of notables approach Jesus and try to bring him down with their questions. For the moment they have banded together to destroy the reputation of this irksome young prophet.

Today they question his orthodoxy. Does Jesus understand the proper hierarchy of God's commandments? Which is the most important commandment? Jesus states the commandments that sum up all of God's revelation: "You shall love the Lord your God (and) . . . your neighbor."

His reply pleases us, but also leaves us perplexed. We feel that we have gotten down to the core of things, but we cannot grasp the concrete import of these commandments.

He tells us that we are to love God with our whole heart, and strength, and mind. But is that possible or necessary, some will ask, in an age when man can fashion and build up the world by himself alone? Do the words, "love God," have concrete meaning any longer? They certainly might have made sense in an age when people thought that the sun and wind and tempest obeyed the arbitrary whims of some all-powerful deity. But what sense can "love" or "submissive obedience" of that sort have today?

"You shall love your neighbor." Now we have something on which everyone can agree. That is a critical and urgent duty. Everyone desperately needs a little more understanding and acceptance. A little more mutual love would certainly help things along. Love of neighbor is on everyone's lips, be he preacher or politician, union leader or social worker. People may not know exactly what the words mean, but they are bandied about by everyone who wants to make his way in the world these days.

Solidarity between human beings has never been as evident as it is today. It is such a commonplace thing that it has become a truism. The means of production and national economies are highly interdependent. The process of urbanization brings more and more people into the confines of a metropolitan area; the organization of urban life is so problematical that the government is expected to protect its citizens from the attendant personal risks. War itself, that old tradition of the human race, is no longer feasible beyond a certain scope because it will entail the simultaneous destruction of both sides. Information spreads through the world with incredible speed, through all the available media. One could produce all sorts of evidence to show that human solidarity has never been so real as it is today.

Some think that this solidarity, growing more intricate every day, signifies progress in brotherly love. To them it means that the world is gathering together more and more in the unity of Christ, even though it may be unaware of this fact.

Thanks to the information media, those who are suffering from hunger and injustice are no longer mythical figures. They are our neighbors, and we must love them as ourselves. The great urban conglomerations must gradually manage to shift from mere collectivities to true communities. The migration of workers and laborers increases our knowledge of each other and breaks down old barriers.

Such solidarity and such mutual dependence should be a harbinger of hope, proclaiming the full realization of the kingdom. But somehow we have the impression that things are not working out that way. The individual feels helpless before the new turn of events. The menacing course of "progress" raises fear in his heart. His work, life, and profession are threatened. A serious strike or a new invention may put him out of a job. If he turns on the radio, he will hear news of some new catastrophe. The pressure of public opinion and the manipulative actions of politicians threaten freedom of thought and constrain him to behave in a predetermined way.

Such threats inevitably lead people to fear that they will be exploited by others; and the fear is all the more intense and insurmountable insofar as the constraining forces are anonymous. Faced with these threatening circumstances, the individual inevitably turns to self-defense and self-protection. He cries out in defense of his independence and comes to reject authority more and more, for he sees the latter as the source of the troubles that assail him.

This gives rise to particularism and individualistic impulses. We hardly know the other people living in our apartment house. We barely greet our colleagues at work. The most obvious and painful note of present-day urban life is loneliness. In the Church there is a proliferation of personal vocations, of protest movements, of more or less clandestine groups of religious and lay people. Things have reached the point where one can talk about "the underground Church."

Amid the hubbub it becomes increasingly clear that man is looking for something. Using all the means at his disposal, he is looking for a ray of light, an added dose of strength, some intervention from elsewhere. He wants some additional possibilities opened up to him, so that he can not only overcome his present troubles but also build a truly just world.

And that brings us back to God's message today. It reveals the cause of man's failure to achieve real solidarity and the new way in which we can bring fulfillment and harmony to all men.

First we are reminded of the first and greatest commandment: "You shall love the Lord your God with your whole heart, with your whole soul, and with all your mind." We must love God with our whole heart: that is, with all our powers of thought and will and emotion.

We must love God with our whole soul: that is, with all the capabilities of our temporal and eternal life. We must love God with our whole mind: that is, with the deepest part of our self where the Spirit of God comes to meet us. Only then, Jesus seems to be saying, will the word of God rise to new heights in our conscious awareness and our will, enabling us to abandon our old idols and to serve the living and true God.

It is our love of God that will determine to what extent we will be capable of loving our neighbor. It is our love of God that will enable us to endure changes in our world and to turn them into positive movements.

Today's selection from the book of Exodus might seem to present a negative teaching. But in fact it is a positive one that is quite pertinent to the obvious difficulties we face today. Put briefly it is this: lack of love provokes violence. Anyone who is familiar with the most elementary lessons of psychology knows that already. Love keeps us from exploiting others and from its harsh consequences. It mirrors God's compassion and reminds us that we must pay heed to every living person.

Jesus Christ speaks to us of God, and the Church was established to proclaim his words. To be sure, we must know how to listen to others. We cannot impose our ideas on those we meet, even by non-violent means. But by some odd quirk, we are in an era when both the clergy and the laity are afraid to speak the message of the gospel. They want to display their solidarity with other human beings, no matter what the cost. Is it not obvious that they run the risk of losing their savor? Human beings today are too distressed, too hardened in their own positions and unable to communicate their real desires to each other, for the Church to be silent. She was created by Christ to proclaim the good news of God's love, and that message is more urgently needed than ever. The Church and her members will not convey that message of love by smoothing over the differences between it and what others think. They must listen, of course. But most of all they must listen to the message of God and transmit it to others.

Some would like to think that the world will reveal God to us. Their motto is: "Christ is other people." But we will be able to meet each other and love each other truly only to the extent that we talk about God and his love, helping each other to trust in him and give ourselves entirely to him. Only Jesus "delivers us from the wrath to come."

31st SUNDAY OF THE YEAR

Mal 1:14b-2:2b,8-10
1 Thes 2:7b-9.13
Mt 23:1-12

Jesus had many run-ins with the Pharisees. He was often challenged and attacked by them, as we have seen in previous weeks. Today he puts the crowd on guard against their teaching—or rather, against their way of acting. He vigorously underlines their perfidy. Then he advises his disciples how to avoid the perverse conduct of these spiritual leaders.

We must admit that when we first hear these words of Jesus, we feel a certain glow of satisfaction. With wit and clear-sightedness Jesus himself takes up our cry for sincerity, authenticity, and fraternity. With a touch of stinging irony he mows down vainglorious, pretentious hypocrites such as those we meet in our own lives. If we suffer some rebuke or setback from a person of that ilk in authority, we feel that Jesus has already avenged us with his words.

The words of Jesus also please us because we readily tend to look for the present-day counterparts of the Scribes and Pharisees. We know they are called "Father." They pass themselves off as teachers, pretend to be spiritual physicians, and expect a certain degree of special consideration and respect. The more recent and treacherous variety pass themselves off as men of simplicity and good fellowship. In a word, Jesus' remarks today fan the fires of anticlericalism that burn within all of us.

Why not accept the truth of the parallel? Why shouldn't priests and bishops accept the fact that people speak thus about them? Are not some of them quite akin to the Scribes and Pharisees denounced today by Jesus?

They are inconsistent. As Jesus puts it: "Their words are bold but their deeds are few." It is true, is it not? As one author remarks, only theologians of the same religion can know the real meaning of the word "hate."

They are lazy. As Jesus puts it: "They bind up heavy loads, hard to carry, to lay on other men's shoulders, while they themselves will not lift a finger to budge them." One must do more than proclaim and teach God's word to demonstrate that one's fidelity is in fact courageous. Conversion is a constant necessity if one is to be an authentic messenger of God's word, but it is not always carried through.

They are proud and vain. As Jesus puts it: "They are fond of places of honor . . . of marks of respect in public." It is often difficult to proclaim God's word, and every human being needs some sign of recognition to assure him. So one is tempted to play a certain role, even though the snobbishness of the moment may be a pose of simplicity.

Let us come right out and say it: there are priests, ministers of God's word who can recognize themselves in the portrait that Jesus draws of the Scribes and Pharisees. Alas, they are not alone. Many other baptized persons, for different reasons and in different ways perhaps, can also see themselves in the same portrait.

In fact, we have had an example of all this in our own experience just now. Insofar as we feel a certain glow of satisfaction from Jesus' words, our own situation is a bit suspect. It betrays a more or less conscious feeling of superiority on our part, as if to say: "I am not like that, thank God." If we think that, we are included in the group portrait Jesus draws.

It is not true that we too, in whatever role we play, claim a right to a certain amount of esteem and approval, if not downright obedience? The father of a family will sometimes say: "You must obey me because I am your father!" In many instances the child should obey him, but that does not mean that the father's motives are always pure. He may not really be trying to inculcate the authentic virtue of obedience, he may simply be trying to safeguard his own domination of his children. He may be using his greater age or strength to protect his personal prestige. Is he not among those whom Jesus describes today?

We often tend to judge or despise others, insisting that they should behave differently. Are we not putting burdens on their backs that we ourselves refuse to carry?

The fact is that we all can recognize ourselves in the portrait of the Scribes and Pharisees that Jesus draws today. The traits are so human and so universal that we all bear them and merit his reproach. The worst thing about it all is our lack of awareness in this area. We bask in the luxury of a good conscience because we are blind to our personal defects.

Today Jesus puts us on guard against ourselves and each other. He gives us a clearer awareness of our personal inconsistencies, and hence of each other's faults. His advice to his disciples will help us to situate ourselves correctly vis-a-vis each other.

Jesus' advice could be summed up in one phrase, but it is rich in content and deserves lengthier consideration. The hierarchy of the kingdom is not to be found in knowledge or personal competence or domination. It is to be found in service. In the kingdom no one is master. We cannot dominate others because we all are brothers. No one fathers anyone else; we all are children of God our Father. No one is teacher or professor because we all are taught by the Spirit.

All that is readily understandable. We know it makes sense because it dovetails completely with the whole mentality of the gospels. But we must make two concrete applications of it in order to flesh it out in our day-to-day life.

First of all, we must develop a certain humility. As Jesus puts it: "The greatest among you will be the one who serves the rest." It is not our natural state; it is something we have to work at to acquire. We will have to fight against our desire for domination, our concern for efficiency, our delight in being important personages. True humility does not put us above others, nor does it make others dependent on us. We cannot seek our own glory and give glory to God at the same time. The vainglorious person is one who does not "lay it to heart to give glory to my name."

True humility has nothing to do with negligence. It makes us gentle, as Paul indicates: "We were as gentle as any nursing mother fondling her little ones." But it does not allow for laziness. Paul himself refers to his efforts and his toil "in order not to impose on you in any way." Thus humility does not mean a multilation of our capabilities or a refusal to develop them actively. It is rather a certain outlook, a conviction that we are merely instruments desiring to be docile to the breath of the Spirit.

This humility will inevitably be accompanied by a certain loneliness. If we are not to be father or teacher for others, they are not to be father or teacher for us either. We certainly are tempted to look around us for people to fill those roles in our lives. It is satisfying and soothing to give oneself into another's hand, to rely on a father or counselor instead of doing one's own thinking. If there are people who play such a role in our personal lives, then we are responsible to the extent that we demand it of them. It is an insidious thing, and it is important that we recognize its presence because it accounts for much of the disorder in our lives today.

Then Jesus offers us a criterion by which we can determine whether we are living up to the proposed standards of humility and maturity: "Do everything and observe everything they tell you." In other words: "Be concerned enough about truth and uprightness to discern what is good, no matter what source it comes from." We often are so childish that we repect the words of another person on the pretext that the person is vainglorious or hypocritical—which is to say, that he is only human. But God can make use of such a person, and we are often tempted to reject everything in sight.

Of course it would be absurd for the ministers of

God's word to take this advice as an encouragement for negligence. They must make every effort to be faithful to what the Lord shows them. But they will never be fully and wholly faithful until we all are gathered together in Christ's kingdom.

In the meantime we must accept the word of God "as it truly is, the word of God at work within you who believe."

32nd SUNDAY OF THE YEAR

Wis 6:12-16
1 Thes 4:13-18
Mt 25:1-13

Today Jesus tells another story related to a wedding. He alludes to certain features of the whole ceremonial and invites his disciples to draw the appropriate lesson from what he says.

To us this story of the waiting bridesmaids may seem a bit odd. We must realize that this wait for the bridegroom, and his tardiness, were parts of the ceremony in oriental countries. Bizarre as the story might seem to us, it did have real symbolic meaning for oriental peoples and for Jesus' immediate audience. Jesus boldly goes beyond the most immediate symbolism and offers an important message.

So we have ten bridesmaids waiting to escort the bridegroom to the wedding with torchlight. The bridegroom is late in arriving, the bridesmaids doze off. Suddenly a cry goes up: the bridegroom is coming. The five bridesmaids who brought oil along with them are allowed to enter while the others are excluded. That is the story.

We may find it hard to picture the event to ourselves in the concrete, but we can easily pick out some of the important points in the story. The bridegroom who is on his way is an allusion to the certain coming of Christ. He will come suddenly and unexpectedly. We must take certain precautions so that we can be prepared for his coming; otherwise we will be excluded from his kingdom. Now let us try to explore these points in more precise detail.

The Lord is coming. The ten bridesmaids have no doubt about that fact; it is a certainty in their minds. They have prepared their torches, arrived ahead of the bridegroom, and now they await him at the specified place. They are so certain that he will come that his delay does not upset them at all. Serene in their certainty, they even doze off to sleep.

Paul proclaims this coming of the Lord in his letter to the Thessalonians. These believers are not to grieve as non-believers might. Paul stresses the certainty of the Lord's final and definitive manifestation, including in the picture those Christians who have already died. He wants to reassure those who fear that the dead will not participate in Christ's imminent return.

So we receive an important reminder here: the Lord is coming. Our expectation of his return sometimes ceases to be a real conviction within us. He is coming, but everything seems to be going on calmly. There is no evident sign of his coming, and he seems to be inactive. The passage of time wears out our patience, and questions begin to crop up in our minds. Doubt begins to gnaw away at us, our knowledge grows hazy, our inner light flickers out, and we become indifferent to predicted future events that seem more and more hypothetical. Then we run into some more terrible shock and our expectations of his coming may seem completely offbase; we give away to despair.

But the Lord really is coming. This certitude should give us strength and peace of mind. It is not an hypothesis, it is the reality that our future will be. Along with the fact of our our bodily death, it is the only sure thing we have. Let us pray that it will fill us with peace and tranquillity.

The Lord's coming will be sudden and unexpected. That is the second point in our story today. "At midnight someone shouted. . . ." It is as if the transition from one day to another were the transition from one state to another. Paul, too, sees it as a sudden thing. It will happen "at the word of command, at the sound of the archangel's voice and God's trumpet." It will be a sudden thing signalized by a clear and shattering warning. Today's divine message tells us that the Lord's coming will be sudden, unexpected, and compelling. It seems to suggest that we would be foolish to imagine that we we will have plenty of time to ready ourselves for it. It will be more like a blinding flash of light on the road to Damascus, unexpected but quite decisive. It will give life to those who are in tune with it, and destroy everyone and everything else.

This is the profound air of expectant waiting that surrounds the believer. Since the time of Christ's Ascension, Christian hope is focused on the promise made to the apostles: "This Jesus who has been taken from you will return, just as you saw him go up into the heavens" (Acts 1:11). But that does not mean that every believer is consciously aware of this fact and lives accordingly, as the rest of the parable indicates.

There were ten bridesmaids, equally attentive in waiting for the bridegroom and equally at peace in the assurance that he was on his way. All of them went out to meet him in the same gay spirit and waited for him with the same assured hope. But five were admitted to the wedding whereas the rest were kept out. The wise bridesmaids brought a reserve of oil with them and were allowed in; the foolish bridesmaids did not provide themselves with any reserves and were not allowed into the wedding. Indeed they were spurned rather brutally: "I tell you, I do not know you."

Their rejection strikes us as rather odd. Their lack of foresight might deserve a mild rebuke, but we feel that total rejection of them is much too harsh. After all, they did believe as the others and displayed the same earnest spirit. Why is the reserve of oil so important? What does it mean?

What seems clear is that every believer must have something in reserve when the Lord comes: an added store of light or strength which will allow him to escort the Lord into the kingdom. However, we also know that light and strength are gifts of God, granted to us through his Spirit. How, then, can someone be condemned for mere thoughtlessness, especially if they remain faithful to the essential things and go out to meet the Lord?

The passage from the Book of Wisdom may help us to grasp the point of God's message here. Wisdom reveals and offers itself to the person who truly desires it. It unveils itself to the person who seeks for it and thus proves his intelligence. It goes out in search of those who are worthy of it.

Isn't that the reserve oil which enabled the wise bridesmaids to replenish their torches when the arrival of the bridegroom was announced? The true believer is alert to the existence of this wisdom. He tries to know it better and live by it. He is imbued with it so that it becomes a way of looking at things and of living his life. Hence it gives him an inner consistency and integrity. It is difficult to define, but we do manage to detect its presence in some people and to bemoan its absence in others. It is evident in a certain harmony and integrity that makes some people seem peaceful and yet impressive at the same time. It is a certain spiritual stance and stature.

Here we have something that is a little more than faith in the Lord or expectant waiting for his coming. Even though a person may believe in the Lord and his return and look forward to it, he can still live the life of a dilettante. He may nurture a false and somewhat magical type of confidence, feeling that there will always be time later on to shape things up and that the Lord will certainly take care of matters in any event. It would be a mistake to see this attitude as humility.

In reality, true certainty about the Lord's coming commits a person to a serious and deliberate effort at gaining wisdom through constant fidelity to the Lord. Wisdom is acquired and nurtured from day to day by cultivating the proper inner attitude. How does it work in our own lives?

Often we are undecided about which course of action we should take. A debate goes on inside us, our human desires fighting against the clearcut will of God and the message he has revealed to us. Our desires may be alluring and even compelling, whereas God's revelation may be intolerable because it will entail total risk for ourselves and for the human group that surrounds us.

We must not vacillate. As soon as the debate begins, we must choose the will of God, whatever cost it may entail. That is how we nurture wisdom and prove its presence in us. We shall then be like the wise bridesmaids who "took flasks of oil as well as their torches."

Jesus will return, and his return will be sudden. May this reminder revivify our hope. May it also revivify our desire to acquire the wisdom that will open the door to us when the wedding of the bridegroom takes place.

33rd SUNDAY OF THE YEAR

Prv 31:10-13,19-20,30-31
1 Thes 5:1-6
Mt 25:14-30

Today Jesus continues and expands the line of thought expressed in the parable of the ten bridesmaids who were waiting for the bridegroom. Approaching the topic in another way, he enables us to gain a better appreciation of the reserve of oil alluded to last week and its importance.

It is the story of a man who entrusts his funds to his servants before leaving on a journey. When he returns, he summons these servants in order to reward them in accordance with the way they utilized the funds he entrusted to them. His treatment of the third servant disturbs us greatly and embarrasses us, for it seems to be cruel and unjust. The servant did not wrong his master in any way; he buried the money and gave it all back later. Solely because he has not made a profit for his master, he is excluded from the joyous abode of his master and hurled "into the darkness outside, where he can wail and grind his teeth."

And the master says something else that shocks us: "Those who have will get more until they grow rich, while those who have not will lose even the little they have." Is it not shockingly unjust to despoil the have-nots for the benefit of the haves?

The answer apparently is "yes." But let us try to follow the course of the story more closely.

The first two servants, each in his own way, saw to it that all the funds received from their master bore fruit. They heightened the value of the whole amount, not just of some portion of it. Then they gave it all back to their master—both the original sum and the increment they had labored to procure. They were men who did not try to keep anything for themselves.

The attitude of these first two servants tells us two

things about our approach to creation. First, we must accept creation as a whole. Secondly, while we are here we must make sure that it bears fruit and then offer it to God.

Accepting creation, all of it, is the first thing we must do. God entrusts creation to man and imbues man with his Spirit. Only one condition is attached: man must not exclude anything. He must invest all that he is and all he can do in the project. He must try to develop all that God has put at his disposal.

The proposition may seem to be very flattering for man, for it appears to be in line with his instincts for wielding power and exerting dominion. Yet if we look at our civilizations and cultures, both oriental and occidental we soon see that man selects certain things to work on and neglects other things. We need only look at some of the more obvious spectacular manifestations of man's work to see the quirk in human affairs.

The flights to the moon are certainly admirable achievements. They may one day help to alleviate conditions on this earth. At the same time they indicate that man, in the course of developing his scientific knowledge and utilizing his precise knowledge of mathematics, has opted for spectacular displays, increased production, and financial profit. Meanwhile, back on earth everything turns hard and dry and icily cold.

People flock into larger and denser conglomerations, yet they have never felt so alone. Soon people will be little more than a number in a computer, and the health-care services will compete for their income.

Art, which should contribute to the transformation of man, has surrendered to the profit motive. The finest works of art are objects of greedy financial speculation.

Man chooses and selects as he pleases, spurning the gift of God's Spirit. As a result, he puts creation seriously out of whack and mutilates himself.

If we admit the truth of these observations, we are forced to make some curious remarks. Consider our scientific knowledge and its technological applications. Our "discoveries" in this area were supposed to improve man's life on earth and his destructive capabilities. It is possible that the whole ensemble is an illusion for which we are now paying the consequences? We call them "discoveries" when in fact they were nothing more than "stock-taking." They enabled us to establish new relationships between the better known elements and hence to produce some achievements that had never been seen before. But in fact they were not creations at all; they were simply extensions or new ways of organizing what had already been given to man. Man blended the elements together in new ways, called that "creation," and was satisfied with himself.

As a result, however, all authentic forms of creation will be discredited because their results will be much more disconcerting. They will compel man to transform himself without being flattered at all. True metamorphosis requires a process of destruction. That is why the real creators, the artists deserving of the name, no longer have any place in the world and are understood by only a small band of initiates. Man has developed his capacity for scientific knowledge and applied technology to an exaggerated degree, at the same time refusing to admit that all his capabilities should be subject to the creative Spirit. His productive work right now is developing into an enormous cancer that will kill him if he does not watch out.

Hence man must accept all of creation. In addition, and this is the second aspect mentioned above with regard to the attitude of the first two servants, he must offer up everything. While he works on every aspect of creation to develop its full potential, he may not do it for his own selfish interests; he must do it so that he can offer it up and redistribute it.

In our present-day world "justice" is set up to do exactly the opposite. It is a set of conventions designed to protect profit. If a salary is in conformity with certain norms, then it becomes one's exclusive property. If we manage to save some money, this money must produce a return for us. We put it where it will bring in the biggest return, not where it will render the most service.

Instead of offering things up, we want to accumulate and use things for our own satisfaction.

Compared with the attitude of the first two servants in today's Gospel, modern man neglects creation and hoards the results of his work. In reality we all are akin to the third servant who buried the funds entrusted to him.

No one, of course, can know or do everything. But the fact is that none of us can really claim that we are modest and clear-eyed enough to take ourselves as we are, to pursue our deepest aspirations courageously, to be faithful to our innermost selves. We all give in to the impulse of the moment. Fearing risk and feeling insecure, we are possessive and self-centered. We close up within ourselves and refuse to share.

That tack is heavy with consequences, and we are experiencing them already. The wailing and grinding of teeth of which the Gospel speaks are the painful consequences of man's refusal to accept creation and to use the forces of the Spirit properly. We are experiencing that harsh fact now, and there is every reason to believe that the time of testing is far from over in the so-called developed nations.

It is certainly dishonest to take what does not belong to us. But it is just as gravely wrong to protect what one has by imposing a system of justice that is really unjust. That tack forces people in need to take back what they need by violent means, and so we get banditry, war, terrorism, and revolution. And it is those who accumulate and hold on to things for themselves who are responsible.

The wailing and grinding of teeth results from the third servant's refusal to make use of the funds entrusted to him. Now we can begin to see why the one thousand silver pieces were taken from him and given to the servant who already had ten thousand. The latter had been willing to accept the whole amount, put it to good use, and return the whole bundle. He is truly poor in spirit, willing to render service to the fullest degree without asking for anything in return. It is to the likes of him that the kingdom of heaven will be granted, as the Beatitude indicates. By giving him the additional one thousand, the owner in the parable merely indicates that the true and honest servant will naturally possess the kingdom in its fullness.

In today's Epistle, Paul warns us not to sleep on the job: "Just when people are saying, 'Peace and Security,' ruin will fall on them." He urges us to be "awake and sober." It is a timely message for us. The Church and human society are being wracked by convulsions, painful events, and anxious questioning. Does it not signify that the Spirit is hard at work, trying to remind us of his existence and urging us to use our store of capital to refashion ourselves?

FEAST OF CHRIST THE KING

Ez 34:11-12,15-17
1 Cor 15:20-26,28
Mt 25:31-46

We have come to the last Sunday in the liturgical year. Having introduced us to all the mysteries of the Lord, today the Church wants to sum up the whole year's message by presenting us with the feast of Christ the King. That is what she does, thanks to the three selections we have just read. Jesus is presented as a king shepherding his flock and looking out for their needs; as a king vanquishing opposing forces and sharing his victory with those on his side; as a king who passes judgment on people and decides in favor of those who accept his rule; and finally as a servant king who gives back his whole empire to his heavenly Father. In a few succint paragraphs we are presented with an astonishingly varied and complete portrait of Jesus. Each feature deserves our attention, for it has much to say to us.

This year the Church presents our king in action. At other times she stresses Christ's origin, thereby indicating that he has a right to rule the whole universe. But today the Lord takes care of us like a shepherd, fulfills our destiny for us, and then brings the work of creation to completion and turns it back to his Father. In a medley of images—now violent, now tender, now exultant—the destiny of the whole universe unrolls before our eyes; it is animated and fulfilled by Christ the King.

Ezekiel begins with the story of the good shepherd. Jesus will pick up the image later on. Today it is meant to show us what sort of a king we are dealing with. He is concerned about each of his sheep. He dresses the wounded, heals the sick, seeks out the lost, and watches out for those that seem to be getting along fine. This king, whose power and dominion should inspire fear in us by rights, is a tender shepherd who keeps careful watch over his sheep. As Ezekiel puts it: "I will rescue them from every place where they were scattered when it was cloudy and dark."

Right away we are inclined to shun such perspectives as these, grandiloquent yet ineffable. We are completely stunned by the revelation of a love like this, in which all the power of the Lord is expressed. We must note that this love is not feebleness or pity of an ineffective kind. It is rich in life-giving impact, so much so that it will in fact destroy death once and for all.

The description in Paul's letter to the Christians of Corinth also presents a dynamic picture. Our king is carrying out a project. His goal is to destroy all the forces that are hostile or contrary to life, to bring all his creatures through death to the final resurrection. This king is Jesus. Crucified, he passes through death and emerges in his resurrection into a life that is no longer menaced by anything. He is the first to make this passage, but he will not be the only one. All the creatures whom he loves and cares for are destined to follow him on this pathway, for he watches over them with the concern of a true shepherd.

To achieve this life that will no longer be threatened by death, he must first win victory over "every sovereignty, authority, and power." Then, "the last enemy to be destroyed is death." The royalty which Jesus attains by his personal passage through death to resurrection is the royalty of a warrior who must destroy the forces which stand in opposition to him. It is clear that we now live in this period of combat. Christ, already glorified, approaches every creature and asks creation to follow him. At the end of this period "he will hand over the kingdom to God the Father." He is the king of a creation that is now in process of mutation. He is the artisan of our passover from this world to the kingdom of God. "When, finally, all has been subjected to the Son, he will then subject himself to the One who made all things subject to him."

His royalty is in the service of his Father. He exercises an authority somehow delegated to the Son during the course of world history. He is to bring creation to its fulfillment and its true goal. That is why "Christ must reign." Human beings cannot possibly ignore him. They must submit themselves to his sovereignty, to his pastoral tenderness. Otherwise they are doomed to utter destruction because no other "mystique" can lead to a successful outcome.

The words of Paul might have seemed a bit abstract at first, but suddenly they take on a note of terrifying urgency. We are not free to accept or refuse. We can refuse, of course, but that will mean failure and ruin for us. The bucolic image of the tender shepherd suddenly takes on new overtones. The tenderness in question is that which comes with spiritual power and spiritual victory. In accepting the royalty of Jesus, we no longer seek some other sort of God besides. For as Paul points out to us, there is a vital and vivifying unity between Christ, the king of the universe, and the almighty Father.

Finally, in today's Gospel we discover another aspect of Jesus' royalty. He is the judge of the universe.

When history reaches its end, the risen Jesus will have completed his work. It will then be time to turn it over to his Father. He will have conquered every other sovereignty and power. Peace and harmony will then be a reality in a new life enjoyed by those who are raised from the dead. Jesus will now appear in all his power and glory. It is the return that has been proclaimed so long and awaited so ardently by each succeeding generation of believers.

That scene of final judgment is magnificently portrayed by Saint Matthew. "All the nations will be assembled before him." All human beings will be there, no matter what their religious convictions have been or what racial and cultural ties they have had. The odd thing is that all those who are going to be judged by Christ seem to be unaware of the fact that they have had an opportunity to serve him or to refuse such service. In the case of those who believe in him, we know that the gospel message provides other criteria of judgment and lays down other specific demands besides. That is only natural because the believers know Christ. His Spirit has revealed him to them. They must be courageous enough to acknowledge him (Mt 10:32). They must obey the will of the Father (Mt 7:21). They must show people mercy and love (Mt 5:7). They must be prompt to pardon at all times (Mt 6:14). It is only natural that these things should be demanded of believers in addition, for they have received more enlightenment than others and they have been predestined to know Christ even during their time on earth. But that does not mean that Christ is not king over all the others too. That is the point which today's Gospel brings out. They, too, will be judged by this king.

We readily recall what the criterion of judgment will be. Insofar as they have shown kindness to the sick, the hungry, and all their fellow men in need, they will have unwittingly helped to forward the Lord's plan of universal love. Insofar as they have noticed to some degree the existence of other persons besides themselves and accepted the evident solidarity of all human beings, they will have been faithful to their God-given nature. So they will deserve to be welcomed by Christ into the kingdom which had been prepared for them from the creation of the world, even though they did not know about it until the day of judgment.

In this text the universal criterion of judgment is revealed to us. There may also be other criteria for believers, but they are not dispensed from this one. It is preliminary to their entrance into the kingdom after their life on earth. It is hard to see how anyone could share in the Lord's kingdom, if he is not now willing to accept all the demands that flow from human solidarity; for that is precisely what the Lord will demand of all those who have not come to know him during their life on earth.

Doesn't this scene offer us a key to solving the whole problem of the salvation of the infidel, which troubles many people. If they truly believe in Christ the king, and if they ponder this judgment scene in the context of today's readings, they should find their fears allayed. God does not exclude anyone from his love. The good shepherd watches over each person, but he guides each in a different way. All will meet in the kingdom prepared for them by the Father to the extent that they are faithful to what has been given to them.

Let us pray that each of us will be faithful to the Spirit and that we will enter the Father's kingdom. Buoyed up by this hope, may we be willing to overcome all the foreign powers within us and remain in league with Christ.

FEASTS OF SAINTS

December 8
IMMACULATE CONCEPTION

Gn 3:9-15,20
Eph 1:3-6,11-12
Lk 1:26-38

Today we celebrate one of the three important feasts of the Blessed Virgin Mary that are commemmorated each year. The celebration of her Assumption and of today's feast enables us to gain better insight into the full measure of her holiness, for she was the first human being to fully benefit from the work of her son. Once again we have a chance to recall the personality of Mary, who was so close to us and at the same time so extraordinary.

Perusing the sacred texts that speak about her, we find that she was quite like all the women of Israel. Her name is not a distinctive one. It had been the name of many women before her, of Moses' sister in particular (Ex 15:20), and it was a common name in her own day. The name "Mary" derives from the name "Miriam," which means "princess" or "lady." It suggests a whole program of femininity that is to be carried out with a truly noble heart. And that is precisely what we find in the personality of this woman who is the daughter of Joachim and Anna.

Her behavior in the gospel texts confirms the promise of her name. She is a pious Hebrew woman, faithfully subject to the Hebrew law. Her most eloquent biographer consistently points up the connections between her behavior and the dictates of the law. However, her acquaintance with Scripture went beyond the ordinary. Her reactions to the important events in her life clearly indicate that she was deeply imbued with the Scriptural message—so much so that its words leapt spontaneously to her lips when she reacted to events. There is her *Magnificat,* for example, which will ever remain one of the most beautiful songs of wonder and praise at God's work. In it we see the influence of the psalms, and of the song known as the Canticle of Anna in the first book of Samuel (1 Sm 2:1-10).

As we meditate further on the Scriptural texts, we

find that Mary is something more than an ordinary Hebrew woman who is faithfully submissive to God's law and quite pious. Some of the salutations addressed to her indicate that she personifies the people of God. She is the "daughter of Zion." The salutation of the angel Gabriel at the Annunication is an extraordinary one. She is the "highly favored daughter" who is full of grace. The salutation recalls the promise of God's arrival in his holy city. In the Canticle of Canticles, this salutation is reserved for the bride, who is one of the traditional images of the chosen people.

All these literary allusions help us to discover Mary's place in the history of her people and in God's plan. In the name of the house of Jacob she, and she alone, receives the announcement of salvation. She alone accepts this announcement and makes its fulfillment possible. Right away she gets beyond purely personal sentiments of gratitude and expresses the joy and thanks of the whole lineage of Abraham. She is totally and unreservedly commited to everything the Lord has proposed to her; she is no longer closed up in the confines of her own individual person. Her heart opens out to cover her whole nation and then the whole of humanity. She will go on to carry out a mystery that seems impossible. She will incarnate a love so personal and absolute that it will be universal in scope.

That is how the personality of the Virgin Mary shows up in the few Scriptural passages that speak of her. We are deeply impressed by the two features that are highlighted. On the one hand she is an ordinary woman like any other woman; on the other hand she is a woman with a singular destiny. Her singularity lies in this fact; she is the first human being to benefit from the renovative power of her Son; thus, in her person is embodied the full, universal salvation of the Church itself.

Here we cannot overlook the intimate relationship, the mystery of communion, between Mary and the Church. To be sure, Mary was called to salvation in faith through the grace of God. As Paul tells us in another of today's readings: "God chose us in him before the world began, to be holy and blameless in his sight, to be full of love." Like every believer, Mary was especially chosen by God; she is the beneficiary of the Creator's love. Like us, she was redeemed by the sacrifice of her Son. And yet she occupies a singular place within the Church.

In her the mystery of the Church is lived out to the fullest. Like the Church, she is the bride of Christ. She is the virgin sanctified by Christ, the "woman" mentioned in today's reading from Genesis. The "woman" could refer equally well to Mary or to Christ's Church. It is this "woman" who will strike at the head of the serpent, the latter personifying the spirit of evil. Finally, in her every Christian soul shares one vocation to holiness and is betrothed to Christ as a "chaste virgin" (2 Cor 11:2).

Thus it is in the person of Mary that we find the first and most perfect witness to the Church's fidelity to her divine call. That is the import of Mary's virginity, which is hallowed rather than diminished by her maternity.

The fact is that in Scripture the mystery of Mary and the mystery of the Church shed light on each other. The Church reveals openly what was lived silently and discreetly in the person of Mary. In both we find a mystery of virginity and of mystical marriage where God is the chosen bridegroom. It is a mystery where maternity and filiation dwell together in harmony. Like the Church, Mary is both the mother and daughter of Jesus Christ—thanks to the Holy Spirit's work.

It becomes clear to us that the mystery of virginity is meant to serve a purpose both in the case of Mary and of the Church. Both are supposed to live in the knowledge of pristine and total purity, a purity that is the result of Christ's grace. As Paul describes it: "a glorious church, holy and immaculate, without stain or wrinkle or anything of that sort" (Eph 5:27).

And so we are presented with the image of Mary,

the mother of Jesus, on this feast of the Immaculate Conception. To some believers this feast may seem to be a bit outdated. The need for ecumenism and the urgency of certain human problems would seem to favor a little more discretion in the celebration of Marian feasts. That notion itself is proof of our own spiritual faintheartedness. If we are thoroughly convinced that only God can save the world and that only his Spirit has the power to move us towards our destiny, then we cannot be indifferent to the way in which God chooses to fulfill this destiny. He chooses to make Mary the object of his own special election. Nor can we be indifferent to the task of discovering what he wants us to become. He takes one of us and makes her Christ's masterpiece; then he offers her to us so that we may contemplate her example and imitate her.

Of course we are not immaculate from the first moment of our conception. Our situation in life is so different from hers that we may find relatively little stimulus in her purity. Preserved from any original complicity with the tempter, she seems to have had a purity that came almost naturally to her. But we must always remember that this purity was the work of Christ, and that Mary fully accepted the presence of the Spirit. Even though we are afflicted with a basic perversion, with a taste for evil, she shows us the road to take and offers us assurance of success. She is far removed from us, yet incredibly near also. She will not abandon us when we strive to be faithful. Her willingness to be a mother, with everything that implies, is a sure guarantee for us. She will never cease to protect those who are wise enough to have recourse to her in their efforts to remain faithful and generous.

March 19
SAINT JOSEPH

2 Sm 7:4-5a,12-14a,16
Rom 4:13,16-18,22
Mt 1:16,18-21,24a

The gospels hardly speak about Joseph, the spouse of Mary, the man entrusted with the task of rearing and educating her son. There are only a few passages about him in the story of Jesus' infancy, and he is almost always associated with Mary. After the story of Jesus being lost in Jerusalem at the age of twelve, the gospels say nothing more about him. Exploring the treasury of Scripture more deeply over the course of the centuries, however, the Church has come to give him an increasingly important place in her effort to understand the mystery of Christ.

Today the Church offers us several readings. The passage from the second book of Samuel talks about the descendants of David: the passage from Romans talks about the spiritual lineage of Abraham; the Gospel begins where the genealogy of Jesus stops. By presenting these three readings, the Church situates Joseph in the prestigious lineage of the patriarchs and kings. With Abraham and David he is one of the three men who are particularly important in establishing God's kingdom, and he also is a characteristic type of the faithful person. Joseph is the spiritual heir of Abraham, the descendant of David. He bears witness in some special way to the revelation that was made to Abraham in Ur of the Chaldees and that developed over the course of centuries. But in what way precisely does he bear his witness?

Reading the gospel narrative, we immediately sense some embarrassment on the part of the author. He obviously is trying to reconcile realities that would appear to be alien to each other. On the one hand it seems quite clear that Jesus is the son of Mary and of the Holy Spirit. On the other hand Jesus must be linked to David's lineage by a man of that tribe who can claim and assert a real paternity.

Today's Gospel mentions the father of Joseph, and then indicates that Joseph himself is the intended spouse of Mary. She will be the mother of Jesus. But although the paternity of his ancestors is stated directly, Joseph himself is not clearly designated as the father of Jesus. We are led to the scene that has often been labelled "Joseph's Annunciation." Joseph is expressly entrusted with the task of taking Mary into his home and giving a name to the child that she will bring into the world. And the Gospel concludes: Joseph "did as the angel of the Lord had directed him."

A closer study of the text indicates that Joseph knew that the expected child was the work of the Holy Spirit—contrary to what many commentators have asserted. How could Mary possibly have kept that news from him? Not wishing to interfere with the unfolding development of God's own plan, Joseph planned to withdraw from the scene and "divorce her quietly" because he was "an upright man." He did not want his own presence as a marriage partner to put obstacles in the way of the exceptional destiny of Mary as mother of the child. But then he too receives a special mission: he is to be the father of Jesus.

With the help of the two Scriptural texts for today, we not only learn something about the person and character of Joseph but also gain deeper insight into the real nature of all fatherhood.

Viewing things from the outside, one might think that Joseph is the father of Jesus only in a juridical sense and only insofar as he links Jesus to the family of David. He obviously was not the fleshly father of Jesus, so we are inclined to conclude that he was not his real father. But there is a little bit more to it than that.

In the first reading for today, Nathan is sent to report what God has promised David insofar as his descendants are concerned. After David is dead and buried, he will have a successor whose royal reign will be solid and perpetual. The promise is reiterated four times: even though David must undergo death and burial, one of his successors will escape this plight. It sounds paradoxical, but two reasons are offered to explain why David's descendant will enjoy perpetual reign. First, he will truly be the Son of the Most High. Secondly, his royal reign will not be a human inheritance but the work of God himself. In the text it is God himself who will do all this. Thus David will have a descendant whose royal reign will not be threatened by the passage of time or potential disasters. It is God himself who will raise up this descendant and who will be his Father, but this king will also be the offspring of David.

In this text, therefore, we are told that a dual paternity can be mysteriously joined in one and the same individual. This individual can be an authentic descendant of David and, at the same time, an offspring of God himself. But how can that be? Paul explores that question for us in today's Epistle.

Paul reminds us that Abraham and his descendants were promised that "they would inherit the world." This inheritance is not a reward for their fidelity to the law. It is not merited by moral uprightness or by obedience to God's commandments. It is not offered on a *quid pro quo* basis: i.e., you obey my commandments and I will give you this inheritance. The promise is made "in view of the justice that comes from faith." It is not merited, it is "grace." All Abraham had to do was to believe in God's promise despite all appearances to the contrary: "Hoping against hope, Abraham believed and so became the father of many nations. . . ." Remember that Abraham and Sarai begot Isaac long after the usual age for childbearing. Paul does not hesitate to say: "He is our father in the sight of God, in whom he believed."

Abraham certainly is the physical father of Isaac. But Paul tells us that the real source of his paternity does not lie in his physical capability which ran its normal course; instead it lies in his faith in God's promise. Thus Nathan's prophecy to David and the experience of Abraham as discussed by Paul offer us images that will help us to glimpse the nature of Joseph's paternity.

On the one hand God himself will raise up a physical descendent to David. On the other hand David's paternity will be real in and through his faith. Starting out as absolute trust in God's fulfillment of his promise, faith becomes actual collaboration in the work of carrying out this promise. But this collaboration is framed within a creation where God takes all the initiative, where God is the only one who can display the required energy. Man agrees to accept everything as a gratitous gift, to be a docile instrument in the hands of God. And when he does agree to do this, he then is associated with God's unique paternity. He is flooded with God's love and becomes a truly upright man. Faith becomes the fountainhead of his own fruitfulness.

It is in this sense that Joseph is truly the father of Jesus, even though he is not his physical progenitor. Indeed, paradoxical as it may sound, we can say that he is the father *par excellence,* the very model of fatherhood. Paternity entails more than physical generation. The latter can be quite accidental, involving no conscious desire to participate in the generative activity of the Creator. On the other hand, the physical activity of generation can be linked with a conscious desire on the part of the father to collaborate with God's paternal activity. In that case it is the sign of a paternity whose ultimate origin is spiritual rather than physical. It is procreative love because it is immersed in the creative impulse of Almighty God. Joseph is the father of Jesus because he "did as the angel of the Lord had directed him."

Joseph's example tells us what true paternity is. True paternity means accepting the role which the Lord assigns to us, thus giving expression to a fecundity whose sole origin is in God. Paternity cannot be the privilege or private property of any human person. All uprightness and all procreative capability is a "grace" from God.

Saint Joseph agreed to be fully a father in the way designated by God. Is it not fitting that he should be designated as the special patron of all fathers of families?

June 29
SAINTS PETER AND PAUL

Acts 12:1-11
2 Tm 4:6-8,17-18
Mt 16:13-19

Today we celebrate the feast of two apostles who have always been regarded as the two most important ones by Christian tradition. Associated in this liturgical celebration, they have also been venerated together in popular piety. For all the differences between them, they have evoked the same response from believers in every age because their lives and activities were so important and necessary in the history of the infant Church.

To help us appreciate what they were in the past and what they might be for us today, the Church has selected three Scriptural readings which present them to us. Meditating on these readings, we will try to see what they have to say to us today, how they differ, how they complement one another, and what importance they may have for the Church in this complex and tormented age.

Right off it is quite clear that both of them were spurred on and animated in their work by the Lord's selection of them and by the help of his Spirit. Paul tells his friend Timothy: "The Lord stood by my side and gave me strength. . . . The Lord will continue to rescue me from all attempts to do me harm and will bring me safe to his heavenly kingdom." We all recall that Paul had been converted earlier by a sudden outburst of fiery light as he was about to enter Damascus and persecute Christians. From that moment on Paul never ceases to proclaim God's liberality in his sermons and letters. He tells us that the Lord flooded him with his grace in order to bind the apostle of the Gentiles to himself and to provide him with the strength he would need to preach the gospel message.

This is even more evident in the case of Saint Peter, for we have Jesus' own words in today's Gospel. Peter speaks in the name of all the apostles, declaring that Jesus is "the Messiah . . . the Son of the living God." Jesus points out that such knowledge could only result from special illumination by the Spirit of his Father: "No mere man has revealed this to you." Peter's faith is a gift from God. What is more, his mission in the world is entrusted to him by Jesus in a particular and personal way: "You are 'Rock,' and on this rock I will build my church." Because of this fundamental situation in Christ's Church, Peter will be the trustee of the Church's spiritual powers and energies.

Both Peter and Paul are fashioned by the Lord and constantly imbued with the energy of his Spirit. But the resemblance stops there. Although God's selection of them is the source of their spiritual and apostolic worth, they are sent on radically different missions.

In today's reading Paul briefly recounts his whole life. He knows that it will soon be over: "The hour of my dissolution is near." His account of his life is a report of suffering and hard work and trials of all sorts. He has fought well, he has finished the race. The accounts in Acts record his numerous journeys, his establishment of churches is difficult circumstances, his frequent misadventures, and his struggles to preserve and solidify the true faith. Paul presents himself as the Church, ever ready and anxious to spend himself and to further the work of spreading the gospel, for this was the mission entrusted to the apostles by Christ before his own departure from the scene. The communities which Paul founds and watches over unceasingly are clearly supposed to embody the leaven of fraternal charity. But Paul himself never ceases to be concerned about their expansion and increase, so he is driven to establish new ones time and again.

Peter, on the other hand, is the rock on which Christ will build his Church. This statement by Jesus conjures up the idea of the Church's stability and necessary perdurance. Jesus then goes on to describe some of the principal characteristics of this Church. It will be stable, permanent, invulnerable: "The jaws of death shall not prevail against it." Freed in advance from all the grave catastrophes one might imagine, the Church is the necessary and decisive precondition for entrance into the kingdom. Peter will hold the keys that open or close the gates of the kingdom; he will be in charge of access to it. He will not preside over the destiny of some particular community of believers. Instead he will be the irreplaceable trustee of the resources which are capable of leading man to his definitive destiny. Thus Peter is presented to us as the power of the Lord living on earth. His prime concern will be to open up to human beings the treasury that has been entrusted to him. With Peter we are presented with the Church, a stable institution that will perdure throughout human history.

The different functions of these two men inevitably lead to different personal experiences and different spiritual adventures.

Paul, who is about to conclude his life here, tells Timothy: "Everyone abandoned me." His is the loneliness of the struggler who has labored hard. His way of life led him around the known world of that day. His audience had been greater and more varied than that of any other apostle. His job of establishing communities led him to know and take charge of many people. Now, at the end of this highly fruitful life, he is alone. He feels stripped of everything and everyone, on the verge of sadness. But he remains at peace because hope in God's grace still throbs in his heart. He is still prepared to fight on and to spend himself further.

Peter, on the other hand, seems to be the object of a very special kind of protection. He is thrown into prison and watched by numerous guards, lest he be freed by a commando raid perhaps. But "the Church prayed fervently to God on his behalf." God sends his angel to free him. The angel frees him miraculously from his chains, unlocks the bolted door, distracts the guards, and restores Peter to freedom. The "jaws of death" must not prevail against him right now because he is the rock on which the Church is founded.

That is what Scripture tells us today about these two pillars of the Church. In their work both men are chosen and animated by the Spirit of the Lord, but they take on different functions and perform different services. While these functions and services may seem to contradict one another, they are in fact complementary. Their diversity and their unity offer us a lesson that is particularly important for us today.

There is no doubt that the faithful are often disturbed greatly by the many different jolts which rock the bark of Peter. Amid the tempest few believers manage to maintain their peace. But the example of the two apostles will help us to appreciate better the full richness and diversity of the mystery of the Church.

We must grasp what the Lord's will is, and it is clearly marked and fulfilled in the lives of Peter and Paul. The Lord wants the Church to be simultaneously stability and movement. As a perduring institution, it is to realize its destiny over the course of centuries, through the unfolding evolution of human civilization. It is not to keep to itself; it is to spend itself unceasingly. No other society has this twofold mission in which opposing functions must dovetail with each other. Without this dovetailing, it will be useless and sterile. The Church must be strong and, at the same time, self-sacrificing. It must perdure, and also disappear in giving freely of itself. The contrasting experiences of Peter and Paul helps us to appreciate all this. The seeming contradictions actually complement one another. They come together in the unique mystery of love that is the Father, Son, and Holy Spirit.

Once we have grasped and accepted the fact that our energies can be utilized in two different directions, we can better appreciate why some believers—by temperament or vocation—seem closer to Peter while others seem closer to Paul. There will be no need to set them off against each other. To the extent that all are equally animated by docility to the Spirit and follow the dictate of fidelity to the gospel message, the contrasts and oppositions will come together in harmony and will reveal the full richness of the Lord's gifts. To unite in communion means to obey the Lord. To point up and criticize differences means to create opposition and to play into the "jaws of death."

August 15
THE ASSUMPTION

Rv 11:19a,12:1-6a,10ab
1 Cor 15:20-26
Lk 1:39-56

Today's Collect alludes to Mary, the Immaculate Virgin and Mother of Jesus, who was taken "body and soul" into the glory of heaven. That is the mystery of the Assumption which the Church celebrates today. Mary, the daughter of Joachim and Anne, was chosen out of all the women of Israel to be the Mother of Jesus. She gave birth to him in a stable near Bethlehem and watched him grow up for about thirty years. Then he left her to start his public life and to gather disciples around him. She saw him die on the cross between two thieves, and then was taken home by John the Evangelist. She took part in the early growth of the Church, which was her Son's chief work. She was an ordinary woman with a singular destiny, whom many people knew and loved. Now she is associated body and soul with the glory of God himself. That is the reality we celebrate, as incredible as any reality we could imagine.

It is difficult enough to believe in Jesus, who is both God and man. But when all is said and done, some people do feel that nothing is impossible for God, that he can manifest himself as he chooses. But it seems downright unnatural that an ordinary woman should be in heaven already—before the end of the world, before the last judgment that will bring human history to its definitive close. Why should she be? How can we justify such a faith, particularly when that teaching is not clearly affirmed in Scripture? Nowhere in Scripture do we find a statement parallel to the assertion in the Collect of today's Mass. What is more, many Christians who do not belong to the Roman Catholic Church refuse to profess faith in Mary's Assumption. And increasing numbers of Catholics feel that this proclaimation is not as important as the liturgy and the hierarchy claim, that there are more urgent questions vying for our attention.

It is true that on the ecumenical plane, in a world growing more materialistic every day, the attitude of the Catholic Church does not seem to be very "reasonable." As many see it today, the wise thing is to be "in tune with" the world, to tell it what it wants to hear. That is the tack for the Church to take if it wants to be successful. This attitude should not be disregarded entirely, but there is another attitude as well: i.e., the Church listens to the Spirit and expresses what it hears even though its words may not please the surrounding world.

That is precisely what the Church is doing today when it proclaims the feast of the Assumption. The world is turning in on itself and choking on its own tortuous lines. The Church cuts through all that, overturning all the accepted data on the human condition. She speaks of a woman who became a mother while remaining a virgin, of an ordinary woman who became the Mother of God, of a fleshly human being whose body now resides in God's own kingdom. What are we to make of all that?

Nothing, really. It is a mystery above and beyond man's reason, particularly when he confines his reason to the realm of material things that can be experienced or subjected to experiment. The Church is of interest to such a person only when it contributes towards the solution of human problems. Mary is important only insofar as she was the mother of a social reformer. Such an outlook mutilates and dessicates everything in the sterile reaches of a reasoning process that has become totally materialistic. It leaves room only for a rather low-level animality, and everything becomes absurd. There is nothing to understand because we are totally incapable of such understanding. And since we are geared to reject any and every spiritual reality, we soon become unable to grasp the fittingness of the mystery proclaimed today: i.e., that the Mother of Jesus is now in glory with him and through him. The Assumption of Mary becomes more and more aberrant in our eyes, and the proclamation of it seems to be useless, if not downright harmful.

The above diagnosis is true for non-believers, and for some believers as well. The more true it is, the more Mary's Assumption is misunderstood and found intolerable, so much the more necessary is it to recall the reality of it. If the Church fails to do this, then she commits suicide; she no longer has any reason to exist. She then becomes nothing more than the witness to an age-old spiritual authority, an accomplice in the further degradation of our humanity.

The Church resolutely refuses to take that course. A vigorous impulse wells up from the depths of her consciousness, compelling her to proclaim the Assumption of Mary with calm assurance. It is true. Mary, the virgin of Nazareth, is now in the glory of the Father—body and soul. The Church knows that if she refuses this assertion, then she is no longer alive; that the more she believes in herself, the more she will proclaim this truth.

If this cry of faith from the Church does not touch the depths of our soul, that is a sign that we suffer from some sort of spiritual deficiency. The mystery of Mary and the mystery of the Church are intimately bound up with each other. We cannot comprehend one if we do not accept the other. Make no mistake about it: here we have a sign that will help us to evaluate the quality of our own life of faith. Rejection of one mystery betokens rejection of the other. And it is only a short step from there to rejecting the mystery of the crucified and risen Christ. They all are bound up intimately with each other.

We can delude ourselves about all this, but we will not be able to halt the inevitable progression. Mary's privileged role in the mystery of her son is clearcut. If the here-and-now reality of God's kingdom is not certain enough for us to believe that Mary can participate in it now, then the Church will soon be nothing more than a terrestrial entity for us. It will cease to be the body of Christ. It will no longer bear witness to the vivifying presence of the Spirit among men. And if it loses its roots and its reason for being in our eyes, then it will no longer nourish us with God's word or with Christ's body and blood. Inevitably we will come to doubt everything it offers to us. We will set at naught the words and gestures it proclaims in the name of the Lord.

These statements may seem exaggerated, but they are not. Whether we are pessimists or not will depend on where we go from here. If we accept the statements, we can turn to Mary and ask her to visit us. We would then be like Elizabeth in today's Gospel.

We must learn to make Elizabeth's salutation our own: "Who am I that the mother of my Lord should come to me?" Mary had "trusted that the Lord's words to her would be fulfilled." How can we help but share Elizabeth's wonderment over her younger cousin! Mary was alone by herself when the angel brought God's message to her, alone when she acceded to the angel's request, alone when she surrendered herself wholly to God's will and agreed to be the instrument of God's birth among human beings. Yet at the same time she is the whole nation of Israel waiting for the expected Messiah over the course of centuries. Alone, she voices the nation's acceptance to God. Alone, she is already the whole Church—the Spouse of the Spirit and the Mother of Christ.

Mary responds to Elizabeth's greeting, which is now our greeting as well. In the *Magnificat* she tells us who she is. And if we let her response flow into our hearts, we will no longer have any doubts about her; we will know that the statements about this woman are true indeed. Her poverty of spirit makes her transparent and docile. She is caught up in admiration of her God and wholly receptive to his love. How could the kingdom of heaven in all its plenitude not be given immediately to such a person!

At this point we can go beyond the events narrated in today's Gospel. It tells us that Mary stayed three months with her cousin. With us it is not a case of three months or three years. She can stay with us always.

As we close our meditation we can only hope that Mary will help us to know her son better, that she will prepare our hearts to participate in the sacrifice we shall now offer. She was present at the foot of the cross, she is now in the glory of heaven. She offers us her help, so that we will be willing to go to her. If we do, then we will deserve the blessing which Jesus pronounced: "Blest are they who hear the word of God and keep it" (Lk 11:28).

November 1
ALL SAINTS

Rv 7:2-4,9-14
1 Jn 3:1-3
Mt 5:1-12a

This is one of the great feasts of the church year. In one festive celebration we honor all God's saints; all those who have reached their true destination after passing their lives on this earth, all those who are willing to let themselves be transformed by God's Spirit. In short, we honor all the baptized in whom the energy of baptism has borne its fruits.

And yet how difficult it is for us to talk about holiness. For all of us the happiness of heaven suggests something that is clearcut yet vague, necessary but inaccessible, tangible yet somehow indefinable. We could not give any precise definition of our thinking about it. Left to ourselves, we are reduced to vague approximations.

But what does God's word tell us today? Let us examine it, without adding or subtracting one iota. Then we will be able to probe more deeply into the mystery of holiness.

Today's divine message clearly affirms certain things, is imprecise about other things, and also offers us some signs whereby we can recognize the Spirit at work in fashioning children of the kingdom.

The first thing that is clear from the passage in the Book of Revelation is that the work of the Lord will be a sure success. All creation, purified and saved by Christ, will find definitive reconciliation and universal harmony. The Book of Revelation tells us this by depicting the gathering of an immense crowd of men and women from every tribe and language and nation. The figure cited, 144,000, symbolizes an incalculable number. These are the people who have been fashioned and flooded by the power of God, and marked with his seal. They have been purified by the blood of the Lamb and made like the Son of God.

We also know that the kingdom is not just something for later on, for some mysterious epoch after this life on earth. In fact Jesus states that two types of human beings possess it already. Speaking about those who are poor in spirit and those who are persecuted for the sake of holiness, he tells us that "the reign of God is theirs."

Those are the points that are stated as certainties.

When Jesus speaks about holiness, however, he deliberately seems to leave certain important points vague and imprecise. The Book of Revelation, too, is mysterious and symbolic in its approach. It prefers suggestion and allusion to clear definition in precise terms, for it is talking about a mystery that opens out to an eternity which we cannot possibly represent to ourselves. And John the Evangelist tells us: "What we shall be has not yet come to light." We know for sure that we will resemble the Son of God, but we cannot possibly describe that in advance or define it in precise human terms. Such a reality escapes our grasp.

John the Evangelist also seems unable to describe clearly what we are right now. He tells us: "Children of God . . . that is what we are. The reason the world does not recognize us is that it never recognized the Son." We know what "world" means to John here: it is everything in creation that is alien or hostile to Christ. In that sense it is not just made up of the apparent enemies of Christ and his Church; it is not just other people. The "world" is in ourselves to the extent that we are only partially liberated, to the extent that our awareness and knowledge of God has not impregnated us to the full. We may know that we are children of God, but we can fully recognize and acknowledge that fact only insofar as Christ's work of regeneration has been effected in us. Our certainty about being children of God vacillates. The place we give it in the conduct of our lives and in the maintenance of inner peace may even shrink. It all depends on the progress of our fidelity, on the relative hold of the spirit of the world over our outlook.

Thus it is impossible to talk about holiness in a sense. Insofar as we are not holy people, it is a reality that is alien and inaccessible to us. To the extent that we have discovered God—and we all have to some extent—we find that human words are incapable of expressing that fact. We can only use symbols, which in turn are accessible only to those who have made a similar journey. And if they have, there is no need to speak about it at all.

We must admit that this is disconcerting. How can we dispense from talking suitably about that which is the real and definitive goal of all earthly existence? Perhaps we can talk about it by exploring the signs which indicate the work of the Spirit. Perhaps that is how we are to view the import of the Beatitudes.

The discourse on the Beatitudes may well be the most beautiful passage in the gospels. It is certainly one of the most important. We must approach it with the respect and sensitivity it deserves.

All the details Matthew injects to introduce this discourse indicate the importance he attaches to it. Jesus sees the crowd, climbs a hillside, and sits down. His disciples gather around him and he begins to teach. In a few brief phrases he will voice all the wisdom of the living God, he will reveal everything that the believer must cultivate in himself, and he will lay bare all the promises given to him by God.

In ten successive phrases Jesus proclaims happiness. But it is a secret, indefinable happiness. We are constrained to silence. We must let Jesus' words echo in our hearts. Here I would simply offer a few remarks.

Two of the Beatitudes refer to the present, the rest refer to the future. The two which refer to the present are among the certainties of which we spoke earlier. Those who are poor in spirit and those who suffer for the sake of holiness possess the kingdom. Yet it is precisely these two Beatitudes that are the most mysterious, the most difficult to comprehend. What is poverty of spirit? If we manage to define it and recognize its presence in ourselves, we will rejoice over the fact; and in so doing we will destroy its presence in us. Our self-satisfaction will clearly be the direct opposite of this poverty of spirit. And who are these people who are persecuted for the sake of holiness? What sort of holiness is he talking about? Finally, what is the reign of God? Jesus does not define it anywhere; he speaks continually in parables.

As we just indicated, the two Beatitudes which refer to the present are the most mysterious ones. By contrast, the ones which refer to the future seem to be commentaries on those two mysterious ones. They explain their content insofar as they offer us signs by which we can ascertain whether the kingdom is possessed or not.

After the first Beatitude, for example, we get a description—or rather a list—of the qualities and states proper to those who are poor in spirit. These people are sorrowing and lowly. They hunger and thirst for holiness. They show mercy. They are single-hearted and peacemakers. All these people will obtain the kingdom, which is depicted here as a promised land of consolation, abundance, and mercy where they shall see God and be called his sons. In six successive statements we are offered signs of our poverty and of the kingdom it gains for us.

Then comes a second series of Beatitudes referring to those who are persecuted for the sake of holiness: "Blest are you when they insult you and persecute you and utter every kind of slander against you because of me." The point is a simple one. If these things happen to us, we should not be disconsolate. Instead we should rejoice because "your reward is great in heaven." Like Isaiah's suffering servant, the persecuted one cannot expect a reward here. He cannot seek triumph or vengeance here. He must trust wholly in the Lord to straighten things out.

Each of us should read these words of Jesus over to himself and let the words sink in. We may not be able to say anything suitable about holiness, but we can discern the signs of the Spirit at work in us. When these signs show up, we must accept them rather than reject them. Our life must be one of solid hope in the promises which Jesus solemnly proclaims today.

May this feast of all the saints intensify our hope in the success of God's work and give us the joy of benefit-ing from it now.

BIBLICAL READINGS

GENESIS (Gn)
1:1-2:2 .... Easter Vigil
2:7-9,3:1-7 .... First Sunday of Lent
3:9-15,20 .... Immaculate Conception
12:1-4a .... Second Sunday of Lent

EXODUS (Ex)
12:1-8,11-14 .... Holy Thursday
17:3-7 .... Third Sunday of Lent
19:2-6a .... 11th Sunday of the Year
22:20-26 .... 30th Sunday of the Year
34:4b-6,8-9 .... Trinity Sunday

LEVITICUS (Lv)
19:1-2,17-18 .... 7th Sunday of the Year

NUMBERS (Nm)
6:22-27 .... Solemnity of Mary

DEUTERONOMY (Dt)
8:2-3,14b-16a .... Corpus Christi
11:18,26-28 .... 9th Sunday of the Year

1 SAMUEL (1 Sm)
16:1b,6-7,10-13a .... Fourth Sunday of Lent

2 SAMUEL (2 Sm)
7:4-5a,12-14a,16 .... Saint Joseph

1 KINGS (1 Kgs)
3:5,7-12 .... 17th Sunday of the Year
19:9a,11-13a .... 19th Sunday of the Year

2 KINGS (2 Kgs)
4:8-11,14-16a .... 13th Sunday of the Year

PROVERBS (Prv)
31:10-13,19-20,30-31 .... 33rd Sunday of the Year

WISDOM (Wis)
6:12-16 .... 32nd Sunday of the Year
12:13,16-19 .... 16th Sunday of the Year

SIRACH (Sir)
3:2-6,12-14 .... Feast of the Holy Family
15:15-20 .... 6th Sunday of the Year
24:1-4,12-16 .... Second Sunday after Christmas
27:30-28:7 .... 24th Sunday of the Year

ST. LUKE (Lk)

1:26-28 .... Immaculate Conception
1:39-56 .... The Assumption
2:1-14 .... Christmas: Midnight Mass
2:16-21 .... Solemnity of Mary
24:13-35 .... Third Sunday of Easter

ST. JOHN (Jn)

1:1-18 .... Second Sunday after Christmas
1:1-18 .... Christmas: Day Mass
1:29-34 .... 2nd Sunday of the Year
3:16-18 .... Trinity Sunday
4:5-42 .... Third Sunday of Lent
6:51-58 .... Corpus Christi
9:1-41 .... Fourth Sunday of Lent
10:1-10 .... Fourth Sunday of Easter
11:1-45 .... Fifth Sunday of Lent
13:1-15 .... Holy Thursday
14:1-12 .... Fifth Sunday of Easter
14:15-21 .... Sixth Sunday of Easter
17:1-11a .... Seventh Sunday of Easter
20:19-31 .... Second Sunday of Easter
20:19-23 .... Pentecost

ACTS OF THE APOSTLES (Acts)

1:1-11 .... The Ascension
1:12-14 .... Seventh Sunday of Easter
2:1-11 .... Pentecost
2:14,22-28 .... Third Sunday of Easter
2:14a,36-41 .... Fourth Sunday of Easter
2:42-47 .... Second Sunday of Easter
6:1-7 .... Fifth Sunday of Easter
8:5-8,14-17 .... Sixth Sunday of Easter
10:34-38 .... Baptism of Jesus
10:34a,37-43 .... Easter
12:1-11 .... Saints Peter and Paul

ROMANS (Rom)

1:1-7 .... Fourth Sunday of Advent
3:21-25a,28 .... 9th Sunday of the Year
4:13,16-18,22 .... Saint Joseph
4:18-25 .... 10th Sunday of the Year
5:1-2,5-8 .... Third Sunday of Lent
5:6-11 .... 11th Sunday of the Year
5:12-19 .... First Sunday of Lent
5:12-15 .... 12th Sunday of the Year

6:3-4,8-11 .... 13th Sunday of the Year
8:8-11 .... Fifth Sunday of Lent
8:9,11-13 .... 14th Sunday of the Year
8:18-23 .... 15th Sunday of the Year
8:26-27 .... 16th Sunday of the Year
8:28-30 .... 17th Sunday of the Year
8:35,37-39 .... 18th Sunday of the Year
9:1-5 .... 19th Sunday of the Year
11:13-15,29-32 .... 20th Sunday of the Year
11:33-36 .... 21st Sunday of the Year
12:1-2 .... 22nd Sunday of the Year
13:8-10 .... 23rd Sunday of the Year
13:11-14 .... First Sunday of Advent
14:7-9 .... 24th Sunday of the Year
15:4-9 .... Second Sunday of Advent

I CORINTHIANS (1 Cor)

1:1-3 .... 2nd Sunday of the Year
1:10-13,17 .... 3rd Sunday of the Year
1:26-31 .... 4th Sunday of the Year
2:1-5 .... 5th Sunday of the Year
2:6-10 .... 6th Sunday of the Year
3:16-23 .... 7th Sunday of the Year
4:1-5 .... 8th Sunday of the Year
5:6b-8 .... Easter
10:16-17 .... Corpus Christi
11:23-26 .... Holy Thursday
12:3b-7,12-13 .... Pentecost
15:20-26 .... The Assumption
15:20-26,28 .... Christ the King

2 CORINTHIANS (2 Cor)

13:11-13 .... Trinity Sunday

GALATIANS (Gal)

4:4-7 .... Solemnity of Mary

EPHESIANS (Eph)

1:3-6,11-12 .... Immaculate Conception
1:3-6,15-18 .... Second Sunday after Christmas
1:17-23 .... The Ascension
3:2-3a,5-6 .... Epiphany
5:8-14 .... Fourth Sunday of Lent

PHILIPPIANS (Phil)

1:20c-24,27a .... 25th Sunday of the Year
2:1-11 .... 26th Sunday of the Year
2:6-11 .... Palm Sunday

4:6-9 .... 27th Sunday of the Year
4:12-14,19-20 .... 28th Sunday of the Year
COLOSSIANS (Col)
3:1-4 .... Easter
3:12-21 .... Feast of the Holy Family
1 THESSALONIANS (1 Thes)
1:1-5b .... 29th Sunday of the Year
1:5c-10 .... 30th Sunday of the Year
2:7b-9,13 .... 31st Sunday of the Year
4:13-18 .... 32nd Sunday of the Year
5:1-6 .... 33rd Sunday of the Year
2 TIMOTHY (2 Tm)
1:8b-10 .... Second Sunday of Lent
4:6-8,17-18 .... Saints Peter and Paul
TITUS (Ti)
2:11-14 .... Christmas: Midnight Mass
HEBREWS (Heb)
1:1-6 .... Christmas: Day Mass
ST. JAMES (Jas)
5:7-10 .... Third Sunday of Advent
1 ST. PETER (1 Pt)
1:3-9 .... Second Sunday of Easter
1:17-21 .... Third Sunday of Easter
2:4-9 .... Fifth Sunday of Easter
2:20b-25 .... Fourth Sunday of Easter
3:15-18 .... Sixth Sunday of Easter
4:13-16 .... Seventh Sunday of Easter
1 ST. JOHN (1 Jn)
3:1-3 .... All Saints
REVELATION (Rv)
7:2-4,9-14 .... All Saints
11:19a,12:1-6a,10ab .... The Assumption